CONCORDIA UNIVERSI

D811.5.L43
TWELVE MONTHS THAT CHANGE

W9-ABE-388

3 4211 000021367

WI

BE FULLY INFORMED

READ THESE BOOKS FOR WARTIME

✦

RETREAT WITH STILWELL. *Jack Belden*

THE JAPANESE ENEMY
GOVERNMENT BY ASSASSINATION } *Hugh Byas*

PRISONER OF THE JAPS. *Gwen Dew*

THE BRITISH COMMONWEALTH   *William Yandell Elliott*
AT WAR   *and H. Duncan Hall*

APPEASEMENT'S CHILD. *Thomas J. Hamilton*

INTO THE VALLEY
MEN ON BATAAN } *John Hersey*

DESERT WAR. *Russell Hill*

CIRCUIT OF CONQUEST. *Relman Morin*

BERLIN DIARY. *William L. Shirer*

BATTLE HYMN OF CHINA. *Agnes Smedley*

LAST TRAIN FROM BERLIN. *Howard K. Smith*

THE LAST DAYS OF SEVASTOPOL. *Boris Voyetekhov*

BORZOI BOOKS

published by Alfred A. Knopf

Twelve Months that Changed the World

TWELVE MONTHS

THAT

CHANGED THE WORLD

LARRY LESUEUR

1943

ALFRED A KNOPF

NEW YORK

CONCORDIA COLLEGE RIVER FOREST ILLINOIS LIBRARY

This book has been produced in full compliance with all government regulations for the conservation of paper, metal, and other essential materials.

COPYRIGHT 1943 *by Larry Lesueur. All rights reserved. No part of this book may be reproduced in any form without permission in writing from the publisher, except by a reviewer who may quote brief passages in a review to be printed in a magazine or newspaper. Manufactured in the United States of America.*

FIRST EDITION

Published simultaneously in Canada by The Ryerson Press

30318

TWELVE MONTHS THAT CHANGED THE WORLD

To my mother

OCTOBER 12, 1941. At dusk a gray mist drifted down from the hills and settled over the bomb-battered Scottish port. Shivering, I wrapped my trench coat tighter and peered through the haze as the motor-boat chugged across the harbor. Then, jutting abruptly out of the fog, appeared our goal — five mud-colored little ships waiting silently at anchor in the oily water.

"So this," I thought, "is a convoy to Russia."

We drew alongside the smallest of the merchantmen, the *Temple Arch*, camouflaged a nondescript gray. From her mainmast whipped the wind-tattered red "duster" of the British Merchant Navy.

Burdened by my two heavy suitcases, containing what I hoped would be a year's supply of clothing and essentials, I struggled up the gangplank of the little 6,000-tonner to be welcomed by a slender, lantern-jawed young Scotsman.

"I'm Captain Sam Lamont," he said with a smile that crinkled the crow's-feet around deep-set blue eyes. "I hope we have a comfortable voyage."

There were six of us, three American and three British correspondents. We divided the cabins by tossing a coin. Four of us went into the narrow sick-bay and 220-pound Eddy Gilmore of the Associated Press shared the two bunks in the purser's tiny quarters with me. There was no room for our bags, so we took out what we needed for a three-week trip and sent the rest of the baggage down to the hold to be stowed away alongside the tons of TNT, tanks and boots for the Red Army of Soviet Russia, enough war material to fill ten long freight trains.

Leaning up against one of the huge fighter-plane packing-cases that cluttered the deck, we discussed our future. Tall, blond Walter Kerr, of the *New York Herald Tribune*, had

3

covered the Russo-Finnish War of 1939–40. As a veteran of winter warfare, he had reduced his equipment to a minimum. He wore a ski suit and had two knapsacks filled with the bare essentials of clothing, a huge sheath knife, and a compass.

"If the news from Russia doesn't get better, we may be spending a large part of our time on skis," he announced grimly.

Eddy Gilmore, from Selma, Alabama, confessed that he had never seen snow until a few years ago and didn't know how to ski. Eric McGloughlin of the Sydney (Australia) *Morning Herald*, had never seen snow in his life. Ralph Parker, of the London *Times* and the *New York Times*, told us in a disdainful Cambridge accent that there never was very much snow in England, but he had brought no winter underwear because he'd heard that all Russian houses were overheated in winter. Alex Easterman of the London *Daily Mail*, wore a handsome fur-lined coat which, he explained, was just the thing for Moscow, but he wasn't sure whether it would do for skiing. We were the blind giving explicit directions to the blind. None of us had ever been to Russia before.

"When do we start?" I asked Captain Lamont at dinner.

The wiry, dark-haired Scotsman was not very informative. "When I get the signal from the Admiralty," he said. "I shall have to ask you all to remain aboard ship until then."

That night we wondered if the Admiralty would ever send the signal. Only a fortnight ago the London newspapers had been black with headlines proclaiming Hitler's greatest boast. "At last," said the Führer, "we have created the prerequisites for the final tremendous blow which, before the onset of winter, will lead to the destruction of the enemy." And next day he had informed the world: "Forty-eight hours ago there began new operations of gigantic dimensions. They will lead to the destruction of the enemy in the east. The enemy has already been routed and will never regain his strength."

That night on the ship's radio we heard that the German Army boasted of a complete break-through on the Napoleonic road to Moscow. "The German communiqué claims that Vyazma, 125 miles from Moscow, is already far in the rear of the battlefront," said the BBC announcer gravely.

We considered our position. There was just a chance that the British authorities might think it inadvisable to land this convoy of war material in Russia for fear that its cargo would fall eventually into German hands. We figured that if Moscow fell before we arrived, we could either go back on this same ship or somehow make our way across Russia to the Soviet Far East and head for America and home from Vladivostok or Tokyo. Even on my small-scale map the distance from Archangel to Vladivostok was tremendous. But I knew the Soviet Union had big radio transmitters at Sverdlovsk and Tomsk and I had eight hundred dollars in a money belt around my waist and an unsatisfied desire to see for myself. The opportunity to see Russia for the last time under Soviet Communism was the greatest adventure that the tottering world had left. No reporter, I felt, could possibly turn it down.

Alex Easterman, who had bid a sad good-by to his family in the cavernous Glasgow railroad station, was quiet and thoughtful. He didn't join the conversation. Suddenly he asked: "Are you fellows insured?"

We told him that our companies had taken out war correspondents' policies.

Alex said hesitantly: "I don't think I'm covered. I've half a mind not to go unless I'm insured. I owe it to my family."

We agreed and advised him to think it over and then try to get ashore in the morning if the ship hadn't left. He could phone his London office and ask them to take out a policy with Lloyd's.

He pondered the question during the night and then explained his predicament to the skipper. By morning the Admiralty's signal had not come, so Captain Lamont gave him permission to flag a cutter and go ashore to telephone. He returned an hour later and said solemnly:

"Boys, I'm not going with you. The *Daily Mail* refuses to insure me."

We helped him pack his bags and I traded him my last English pounds for some extra American currency. Then

silently we watched his launch return to the Scottish dockside. He turned to wave for the last time, and someone said
gloomily:

"This is like one of those tragic entries in Scott's diary
at the South Pole. 'Easterman disappeared today.' "

At one o'clock in the morning the ship trembled with the
beat of the engines, and the anchor chain clanked in the
hawsehole. I threw an overcoat over my pajamas and hurried out on the cold deck. The dockside was blacked out, but
I could dimly make out the loom of the land slipping slowly
away off the stern. We were on our way to Russia.

October 14–31   During the night we passed
down the Clyde and were joined by two more heavily laden
freighters from Liverpool. British reconnaissance planes on
U-boat patrol picked us up at dawn and I watched them chase
one another's tails through the skies over the convoy until
nightfall. Two destroyers and three minesweepers cut white
swaths around our plodding ships like a pack of incisive
little terriers guarding a flock of slow, cud-chewing cows.
The RAF pilots overhead enlivened our long vigil by going
through elephantine mimic dog-fights with their huge planes
as the ships steamed down past the green hills of the North
Channel.

I wondered when I was going to see green hills again. As
we threaded our way past the soft outlines of the Hebrides
and the Isle of Skye, all desolate green and silvered with a
thousand lacy streams, I thought Scotland was the handsomest country I had ever seen. We were on our way to
Scapa Flow to pick up the rest of our escort.

We entered the main base of the British Navy at dawn
and anchored in the midst of the most barren region in the
British Isles. Low green hummocks emerged from the deep
blue waters with only a small cluster of white houses on the
Pomona mainland. All around us were sleek, pugnacious
warships. At our side a British submarine was nuzzling close
to its mother ship, a reconstructed freighter fitted out with
dormitories and a gymnasium where the submarine crew relaxed until the next underwater patrol.

At dusk a black flag rose on the barracks flag-pole on the Pomona mainland. It was the air-raid alarm. On every ship we saw British gunners run to battle stations, and the misty gray sky was suddenly filled with black and white smoke blobs. The raving of the anti-aircraft guns was hideous. Three Hurricanes roared off from a near-by field, but darkness closed in before the guns or planes could down the lone German reconnaissance plane sent over from Norway. It looked like a bad omen for our convoy to Russia.

That evening, under heavy skies, we left Scapa, passing through the intricate series of anti-submarine booms in the tide rips of the Pentland Firth, which opened for only one ship at a time so that enemy submarines could not creep in unnoticed. Added to our two destroyers and three mine-layers was the County Class cruiser *Norfolk*. Trim and majestic, she wore the war-paint of the Northern Patrol, sky-blue with jagged streaks of black and gray — a striking camouflage blend for the ice floes and snow squalls of the Arctic seas.

I remembered that the *Tirpitz* had been reported sheltering in a Norwegian fjord. The slim, gray cruiser around which our slow merchantmen huddled would be no match for a battleship of the class that had sunk HMS *Hood*. I asked Captain Lamont what he knew of the *Tirpitz*.

"She's around," he said, "but don't worry, boy, the British Navy will take care of you." He grinned as though that were enough to satisfy my curiosity about the *Tirpitz*.

Then at lunch one day someone asked the captain how long the *Temple Arch* would stay afloat if a torpedo hit it. "It's not a matter of how long she'll stay afloat," he replied. "It's a question of how high we'll go. Remember there are two thousand tons of TNT under us."

We smiled at his answer, but the eyes of the captain of the *Temple Arch* were unsmiling. I knew that any talk of harm to his ship touched him deeply. He knew every bolt and plate in her. He had watched her grow from steel and sweat in a Scottish shipyard. She was his first command, and his ship was part of him.

Captain Lamont called the correspondents to his quarters

and told us that we were entering a dangerous stretch, the waters between the Shetland Islands and the Faroes, where German U-boats plied on their way from the Baltic and Norway. "We'll pass at night," he said, "to avoid land-based German bombers. I advise everyone to sleep in his clothes for the rest of the trip." He called attention to our carelessness about the blackout. There was too much delay in shutting the door of the main cabin at night. The light shone out over the dark northern waters too long and too often. If we weren't more careful, he told us, we'd have to keep off the deck at night. That would be just another restriction. We couldn't even listen to the radio. The squeal which just meant static on land was a signal to the enemy in these U-boat-infested waters. All receiving sets belonging to the crew had been sealed. Only the captain and ship's radiomen with their specially shielded sets could listen in.

The radiomen stayed constantly tuned to the international distress wave-length. Day after day they picked up feeble calls for help. There was nothing we could do about them. We were too far away to help and we couldn't break convoy. All we knew was that somewhere other ships were sinking and that we were safe. I wondered if we would ever receive help if we sent a distress call from the middle of the forgotten Arctic.

There was a nip in the October air as we headed for the North. The key men of the crew were issued their Arctic clothes — camel's-hair duffle coats with hoods, and long cashmere underwear. The rest were told that the daily rum ration would begin at the Arctic Circle.

For the correspondents life was mostly eating. Breakfast of curried rice, oatmeal, and tea, with bacon and eggs once a week. A heavy lunch of meat and potatoes; then at four o'clock tea, bread, and jam, and for supper sandwiches and cocoa. The food was better than I had hoped for; the *Temple Arch* had restocked on her previous voyage to America.

Exercise was almost out of the question. The decks were made almost impassable with tons of war material. We rigged a line between two of the airplane crates and tossed a rubber quoit for deck tennis. Unfortunately, the quoit was pitched overboard into the heaving sea in the very first game. That ended our attempts at exercise. We settled down to reading, studying Russian, and playing checkers.

The convoy skirted Iceland and crept up along the Greenland coast. The dull green of the North Sea gave way to the icy green-blue shades of the Arctic Ocean. The raucous seagulls that had followed us from Scotland departed, and their place was taken by slender, graceful kittiwakes, vagrants of the sea, soaring endlessly in our wake, white wings tipped with black.

The monotony was peculiar. We were always waiting for something to happen. Suddenly a black flag would run up on the halyards of the cruiser. It meant: "Unidentified aircraft sighted." A seaman would run through the ship clanging a bell madly. We'd rush to our cabins, grab our life-preservers and tin hats, and take our positions beside the lifeboats, with a tight feeling in the chest and hearts pounding. The naval gunners stood at battle stations. The eyes of the Luftwaffe had sighted us, but the reconnaissance planes carried no bombs. They were reporting our position to cruising U-boats. Here at the edge of the Arctic icepack, we were too far away for torpedo bombers to strike from Norway and Finland.

It occurred to me that perhaps the Germans were not particularly interested in sinking our convoy. Captain Lamont had revealed to us that Finnish-German troops had already cut the railroad line leading from Murmansk to the Russian interior, so Archangel would be the only port open to us. And east of Leningrad the main forces of the German Army were within striking distance of the railroad junction of Valogda. Capture of that railroad hub joining Moscow with Archangel and the Trans-Siberian railroad would mean that we and our supplies would be cut off from the rest of Russia. The previous small convoy had got through unharmed, we learned. The Germans were making no large-scale effort to cut off the trickle of Allied supplies to Russia because they obviously thought that this war aid could have little effect on the outcome of the great battle. Moreover, since the German Army was scoring such tremendous successes, a Soviet capitulation would mean the surrender of all war material in Russia anyway. The Germans appeared to have little to lose in allowing our convoy to proceed safely to Russia.

We plodded along the 75th meridian, some 900 miles from the North Pole. We kept driving north. Ice covered the decks, the guns, the halyards. Once a day the seamen lined up for their daily ration of heavy Jamaica rum. They didn't drink it for the taste alone. They needed it to keep their blood moving.

One afternoon I noticed Mr. Curry, the gray-haired chief engineer, come waddling along the snow-lashed deck bearing in his arms a load of what were unmistakably Christmas boxes.

"This is the Mohammedan Christmas," he said. "Tonight is the Feast of Ramadan." The chief explained that his Arab stokers from Saudi Arabia had been with him for years. "And no matter what part of the world we're in, I always have presents for them." But it was the first time, he recalled, that his crew had celebrated the Feast of Ramadan above the Arctic Circle. That night the Arabian stokers from sun-washed Aden were mentally transported nearer home. Small swirls of pungent incense curled from their porthole past the icy white masts. At dusk I passed Mohammet Ali, the silent, hawk-nosed little man who was assigned to pull an oar alongside me in the lifeboat drill. He pulled a tarpaulin off a chicken-coop that I'd never noticed before on deck. Inside were three live chickens and a seagull. The chickens had been bought in Philadelphia on the last voyage. The seagull had been captured when it fell exhausted on deck during a gale. All would be eaten at the Feast of Ramadan. Swarthy Mohammet Ali showed his white teeth in anticipation.

During the long days I boned away at *Hugo's Easy Russian*, a concentrated course. According to the optimistic introduction, if each lesson was studied for an hour, within one hundred hours a pupil would be able to speak, read, and write Russian fluently. I started out ambitiously and learned the Russian alphabet. Then I discovered that it was taking me two or three hours a day to absorb one lesson and next day I had forgotten much of what I had learned the day before. It was almost impossible to picture the words in my mind because of the strangeness of the Russian letters.

Spurred on by the thought that the language would come in handy on the long trek across Siberia, there was some competition among us to master our textbooks. Unfortunately, it was soon evident that everyone had a different idea about the pronunciation of the simplest Russian words. We were compelled to abandon the idea of conducting conversations in Russian among ourselves because none of us understood what the others were trying to say.

The afternoons were spent reading or playing checkers. I alternated between *The Wind in the Willows* and *Gone with the Wind*. The rest of the time we spent on the bridge or in the chartroom trying to reckon our course. Not even the skipper knew what it would be. He followed closely in the wake of the leading ship of the convoy. Changes of speed and course were signaled by flags from the commodore's ship. Captain Lamont, a highly efficient master, was boyishly eager to get his answering signal flags up before the regular sailors on the cruiser *Norfolk* could send theirs to the halyards. At times he grew annoyed at our amateur efforts to help, especially when we plucked the flags from their case on the bridge and hoisted them upside down. One afternoon I watched his face contort in silent anger as a correspondent dropped the ship's best pair of binoculars on the cement floor of the bridge. We knew that the captain would have no chance to get them repaired in Russia.

Sometimes in the evening Captain Lamont let us listen to the BBC on his special receiving set. The news from Moscow wasn't good. "The Russian High Command announced that fighting was particularly fierce around Kalinin, 95 miles northwest of Moscow," said the British announcer. "Fierce battles are taking place at Mozhaisk, 60 miles west of the capital, and Maloyaroslavets, 65 miles to the southwest." Grimly the voice from London added that "the Germans are said to be throwing in masses of fresh troops and have forced the Russians to give ground just east of Mozhaisk. The Germans were halted and heavily counter-attacked, but the Red Army has failed to dislodge them on the central road to Moscow."

We began to wonder if there would be a Soviet Russia

by the time we arrived. I remember the almost audible sigh of relief that arose from the British Isles on that Sunday morning in June when Hitler reluctantly turned his face from England to seek his destiny in the East. England's back had nearly broken under the weight of fire and rubble heaped on her cities by the flaming attacks of the Luftwaffe. Every American knew that a German invasion of the island would meet with such a fanatical resistance as the Nazi Army had never before known, but every clear-thinking person realized that the little island would be left a wasteland by an invasion, win, lose, or draw. With much of the British fleet sacrificed in the narrow waters of the Channel, the island would have been at the mercy of successive waves of bombers and gray-green-clad invaders from a nation which boasted twice the manpower of England and many times the industrial power.

But the English spirit of stout-heartedness had been kept unwavering down the years by the unconscious indoctrinization of great traditions. An England made homogeneous by the tragedy of Dunkirk and the brutal night bombardments was living on hope and faith — hope that America would enter the war sooner or later, and a profound conviction that the England of King Arthur and the Knights of the Round Table would never be conquered by an upstart German paper-hanger. Even to discuss in public the odds against England facing a Germany in control of the vast industrial resources of western Europe *and* Russia was considered to be defeatism and "spreading despondency and despair." Every RAF station had posters on its walls reminding the hard-pressed, overworked pilots to "Think, dream, and talk Victory, or, for God's sake, shut up! "

Only a few weeks before Germany had turned on Russia, Whitehall's inner circles held little hope that Russia could stand for long against the invincible German dive-bombers and tanks that had overrun France and driven the British from their last European bridgehead in Greece. I had talked with Sir John Dill, Chief of the Imperial General Staff. The then highest-ranking officer in the British Army held a low opinion of Soviet Russia's strength or resolution. "If Hitler seeks the rich wheatlands of the Ukraine," he said, "Stalin will never fight back. Russia is still licking her wounds from the Finnish War." Miraculously, Russia had now been fighting back for three months in a way that astonished and elated her new British allies. The plea "if Russia will give us only three months to prepare" had given way to almost public prayer that the Red Army might "hold out until the snow flies." Yet Hitler's uncontradicted bombast that the "Stalin Line" had been broken at all points and the "last Russian Army" was "in the process of being destroyed" left hope for the survival of Moscow almost too much to yearn for.

I wanted to see Russia more than I wanted to do anything else in my life. Assignment to Moscow was the Ph.D. for a foreign correspondent. Many stories I had heard of the enigmatic and iconoclastic land. Not many people in the Western world really believed the news sent out from Russia. The Soviet was the land of propaganda, where censorship prevailed even in times of peace.

A British censor, when he learned I was going to Russia, had warned me seriously. "Be careful, Lesueur," he said. "Don't get tough with the Russian censors. Remember they shoot people over there." I laughed, but I was impressed.

I, too, had heard the stories of the bloody purges and the secret police. Of how the Russians were trying to change human nature by taking children from their mothers and rearing them in Communist institutions. Of "Godlessness" . . . "Free Love" . . . "Share and share alike" . . . "What's yours is mine and what's mine is yours." This might be a last-minute opportunity to see the gigantic Russian "test-tube" and to examine the Russian experiment before it burst like a bubble in front of the German tanks.

I still had a fifty-fifty chance, I figured. The failure of the Russians to collapse in the first three months had made me realize that the only people who really knew anything about Russia were the Germans. But they had not attacked until they added the immense military stores of captured Europe to their own tremendous stocks, not until the entire war production of western Europe was feeding arms to the battle-hardened veterans of the campaigns in Poland, Norway, the

Low Countries, France, the Balkans, and Crete. But still, having made their judgment of Soviet Russia, the Germans had chosen to attack.

Our convoy slid slowly past Jan Mayenland, one of the northern stepping-stones between Greenland and Scandinavia. As we drew closer to its icy sheerness, I heard the cries of tens of thousands of sea birds, sounding like the roar of a cascade. The northern lights were brilliant. They danced like frozen edges of prismatic color: amber, rose, light blue, and palest green, flashing on and off among the stars. We traveled in waters unvisited by merchantmen for years. Bear Island was picked up in a snow squall, so heavy that our ship seemed to be pushing through a corridor of white flakes hidden from the rest of the convoy. Off the North Cape came an excited sparkling of blinker lamps throughout the convoy as one of the destroyers caught the underwater hum of a U-boat engine. We zigzagged south like frightened sheep. Everyone felt bad when the fifth ship in the convoy lagged far behind, flashing a signal that meant: "Not under command. Keep away." Her engines had broken down. When she reappeared two days later, we were all greatly relieved.

The entire trip was like that — a sense of foreboding doom, apparent tragedy; then the uncomfortable anticlimax.

The days went by, one after another. I don't know which were worse, the brilliant, silent days when the sun broke over the ice like cracked glass, or the gray, foggy days when sea and sky met like a vast, silent bowl in which we plodded endlessly. Sometimes one of the men would spot a whale and everyone would rush to the side to make sure it wasn't a U-boat. It was something to do — some activity to break the monotony. Then again the cold, endless seas and the long, black nights. It was five below zero.

Our cargo of war aid to Russia was in danger from the cold. One noon the cruiser flashed a signal to all ships to drain the radiators of all tanks and trucks aboard. They were under tons of cargo, however, and we could do nothing. A gale hit us as we entered the White Sea. All night the *Temple Arch* tossed and twisted like a tormented elephant trying to waltz. Mountainous waves lifted her stern out of the sea, the ship shuddering as her screw raced in the air. Every plate groaned and shrieked with the strain. Sleep was impossible. Finally a heavy shock brought me out of bed with a start. A Bren gun-carrier had broken loose below decks and was madly charging into the ship's side. Wide-eyed and pale, the mates broke open the hatches and tumbled into the hold. Hours later they tamed the charging scout car with lassos of steel cable. We all had a drink when they came up. Next morning we discovered that the seas had stove in two of our packing-cases loaded with war-planes. Another ship of the convoy had pitched a $100,000 Hurricane overboard. The Arctic gale left my cabin a shambles of books and clothing. The wash-basin support had cracked and the porcelain lay shattered on the floor.

Dropping a bucket overside on a rope, I drew up a sample of the Arctic Ocean. It was so cold that I realized that the difference between getting torpedoed fully dressed or in my pajamas was of only academic interest. I recalled the captain's warning about sleeping in our clothes, but I decided to sleep and die comfortably in pajamas.

And then one day, just like any other day, out of the same cold, gray endlessness of sea, sky, and silence, we saw land! It was our first sight of Russia — a huddle of snowbound huts on a desolate point of land sticking out into the lead-colored waters of the White Sea. A line of snow-shrouded telegraph poles skirted the flat tundra. The second mate stared at it through binoculars. I turned toward him, my eyes an eager question mark. "It's a Soviet wireless station," he said. ". . . Lonely sort of place, isn't it?" It *was* a lonely sort of place. There were no signs of life, just hummocky, snowy tundra, the cluster of rude huts, and a wireless mast sticking out on the top of the world. The wind blowing off the tundra was icy and untainted. It had a peculiar sweetish flavor, like medicine. I watched a hunter's moon come up on the same side as the sun, as we steamed down the coast of Russian Lapland. It was as bright as new gold. We were plodding toward Archangel.

This was one of the most dangerous legs of our journey. Here the White Sea narrowed down to a slender mouth, bringing us within range of German bombers operating from Finland. U-boats could control these constricted waters easily, knowing that our convoy could no longer hide in the wastes of the Arctic.

The commodore's ship of the convoy sent out a call to Archangel for additional escort. We wondered when it was coming. Then suddenly we heard the whine of planes, coming louder and nearer. We gathered on the bridge, straining our eyes against the blue Arctic sky. I wondered if the Germans were going to get us after all. The tension on the ship was electric. The men stood ready at battle stations, training their guns. Would the oncoming drone turn into the shock of an exploding torpedo?

And then the black dots grew larger and turned into seaplanes, silver and gleaming. It was a Russian escort, the first time in my life that I saw the Red Star. It circled protectively over us on the wings of the Soviet planes. The skipper of the *Temple Arch* pulled a red flag out of his pocket and ran it up on the halyards. It was his secret. He had ordered the bosun to sew it during the night. We were the only ship in the convoy that possessed a state Soviet flag to run up in honor of our hosts.

The light-green water of the White Sea was whipping over the deck in an icy, frothy spray as a tiny motorboat chugged through the choppy waves toward us. It held three people. A girl was steering. The others were men in the blue uniforms of the Red Fleet. They were the Russian pilots.

The girl brought the motorboat close alongside and the pilot clambered up the rope ladder we threw down. As he climbed up to the bridge to take over, we turned our attention to the girl. She was the first woman we had seen since leaving Scotland. She wore a fur hat and rubber boots and was bundled up in a big sheepskin coat, looking for all the world like a small blond bear. Eddy Gilmore, the only correspondent who had declined to study Russian aboard the ship, was trying to talk to the girl in his Southern drawl. They had some difficulty until he began the international language by tossing down some cigarettes and chocolate to her. She said: "*Spasiba bolshoi* (Thank you, very much)." We gathered from the rest of her talk that she was an apprentice pilot. Her round tanned face was lit up by a good-natured smile as she waved good-by and the Russian pilot took over the helm of our ship.

We threaded our way down the tortuous channel of the North Dvina. The Russian officer gave commands to his helmsman in the international language of the sea, calling out in English "port" and "starboard." All day we grated against the ice floes that hid the channel. I kept thinking: "You're in Russia at last. A few minutes more and you'll be in Archangel." The giant ice-breaker *Stalin* battered its way through the floes ahead of us, and as we passed an icy headland, I caught my first sight of Archangel.

It was a sprawling city of wood. I could see the shining gold onion dome of a church amidst the snow-covered shacks. Piles of timber covered the immense wooden docks on both sides of the harbor. The skipper said to me: "This is the largest timber port in the world. Russia has plenty of wood — and plenty of space."

We put our line over on Russian soil as dusk fell over Archangel on the last day of October. All night long the skipper remained on the bridge trying to force the ship to the wharfside against the fresh-forming ice pans. Russian labor gangs worked unceasingly to get the ship alongside. I spotted an Englishman standing on the dockside. He was easily distinguishable because his blue British ulster stood out like a lighthouse among the dark-green overcoated Russian labor corps.

"I'm an American correspondent," I shouted. "What's the news?"

"There's plenty of news, but it's all bad," was the answering shout. He came closer and told me that Odessa, Kharkov, and the Crimea had fallen. "Moscow," he said, "is under a state of siege, with the Germans only sixty-five miles away. You fellows won't be able to go to Moscow, because the correspondents and the embassies have been evacuated to the rear."

"Where to?"

"I think it's a place called Kuibyshev, back on the Volga," he answered.

I passed the bad news around to the rest of the correspondents and we searched in vain for Kuibyshev on our maps. Finally we determined that it must be the Volga city once called Samarra. All that I knew of Samarra was its use as a part of the title of the book *Appointment in Samarra*, and after the weeks of worry on the ship that somehow didn't seem like sufficient information. It had an ominous sound.

A muscular Red Army sentry posted at the gangplank barred our way from the ship with his rifle. We would have to wait until the Russian customs men arrived. They didn't come until the afternoon, after darkness had already fallen in the Arctic Circle. They went through our baggage, surprising us with their leniency. Nothing was taken from us nor was there any customs duty. The officials only admired our possessions. One of them had red hair. I don't know why that seemed strange to me, but somehow it was surprising to find out that there were red-haired Russians as well as red-haired Americans.

The man with the red hair shook his head in admiration at my noiseless typewriter. In English he said: "What a beauty!" Then he noted down its number in my passport. "You must take it out of the country when you leave," he explained. "Otherwise, by speculation, you might sell it for an enormous price in Moscow." He looked at my wrist watch, too, and asked if I had any other jewelry that could be sold at speculator's prices. I hadn't.

My passport stamped, I didn't wait for another word. I grabbed my hat and coat and hurried down the snow-covered gangplank. The Russian sentry read every Russian word in my passports and then motioned me on. I was on Russian soil at last.

I lit a cigarette, but within half a dozen steps I heard an officious voice behind me. It belonged to a heavy-set, middle-aged Russian woman. It seemed she was a watchman, and smoking was not permitted on the TNT-cluttered docks.

The unloading of our ships began immediately. A large floating dock had moored alongside and the holds of the *Temple Arch* were opened to let the big chains lift out the tanks and gun-carriers. After the monotony of ship life, the floodlit dockside scene seemed high drama. It was Russia's hour of supreme crisis. She needed so much, and even the little we had brought was a help. I noticed that the long, silent lines of laborers, dressed in green-gray army overcoats and peaked cloth hats, were being guarded by armed sentries. The British dock officer explained that they were prisoners working off their crimes and breaches of discipline. Their unceasing toil had etched lines of hopeless exhaustion in the patient, wooden faces of the prison corps. Even the faces of their guards wore a look of weary resignation to the futility of life. It could have been a scene from Dostoievsky.

I remembered how it had been a little more than a year ago in France during those bright June days when the Germans were driving on Paris. Panic and fear were written on the faces of the French. Work had come to a standstill. Yet here in the Arctic, I could see work going on with ruthless energy as the Germans advanced on Moscow. The grim knowledge of the life-and-death struggle outside the Soviet capital was stamped on every movement of the labor gang. They looked not only as though they realized that they could see no end to their toil, but under the inexorable direction of the State, they, too, were responding to Russia's terrible reverses with new efforts. The brutish straining of the men hauling on ropes on the bright yellow floodlit snow was in its way a terrible sight, but an awe-inspiring one. It carried the answer to great questions in my mind. The war was not over. Russia was not giving up.

November 1   ✉ Today we crossed the ice-packed harbor to the city of Archangel. I found myself looking at a typical American frontier town of a hundred years ago. The snow-filled streets were jammed with round-faced men and women in fur hats, felt boots, and dirty, serviceable sheepskin coats. They needed only coon tails on their caps to make them look like an army of Daniel Boones.

The trolley cars, clanging their way along the ice-bound main street, looked as incongruous to me as they would have in Kentucky in 1800. The cars were so packed that people clung on the sides and stood three deep hanging on the steps. People were hurrying along the crowded sidewalks. There seemed to be a kind of irresistible urge to go somewhere. We were carried away in the throng. There were a great many soldiers about, part of the Red Army from the Finnish front. A bus full of wounded was being unloaded in front of a long, wooden hospital building. We foreigners were the only ones who stopped to watch. The cold was so intense that the snow drummed like dry sand under the feet of the stretcher-bearers.

Three little boys brushed past us, bundled up to their ears in handsome fur coats. They were skating along the icy street and each of them was carrying a brown leather briefcase. I thought it was funny — school children with briefcases on the edge of the Arctic Circle. Bearded hillbillies plodded through the snow. I was very conscious of an unpleasant sour odor when they were close. Later I learned that this was the characteristic smell of the Russian backwoodsmen. Their clothes were impregnated with the smoke of a popular tobacco substitute, mahorka. Some of them hadn't shaved since boyhood. I felt my own face ruefully. Gone was the carefully nurtured three weeks' beard of the Arctic voyage. The chief engineer of the *Temple Arch* had forced me to shave. Wielding a clipper and muttering in a voice slightly thickened with the rum of our arrival celebration, he had backed me into a corner and clipped a white swath across the beard which I fondly imagined made me look like a Viking. Now I saw that in Archangel clean-shaven faces were clearly out of place.

The Arctic city was a jumble of gray, unpainted wooden houses and log cabins, interspersed with brand-new yellow wooden dormitories. It was a city of wood. As I reached the main square, I saw my first statue of Lenin. It was a small, snow-shrouded granite figure in civilian clothes, pointing in the traditional fashion toward the future. The statue dominated the public square. Near by were new gray stucco buildings — a library, a theater, a three-story schoolhouse, and a newspaper office. Here was the evidence that the famous Soviet five-year plans had reached even the Arctic. My interest quickened at the sight of a tall, snow-encrusted radio mast. I noticed several men in European clothes and felt hats, carrying briefcases and looking as foreign as we did, walking out of the government buildings. I decided that they must be Communist Party members.

We ate our lunch in the public café as our first adventure, making our way through the double storm doors of the Northern Restaurant, after laboriously translating letter by letter the Russian sign over the door. The hubbub of conversation died down as we entered the warm, close atmosphere. As we checked our coats I got my first sight of the inevitable Russian cloakroom, a necessity in a country where people wear such heavy clothes. The waiting lines of soldiers and their girls gave way before us and they beckoned us to go straight ahead. Our clothes stamped us unmistakably as foreigners, and this unusual, automatic courtesy was to become part of my life in Russia.

Russia, I decided, was a land of the primary colors. The restaurant was decorated in unsubtle shades of red. We sat down and ordered vodka. The waitress, a pure Slavic type, was blonde and broad. Her nails were emblazoned with ox-heart red paint. She left us and came back with the manageress, a woman with horn-rimmed spectacles. She, too, shook her head over our request for vodka and explained that none was being sold these days because it was all going to the front. Then she hesitated, looked us over thoughtfully, and, deciding that we were really foreigners, changed her mind and told the waitress to bring us a full carafe. We ate a hot meal of cabbage soup, browned beef and potatoes, and stewed fruit. The food was good, but the bill was staggering. At the rate of five rubles to the dollar, it cost us each four dollars. I included an English sixpence in the tip. The waitress looked at it coldly. Apparently she was not a coin-collector. It was my first recognition of the fact that coins have small value in Russia. There is very little that you can buy for less than a paper ruble.

As we left the restaurant I wondered where some of the men sprawled on the sidewalk were getting their vodka. Several had fallen peacefully asleep in the snow. The marching peasants circled them carefully with glances that held only amusement tinged with envy.

It was getting dark as we made our way back to the ferry. I asked a blue-uniformed militiaman on traffic duty where the ferry landed. He looked me over carefully and then directed me up some wooden stairs to an unpainted frame house. I thought it must be the ferry office. Pushing aside the heavy door, I entered a bare room where a hard-looking military man was questioning a group of peasants. I wondered what I had got into and decided to retreat, but the door was locked. Nervously I waited. I knew I had wandered into the Archangel headquarters of the Russian secret police. Suddenly the door opened again and a Red Army girl strode into the room. I backed around behind her, got my foot in the doorway, and left in a hurry.

We heard the tooting of a launch. It pulled up to a nearby dock and disgorged a mass of sheepskin-coated peasants. It was the ferry. While we waited to embark, a strange shambling figure came wobbling down the wharfside. It wore a British sailor's duffel coat, topped by a shock of flaming red hair. We recognized a Scots sailor off our ship. With a seaman's sure sense of direction he had gone directly to the source of black-market vodka. He could still talk, but had lost control of his legs. We propped him up and led him across the tottering gangplank. He stumbled into the aft cabin, followed by a mob of pushing peasants. We never saw him again. He missed his ship. Every type of peasant jammed his way aboard the tiny wooden launch — slant-eyed Eskimo types, Samoyeds, Mamalukes, Tatars, Kirghiz, Poles, Letts, Finns, Estonians, Ukrainians, and snug-nosed Russians. Everyone carried something — a balalaika, a knapsack, a skinned and frozen sheep, even a log or two. The passengers seemed as laden with burdens as energetic ants.

A gloomy dusk settled over the frozen harbor as the launch pulled out. The icepack had become thicker during the day. The small, overcrowded ship smashed against the barriers of heavy pack ice, with a tearing crunch as though her wooden bottom were ripping off. At times the bow of the launch slid half out of the water across a solid floe, tipping the ship up until the ice sank under the weight of the hull.

I began to wonder if I had braved the perils of a convoy

to Russia only to sink miserably in the harbor of Archangel. Even the ferry pilot seemed concerned and posted a lookout atop the wheelhouse to search for leads in the icepack. The launch followed these until they ended in barriers of heavy ice. Time after time the launch lost steam and the crew piled more wood into the firebox.

A peasant sitting next to me said: "Cigarette?"

When I reached to offer him one of mine, he shook his head vigorously, tore a strip off the newspaper he carried in his pocket, and carefully rolled me one out of mahorka. The correspondents seemed to be the only passengers who were worried. As a form of whistling in the dark, we began humming: "I Love to Ride a Ferry." The response was instantaneous. A half-dozen sheepskin-coated peasants who had imbibed freely of vodka clambered over their fellow travelers to join in a Russian version of the song. The boat listed perceptibly. Nervously we stopped singing for fear that all the passengers might want to gather on our side.

Finally only a hundred yards of new-formed ice separated us from shore. The launch ground to a halt, the crew threw a couple of planks over the ice, and we waited to see who would make the first crossing. It was a man with a wooden leg. With his crutches he hobbled along the planks, slipped, and fell headlong. Several peasants rushed overside to help him, and they led a strange procession to the snow-covered dock. After several husky peasant women, balalaikas on their backs and babies in their arms, had made the precarious crossing, we decided it was safe. Land never felt so good under my feet.

We stayed on the ship that night, too gloomy to read or play cards. If the rest of Russia was like Archangel, I knew my assignment here was going to be an ordeal. I had visions of living in a log cabin for a year trying to interpret Russia through the minds of 193,000,000 hillbillies who didn't look as though they had many reactions. I had been prepared to visit a primitive country, but the sudden shock of being transported back a century or so was depressing.

I asked the skipper if any Russian officials had inquired about our presence. No one had. It was obvious that with Moscow besieged and the fate of the State in the balance, the Soviet authorities had other things on their minds besides the welfare of a group of newly arrived foreign correspondents.

November 2–3 ⚡ The work of unloading the tanks went on day and night. The men of the British tank school helped in the ceaseless work, but the English tank officers were obviously disappointed. The Russians wouldn't hold the tanks in Archangel until the British taught the Russian crews how to run them.

One British officer said to me with a shrug: "All these Russians want to know is 'Where is the clutch?' It looks as though our tank school came to Russia for nothing. They seem to know all there is to know about a tank and they need these on the Moscow front immediately."

I asked him when a train was leaving for Moscow. He said: "I hear there's one leaving tomorrow night."

With this news, we decided not to wait for the Soviet authorities to look us up. We would get out of Archangel somehow. We told our plan to Captain Lamont and with a sailor's foresight he warned that we'd better take at least a week's supply of food with us. He generously agreed to supply it out of the ship's stores.

Faced with the problem of lugging two heavy suitcases into the unknown, I approached the bosun with an appeal for a handmade knapsack. He stayed up through the night sewing one out of heavy sailcloth. Next morning I put all my essential clothing into the huge sack, gave one of my suitcases to the ginger-haired mate, and packed the rest of my outfit into my remaining handbag, to be discarded in case I had to make a run for it somewhere in the interior of Russia.

November 4 ⚡ The ice became so thick over Archangel harbor in the past twenty-four hours that all ferries have stopped for the winter. The first of the intrepid Russian peasants have started to walk over the mile of ice afoot with their ever present bundles on their backs.

It didn't look as though it would be possible for Allied ships to force their way into Archangel this winter. The British dock official said to me: "Don't worry, the Russians have provided for that. They have two big ice-breakers, the *Stalin* and the *Lenin,* both 10,000 tons and as big as cruisers." He spoke of a new port of Molotovsk, about twenty miles down the bay. "It won't be on your map," he added. "A month ago there was nothing there. Since then the Russians have sent in ten thousand workers and it has become a thriving city."

We took our farewell of the ship's crew and put our bags and food aboard a small truck already loaded down with British diplomatic mail pouches. It was midnight when I left the ship, knapsack on my back and typewriter in my hands. There was a blinding snowstorm, but the labor corps was working through the night under the floodlights. Shivering, insecure, and worried, I walked along the tracks to the station, trying to imagine what the rest of Russia was like and where I would be within the next week.

The rest of the baggage and the diplomatic pouches had been dumped in the snow of the railroad yard, but there was no one there to direct us. We decided to post a guard over the baggage while the rest of us took shelter from the cold within the station. An hour passed and no one came to claim the diplomatic mail. I helped drain a bottle of sickeningly cold gin that we placed in a snowdrift to keep the "baggage guard" from freezing. Finally the life-giving gin gave out, but greatly heartened, we decided to lug the baggage and pouches inside the station. We did it in exhausting relays, dragging the bags through the crowded Archangel station, unavoidably bumping into sleeping peasant families stretched out on the floor. There had not been a train for the past three days and most of the sheepskin- and sackcloth-clad peasants had been living in their places in line in the warm, close station. They muttered in their sleep as we stumbled past them, and a baby began to cry. With remarkable dignity and unconcern its mother opened her quilted jacked and nursed it.

I entered a less crowded room over which hung a sign: "AGITPUNKT (Agitation Point)." It was filled with young soldiers, from twenty to twenty-five years old. These members of Soviet Russia's first generation were alert and bright-looking. A group of them was playing pool. At one end of the room was a moving-picture screen and at the other end hung red muslin banners emblazoned in huge white letters with war slogans.

An hour passed and finally a British officer arrived, Colonel Hulls. We explained our situation and told him that we'd been guarding the mail pouches. He thanked us and without blinking an eye heard our confession that we had no Russian money, no railroad tickets, and only an ambition to get somewhere to see the war. He, too, was trying to reach Moscow to get some of his possessions left behind in the evacuation of the diplomatic corps. He argued with the station master to get us seats on the train, but was told that there was no room for us. Then he called the Soviet Foreign Office representative in Archangel on the telephone and left a message with the secretary on duty.

While we waited, I questioned him about the *"Agit-punkt"* room. He said we would see those in every station and in every city in the Soviet Union. "Those are the places where lectures are given by prominent Communist Party members," this veteran of Russia explained. "They talk about international affairs, internal economy, and the course of the war." Colonel Hulls said this information was carried by the politically and socially active Russians to the other 190,000,000 members of the public who do not belong to the Communist Party. It was the first time I had ever heard anyone refer to the bulk of the Russian population by their Soviet title: "Non-Party Bolsheviks." The colonel added that the Agitation Points were a kind of town-meeting halls, but since the war all foreigners were barred from attendance.

Then the phone rang. It was the Soviet Foreign Office representative. The scowling station master answered and suddenly changed his mind about the availability of seats on the train. He assured us that there was plenty of room if we hurried. I did hurry, rushing our bags through the sleeping crowds on the station floor and waking the baby once more. The diplomatic mail pouches were placed in a sealed freight car, for there was no room in the narrow train

compartment. Parker, Gilmore, and I took advantage of this
and put our extra suitcases in the freight car with the mail.
We were assured it would get to Moscow or Kuibyshev before we did, but my clothes were to have many adventures
before I saw them half a year later.

November 5–22   🏴 The train left Archangel at
two in the morning. We found ourselves bunked four to a
compartment and we undressed in the dark. The food and
baggage were stowed in a large compartment over the train
corridor, built for just such a purpose. Distances are great
in Russia and travelers are expected to come prepared.

When I awoke in the morning, the great adventure had
begun. The train was clicking smoothly over the Russian
wide-gauge tracks south toward Moscow and the battlefront.

I was passing over the top of the world and I felt that
way. On both sides of the train flat, rolling tundra stretched
limitlessly. I rose from my berth and broke into the food
stores, carelessly biting into an apple from our slender
stocks. The conductor, a simple, smiling peasant, eager to
please, got his samovar going and we breakfasted on tea,
bread and butter, jam — and the apple.

After a hundred-mile run our train stopped almost every
fifteen minutes at a siding to let more important trains go by.
The subarctic villages were of new yellow wood, one-story
shacks with the snow piled high against them. In every village ran small packs of half-breed Samoyed sled dogs. Their
tails hung wolflike. When I got off the train to stretch my
legs, I approached one pack with a piece of bread. They
backed away slowly, riveting me with a cold, yellow stare.

I walked up to examine our engine. Although manufactured in 1934, it was extraordinarily high and its awkward
drive-shaft made it look like a gigantic sewing-machine. It
was a wood-burner. But these Soviet locomotives were powerful, I noticed as I watched long freight trains run past us.
It was military traffic. The freight-car roofs were camouflaged with pine branches, and some trains were pulled by
giant Diesel engines that read: "Archangel to Baku" — the
Arctic to Persia, I thought, and all of it Russia.

As I watched the ammunition trains go by with the pine branches atop, I curiously remembered one of the most pathetic sights I ever saw. It was in France during the June retreat. On a hot, dusty roadside, clogged with weary refugees, a young French girl wheeled a baby-carriage. Her face was streaked with dust and perspiration, her forehead creased with worry. She had placed several branches around the baby-carriage. She, too, had seen this form of camouflage on the trucks going up to the front and she hoped it might save her baby from being dive-bombed.

The conductor, or *provodnik*, assured us that the trip to Moscow would not take longer than a week, so we dug heartily into our stores for supper. The sunset over the tundra was a wild debauch of color. Reflected back by the snow glare, the sky flamed from yellow through salmon and finally to deep purple as the sun sank in exhaustion. As we traveled south from the flat top of the world toward Moscow, the scenery changed from hummocky tundra to clumps of dark-green pines.

I saw whole families working at the roadside — men, women, and children turning the frozen ground into earthworks with picks and crowbars. We knew the Germans were already east of Leningrad, only 150 miles away from us at Tikhvin.

Colonel Hulls, tacitly in charge of our group, organized us with semi-military discipline. We took turns preparing the food and cleaning the car. He was singularly undisturbed by the German advance. We learned that he had already escaped from the Germans once in this war and once before in 1917. I coaxed his story out of him. He had been stationed in the Maginot Line with the 51st Highland Division during the invasion of France. His regiment held off a German feint at the Maginot Line while the main Nazi force plunged through the Forest of Ardennes and outflanked his troops. The Scots Highlanders were marched back toward the Channel. They went into action on the Somme and gained some ground. One morning they awoke to find that the French Army on their flank had been withdrawn. The Highlanders had to fall back, too. Then they received word to retreat on Le Havre for embarkation to

England. Destroying their heavy arms and equipment, the Scottish division marched afoot to a rendezvous at Saint-Valery-en-Caux. When they reached it, they found the Germans already in possession of Le Havre. The 51st Division had arrived just one day too late. The French Ninth Army surrendered and the virtually unarmed 51st Highlanders could do nothing but surrender too. Colonel Hulls related grimly that although they were disorganized by their heady triumph, the Germans nevertheless had prepared a prison camp in advance to receive the retreating Scotsmen.

Then the prison march of the Highland division began toward Germany. Guarded by infantry and armored vehicles, they were moved east, stage by stage. The colonel knew from his experience in the last war that if he was going to escape, this would be his best chance. With a naval liaison officer who had been sent to assist in the evacuation, he planned his break. He could speak French and the naval Officer knew German. One night as they were being moved to the next camp, they loitered behind and escaped into a wood unnoticed. They resolved to go back to Rouen. Since they both wore British uniforms, they slept by day in forests and walked by night through strange country, by compass. One night they got tired of crossing the fields and barking their shins on fences, so they walked after dawn through a big park and ran smack into a house guarded by a German sentry. It was still half dark and they hurriedly talked loudly in German. The sentry failed to recognize their uniforms in the semi-darkness. But they vowed never to take such chances again. They continued at night through woods and fields and kept away from the roads. Running upon a young French woodchopper, they told him their story outright — how they were half-starved and living only on potatoes they dug from the fields at night. He told them to wait in the woods until he returned with his brother, a French barber. Again they explained their plight and the friendly barber promised to bring them civilian clothes. They put the French jackets on over their uniform blouses, because they wanted to keep their identity as military men, should they be taken prisoner. The barber directed them to an inn at Rouen. They walked there that night.

30318

The frightened innkeeper remained doubtful for a long time, but finally he broke down and took them in, hid them in the attic, and fed them. He even took the precaution to show them the best way out over the roofs if trouble arose. That night Colonel Hulls and the British naval officer conferred with the innkeeper over the bridges of the Seine. They learned that all the bridges had been blown up, but there was a little rowboat being operated by an old fisherman for the benefit of refugees. The loyal innkeeper gave them some food, some francs, and even bicycles. They paid their two francs fifty to the ancient fisherman and crossed the Seine undetected on the refugee ferry. Pedaling over the exploded bridges, they watched the bodies of French soldiers being dredged from the river. Some bridges had been blown up while the French were still retreating over them.

The going was easier when they got on the other side of the river. Food was more plentiful and some towns had been completely untouched by the war. At last the two British officers reached the coast at Le Havre and searched for an unguarded boat. The French-speaking Colonel Hulls decided to do a bit of reconnoitering and told the British naval officer to keep under cover. When he returned late that afternoon, he was shocked to see his friend standing in the midst of a group of German soldiers. While he watched, horrified, the group broke up and he saw his friend walk back to the rendezvous triumphantly puffing a cigarette. He confessed to Hulls that he was so hard up for a smoke he decided to approach the Germans and tell them that he was a Dutchman. They had accepted him as such, with his badly accented German, and asked him to point out the sights of Le Havre to them. He gladly accommodated them and they rewarded him with a cigarette.

Days of searching and starving followed until the two Britishers found a battered sailboat. They repaired it and crossed the English Channel from Cherbourg to the Isle of Wight. It took them four days, and at one point they had become too weak to raise the sails. Hulls said the two hours he spent lying on a bed in an English cottage called Seaman's Rest, on the Isle of Wight, were the happiest hours of his life.

In the next car of our train were a colonel of the Red Air Force and several naval officers who had been on a military mission to Britain. I had first noticed them, looking lost and bewildered, on the station platform at Glasgow. Although they spoke little English, no one had accompanied them to the convoy port from London. Now in their homeland they were exceedingly pleasant and helpful to us foreigners. Colonel Fedrovi told me proudly that he had bombed Germany from the west on several occasions as an observer in a British warplane. It was the first chance I had had to examine a Russian officer's uniform closely. The loose blouse of finely woven dark khaki extended half-way down to the knees in traditional Russian fashion. There were two large pockets at the chest and a dark Sam Browne belt gathered the blouse in at the waist. It looked comfortable and practical, since there were no buttons to tear off in front. An officer's cap with a light-blue band denoting the Air Force and dark-blue breeches and well-polished Russian boots completed his outfit. He wore a smart brown leather coat.

The third day out of Archangel our train waited on a siding for two hours while the tanks we had come with from Britain hurtled past toward Moscow. They still bore the painted inscriptions put on by British workmen: "Here's one for Uncle Joe" and "Another one for Iron Mike Molotov." The tank train was at least a mile and a quarter long, but I could see that in relation to the vast distances to be defended, those tanks would have to be stretched out mighty thin. I knew this was certainly a change from the last war, however, when, historians said, war materials were piled on the Archangel docks for months in the great confusion.

As we traveled farther south, the country changed to thick, trackless pine forests. The burning sunsets colored the snowy tips of the trees like a forest fire. The peasant huts I could see from the train had obviously not changed their architectural style down the centuries. Gesturing toward the wilderness, the Russian colonel explained that this was some of the finest hunting country in all Europe. The old peasant woodsmen, he said, still hunted bear with dogs and spears in these dark forests.

At the city of Yaroslav we met out first luck. Colonel Fedrovi telephoned to the Intourist Hotel to prepare us a hot dinner. Unfortunately, it was not until two a.m. that we arrived at Yaroslav, but the obliging commandant of the station produced a hot meal out of nowhere. Then Colonel Fedrovi announced that there was room for only four people at the Intourist Hotel, so Gilmore, McGloughlin, and I stayed behind to guard the baggage. I huddled on a bench near the station coal stove. Refugees from the near-by front stretched out on the floor beside me. They were mostly women and children, carrying the inevitable loaves of brown bread.

The warmth soon put me to sleep. I was awakened by an extraordinary conversation. McGloughlin and Gilmore were making signs to two strange Russian men. Apparently the Russians wished them to go somewhere. By way of answering them, I saw Gilmore flap his arms and questioningly repeat: "RAF?" Sleepily I gathered that he was trying to find out whether the men had been sent after us by the Red Air Force colonel. McGloughlin, the Australian, was also going through a difficult pantomime. He was trying to act out the word: "Now?" He kept repeating it with wild gestures. The Russians understood not a word nor any of the pantomime, but agreed to everything. We clambered into their car and drove off into the night. I was greatly relieved when they led us to our companions, sleeping on small cots in a hotel dormitory. I felt a lot better, too, after a breakfast of raw herring, cheese, brown bread, hunter's vodka, and tea.

It was November 7, the first wartime anniversary of the Revolution in a quarter of a century. The refugees in the hotel clustered around the radio loudspeakers, listening to the voice of Stalin making his first speech from Red Square since the war began. The refugees were delighteded by the gesture of a daring Red Army parade before the Kremlin under the very noses of the German bombers. They didn't know it would be followed by the heaviest mass air raid Moscow had ever suffered.

Stalin's speech was unintelligible to me, but I was deeply impressed by the cheers which followed it. For fully ten minutes they resounded throughout the hotel as the loudspeakers trembled with the noise. When it was over I could see that the Russian refugees were measurably heartened. I gathered that they had come to the tragic conclusion that Stalin had left Moscow and the city was lost, but now they heard the voice of the leader once more from the very walls of the Kremlin and the lusty cheers of the gathered Red Army. I felt greatly reassured about my own immediate future.

Colonel Fedrovi grinned delightedly and told me that Stalin had declared that everything was going to be all right within another year, and that in six months or twelve the Germans would collapse from the strain. I was pleased and yet a bit astonished at this Russian officer's unquestioning belief in Stalin's words. Skeptical myself, I could see that the Russians had complete faith in their leader.

The hotel was crowded with refugees. Scores of tow-headed little boys and girls played in the corridors, unconcerned about their futures. I looked at them curiously, wondering what the coming years meant for them. Their fate was being decided just 150 miles away where the German tanks and flame-throwers were battering their vicious way toward Moscow. I wondered if they would be Soviet citizens or a part of the nameless population of conquered Europe. There was no doubt on which side the little boys were. A number of them wore tiny Red Army uniforms like those of their fathers at the near-by front. I watched them play "Russians and Germans" up and down the halls. The results were the reverse of what was happening at the real front.

At dusk we drove back to the station to find out whether we could go into Moscow. The station commandant had just returned from the front. Squat, thick-chested, and broad-shouldered, he was uncompromisingly optimistic, but when he remarked that he had organized the last train out of Mozhaisk, bringing 1,500 German prisoners with him, I realized for the first time that the last big town directly in front of Moscow must have fallen. The Germans, I knew, must be marching up the Napoleon Road, less than fifty miles from Moscow's gates. I felt a pang of despair.

The commandant deepened my pessimism by declaring that we could not enter the besieged capital. He would give us a car of our own and reroute us northward again to the Valogda junction, which we had passed two days ago. There we would connect with the Trans-Siberian railroad, go east to the northern Urals and Asia, and then recross the southern Urals to join the diplomatic colony at Kuibyshev on the Volga. He sent a soldier to conduct us to our new railroad car. I helped lug our food stocks across the snowy tracks, deeply thankful that I could carry my belongings on my back in the already invaluable knapsack.

Our new traveling home was a disappointment, but we were glad to get out of the snow and the ten-below-zero cold. It was the Russian "hard," third-class coach with no upholstery on the seats — just eight hard wooden bunks. A small compartment in the rear housed the toilet and washbowl. The conductor slept in a tiny broom closet next to his samovar.

Colonel Hulls looked around drearily, then shrugged his shoulders and reminded us of an old axiom of war: "Every change is for the worse." The conductor gave us our bedding — a sheet and a thin rocky mattress with slate-colored blanket that felt as cold and hard as a stone shingle. Before I settled down to sleep there was a commotion at the station. From the half-frosted windows I saw colored lights arching skyward out of a near-by wood. Colonel Fedrovi pulled out his revolver and jumped from the train, followed by the naval officers. He came back a half-hour later, tired and disappointed. He explained that German parachutists had been firing the signal lights to inform their Nazi bombers that the station was crowded with military traffic.

The train had not moved by morning and the bombers finally arrived. Anti-aircraft guns slammed with a strange hollow sound in the sub-zero air. Five German planes dropped twenty bombs into the snow along the tracks, hitting only one freight car. Unfortunately, the damaged car was one carrying evacuated factory workers to the east. I watched the wounded being carried away from the burning wreckage.

I was glad to get moving even though it took us three days to retrace our way to the Vologda junction. As the train passed finally onto the tracks of the Trans-Siberian toward the Ural Mountains, the scenery began to change. The dense pine forests of the north gave way to silver-birch forests interspersed with great clearings that marked the extreme limits of the great southern steppes. The trackless snow, glittering like a wedding cake, was even heavier as we moved east. The temperature clung to ten below zero.

We began to pass mile after mile of loaded flat cars and box cars standing motionless on the sidings. The cars were of a strange type, not seen in western Europe. They were peculiar because of the number of little smoke stacks that sprang out of the roof. People were living in them. These were the evacuated factory workers moving from the conquered west to the safety of the Urals and Siberia. The flat cars that interspersed the inhabited box cars were piled high with refugee machinery. The workers were traveling with their machines in complete units. Snow draped the machines and rolling homes alike. Unfortunately, some of the giant lathes, generators, electrical equipment, and stamping mills had been moved from their threatened factories too quickly to throw canvas over them. The snow was seeping down into their finely polished precision gears. Some of the machines had come a long way. Stamped in steel were the words: "Bullard, Bridgeport, Connecticut," and "Cincinnati." At dusk we stopped at a siding where the slow-moving factories had evidently been waiting for days while military traffic took precedence over the single-track road. It was a refugee encampment. I hadn't had a bath for a long time, but I hesitated to emulate some of the refugee workers. The men had stripped to the waist and were rubbing themselves down with snow. It was fifteen below zero at nightfall.

They were the perfect refugees, as adaptable as pioneers. The women were cooking over campfires that dotted the snow. Small children were dragging dead branches out of the near-by forest. All seemed cheerful and healthy. The future of half the population of Russia was being decided in front of Moscow, but they knew that they would be safe soon in the Urals and Siberia. Like the toilet facilities in our car, theirs, too, were frozen in their refugee box cars. The tracks and woods were their latrines. They were unashamed of

their natural functions. Several women squatted near campfires nursing newborn infants. The babies were wrapped in
flashing red blankets like papooses, only their faces with
big eyes and wet mouths showing.

I recall the surge of refugees in France, little more than a
year ago. It had been completely disorganized. All central
France was a great traffic jam. The roadside had been littered with furniture, mattresses, and broken-down jalopies.
Food was a rarity. Every restaurant in central France was
sold out before more than a third of the long lines of refugees
could be fed. It was obvious to me that the Russian evacuation was part of a well-organized plan. I felt less pessimistic
at the sight of these well-fed, happy-go-lucky people. They
had none of that look of inward, searching worry of the
French refugees. Despite their plight, they didn't seem to
feel any insecurity. It was becoming clear that the German
advance into the heart of Russia had long been considered
by the Soviet Government.

We kept our dwindling supply of candles lit long enough
to prepare supper that night. Later, as we sat in the dark,
Colonel Hulls said cheerfully that the Russians were carrying out one of the most important strategic methods of
resisting enemy attacks. He quoted the hundred-year old
counsel of Clausewitz and explained that he thought the Red
Army had fallen back deliberately, deciding to put up resistance in the interior. In his Scottish brogue he explained
that although a great part of the country was falling into
German hands, the Germans would sooner or later find
themselves in difficulties as they moved farther from their
own native land and bases. "If Moscow holds," he said,
"sooner or later the German offensive power will shatter
itself against the planned Russian defense." He pointed out
the window and said: "There's your answer. Do you think
that whole factories and their workers could be moved like
this if it weren't planned?"

Next morning we followed a band of young Russian girls
over the snowy fields to an isolated peasant's cottage. There
was an ancient ice-covered well in the yard, equipped with
a long peeled log boom that had to be tilted to bring the
water from the bottom. We filled our water jugs and looked

at the high-bosomed ruddy-faced refugees. Their bright scarves wrapped round their heads were a colorful splash against the sunlit snow. Even the padded jacket of one of these eighteen-year-olds did not conceal the fact that she was pregnant. Her baby would certainly be born before she reached the haven of Siberia. But her rosy, good-natured face was unlined by worry. She took her turn tilting the heavy log boom. On their return the laughing girls halted to help a wounded Red Army man re-dress his bandaged foot. They sat down in the snow with him. Back at our stalled train, I walked over to talk to a family boiling water over a campfire. I wondered why they left the warmth of their box cars for the sub-zero out-of-doors, but although I shivered, they were talkative and cheery.

The setting was as attractive as an old-fashioned Christmas card. Slender silver birches were weighted down with snow and the dark pine clumps were tipped with gleaming silver from the pale yellow sun. In the frosty ice-box air the family munched on dry and heavy whole-grain rye bread. In a pot cooked the inevitable Russian "kasha" — whole grains of brown barley. The beshawled mother drew a dried fish from a canvas bag and shredded it over the boiling barley. Their little daughter jumped out of the open doorway of the near-by freight car, her brown hair hanging in braids. She wore felt boots, but no hat and only a thin cotton dress. Her mother ordered her back into the freight car to get fully dressed. I offered them cigarettes and they took them with a smile of deep appreciation. They motioned for me to squat down next to them. The father said they had been on the road for five weeks after being evacuated, bag and baggage, from Pskov on the Estonian frontier. "We brought along all the food we could carry," he said, "but our apartment, the Germans have it now." His wife murmured: *"Nichevo* (No matter)." I was soon forced to straighten up from my awkward position squatting on my heels. The Russian family remained comfortable and motionless. I recalled that the only other person I'd ever seen remain comfortably in that position for a long while was a half-Indian guide in the Maine woods.

The Russian small fry enjoyed the escape from city life

most of all. They were earnestly dragging branches across the snow to replenish the fire. The clink of hatchets rang out under the cold platinum-blue sky. They reminded me of a Boy Scout troop out on a winter hike. The sun had warmed the snow to excellent packing quality, so I fashioned a snowball and chucked it at the kids. It was a signal for fun and laughter. The tall foreign-dressed strangers in their midst were met by a storm of snowballs. Our American baseball experience gave us the edge and we had little trouble holding off the pack of bright-eyed youngsters. During the excitement I noticed that the ranks of the children in front of us had become depleted. I thought they had grown tired of the snowball fight, but suddenly I was hit by a chunk of icy snow in the back of the neck. I turned around to discover that we had been surrounded. One of the fathers smiled at me and said: *"Kak partizans* (They fight like partizans)!"

Then our engine whistled and we rushed aboard, bound for the Urals. As we rolled on through the heavy pine forests that closed in on each side of the track, I remembered that I saw no signs of an all too familiar sight in America — the ugly scars of forest fires. I couldn't figure out why. As we neared the Urals, the countryside began to resemble the rolling hillsides of New England. The tracks of the Trans-Siberian ran through gashes in the old worn-down mountain range dividing Europe from Asia. Ancient and eroded by the centuries, the Urals seemed to be only a series of foothills compared to our own Rocky Mountains. I could see that in themselves they would scarcely be much of a barrier to a mechanized army.

Our engine breathed heavily in the cold air as it puffed up over the grades and the brown and white smoke quickly condensed in great clouds over the train, coating the windows in frozen vapor an inch thick. A diner had been attached to the train at the last stop and I looked forward eagerly to a hot meal again. As privileged foreigners, Colonel Fedrovi led us for the first serving. Middle-aged, kind-faced peasant women served and did the cooking. The plates were heaped high with the excellent home-cooked food, but it was very expensive at our ruble exchange. For seven days we enjoyed a single hot meal daily: cabbage soup, fresh caviar, chicken or other meat, potatoes, stewed fruit, and tea, for an average price of thirty rubles, or six dollars at the official exchange rate.

Sitting opposite me every day in the diner was a grizzled old Russian named Maraga. He knew some English and German, for he had been an animal-trainer all his life and had traveled throughout Europe before the Russian Revolution. He told us that when his wife and daughter were killed in the bombing of Leningrad, he had volunteered as a guerrilla behind the German lines. Crunching a chicken bone between his strong white teeth, he said between mouthfuls: "I had revenge. I killed two Germans myself with a hand-grenade."

In his last raid on a captured village the Germans had countered with mortar fire and the gray-haired lion-tamer was knocked out by the shell explosion. Dragged away by his comrades, he had partially lost his hearing and suffered a spine injury. He hobbled to the dining-car each day on crutches.

Yet his speech had lost nothing of its vigor. Pounding his hand on the table with a force that made the plates jump, he said: "The doctor told me I would need a few weeks more." Then he showed his handsome teeth in a wry grin and added: "It's hard to do nothing at a time like this."

With a distant look in his shining black eyes, he talked about Leningrad. "It is very cold there," he said. "People are dying in the streets. Sometimes the old ones like me don't wake up in the morning. And sometimes their families just let them lie there. If they report their death the ration card will be taken away. The mothers divide the extra slice of bread among the children. That is all they get now. We were chopping down the small wooden buildings of old Leningrad, so we could heat our homes, the hospitals, and the factories. But it's not enough. Still we have never stopped the movies or the theater. It is worth chopping down our old houses to keep them alive.

"You are a young man," he went on with feeling. "Listen to me. A man fights better if he keeps alive the things he is fighting for." Pouring his hot tea into a saucer and raising it to his lips, he drank thirstily and said: "We have no water there. The women and children carry their pails for miles through the street to get water out of a bombed water-main. It's hard, but we fight back — all of us, the workers in our factories, the clerks, the student. They all have taken up arms and they drill every day in the week and then they replace the fallen at the front." The old guerrilla's face glowed and he said pridefully: "We have a great musician there, a composer, Shostakovich. He's writing the song of Leningrad. You have heard of him, eh?" He grinned.

Then his lined face saddened. "No one works and suffers more than our women. They went out to dig tank traps. The ground was frozen hard. You could see little fires all over the suburbs — fires that the women lit to thaw the frozen earth. We in Leningrad walk miles and miles to work every day in cold factories. There are no street cars or buses any more." Thumping the table again, Maraga almost shouted: "But Leningrad is still Leningrad! "

There was another diner who attracted my attention, but I never got a chance to sit next to her, for our fellow passengers, the Soviet naval officers, recognized a pretty girl when they saw one. She, too, was from Leningrad, recently evacuated from the city with her two-year-old son. She wore silk stockings, galoshes, and a smartly-cut blue coat, her bright blond hair wrapped in a silk scarf. It was remarkable how well groomed she was each day, although she lived with her baby son in a two-by-six-foot wooden berth with people sleeping on the floor alongside. The young officers hurried every day to her car when we stopped at a siding, to escort the girl up and down the snowy tracks or into the dining-car. She had deep blue eyes with a singularly serene expression and rewarded us with a smile each day when we entered the dining-car.

Maraga, the lion-tamer turned Nazi-tamer, told me that her husband had been killed at the front, but she didn't know it. He begged me not to mention it. I found out that everyone in her car knew of the tragedy except herself. We gave our cans of condensed milk to her for her baby.

We had been two weeks on the train when the dining-car was taken off. It meant going back to nothing but cold meals of corned beef, canned herring, bread, and jam, but every

morning was an adventure. We took turns running down to
the nearest station to fill our kettle with water for tea. Every
station and almost every siding had its *"kipitok,"* a line of
faucets giving hot boiled water. The lines were long in front
of them and the waiting was cold. Many times the boiler was
dry when it came my turn, and nursing tingling ears I'd run
back to the train with an empty kettle to meet the black look
of the others, who had sliced the bread for the meal.

Every city in Russia seemed different from the others.
Yaroslav was a city of ancient churches. Most of them had
been converted into museums. Perm, as most Russians still
call the renamed city of Molotov, had hundreds of old Russian homes with their windows and doors trimmed in bright
blue or red paint.

Now as we passed through the Urals, dozens of lumber
camps were scattered everywhere. On the open slopes I saw
a number of Red Army training camps. Most of the men
seemed to be practicing on skis. This rather amazed me, for
I thought if the situation was so bad in front of Moscow and
most of the Russian armies were destroyed, even these half-
trained men would be thrown into the battle. I reflected that
the Soviet Command either thought they could hold the capital or did not regard the battle as completely decisive.

Several of the Red Army skiers glided down to the tracks.
Dark and wiry, they were pointed out by Colonel Fedrovi as
Uzbeks and Turkmenians. Smiling, he said: "Those fellows
never saw snow where they come from, but they see plenty
now." I realized that the German hold-up in front of Moscow
was giving Russia a great chance to train new armies, and
furthermore many of the Soviet soldiers were as unfamiliar
with the famous central Russian winter as the Germans they
were fighting against. But these southern Russian soldiers
were learning fast.

That night, to our surprise, we began to speed past modern floodlit towns. At four o'clock in the morning I looked
out the frosted windows on a large collection of new yellow
wooden factory buildings and dormitories crouching on the
wooded hillsides of the Urals. Although dawn would not
come for another four hours, the snowy streets of this new
city were crowded with pedestrians. I knew it must be one

of the newly founded cities of the Urals, working right around the clock on war production.

We passed another and another of these mushroom towns, and although I possessed an excellent *National Geographic* map of Soviet Russia, they were uncharted. I knew we were among the shadow cities of the Urals, hastily thrown up to house the factories and workers which were leapfrogging across the plains of Russia. I saw carpenters clinging to the snowy roofs slapping up the newly finished pine boards. Work was going on throughout the night under the golden gleam of powerful arc lights. New railroad spurs were laid through the center of the towns, and the refugee factory workers and dismantled machinery were arriving from the conquered west. I saw whole families of workers down to the small children hauling the heavy machinery off the flat cars onto trucks and sleds. We could actually see the new cities coming to life before our eyes.

In the absence of the diner our food situation grew serious. The stocks we had taken from the ship were running out. We rationed ourselves to two pieces of bread a day and two hunks of cheese or corned beef and plenty of hot tea. One morning, dirty and wearied by the endless train ride, everyone sulked after a heated quarrel in which "certain persons" were charged with sneaking an extra slice of bread from the slender stores. The Russian passengers bought bread at every station, but we were denied this resource because we had no ration cards. Colonel Fedrovi and the Soviet naval officers kindly donated some bread and bologna to us.

On the downgrades of the Urals leading to Asia we were gratified to see that the Russian peasants had not forgotten the old custom of meeting the trains to sell food. I had read that in the old days they met the trains with roasted chickens and wine, but these peasants were selling potato cakes, milk, pickles, eggs, onions, and a curious matted substance composed of dried and pounded berries. I bought a long rolled strip of it and divided it among the boys to eat as a substitute for fruit. The Russian passengers who saw us munching it laughed and told me it was really to be used to brew berry tea.

As our train slid down the grades of the Urals into Asia we saw a vast flat snow-covered plain unrolling in front of us. Siberia did not look much different from European Russia. Then we chugged into the great railroad yards of Sverdlovsk, the former city of Ekaterinburg, where Czar Nicholas and his family met their death. It was a busy boom town. The freight yards were an impressive sight. I saw that many of the countless refugee factories had reached their destination. The workers who had camped for weeks on sidings all the war across Russia jammed the station. Many were busy unloading the snow-covered machinery. The yards were piled high with odd bits of machinery like a gigantic jigsaw puzzle. Crowds of men and women refugees wearing black, shapeless overcoats whose drabness matched the grimness of the Russian landscape stood in line before makeshift canteens waiting to get their first good meal since they left their homes, thousands of miles to the west.

There were hundreds of unshaven, sheepskin-coated backwoods nomads, thrown into the turmoil by the mighty upheaval in the west, walking up and down the tracks in bands. They had ridden the rods to Siberia. Their clothes were in rags and many wore burlap wrapped around their feet. They were jobless and homeless. Corps of blue-overcoated Soviet militiamen were busy rounding them up from their hiding-places under the trains, prodding them with rifles and marching them away under the guard of well-trained police dogs. The dogs trotted alongside the hobo gangs, ready to nip them if they tried to make a break away from the guards. Some of the ragged hoboes were only youngsters, made homeless by the war. They, too, clung together in bands, their meager possessions slung on their backs in brown canvas bags. I wondered where they had found anything to eat on the inhospitable road.

Colonel Fedrovi looked at them grimly and remarked: *"Bisprizorni"* (homeless boys). He said emphatically: "This time our children will not be driven wild by the war." He explained that the fourteen-year-olds were being rounded up by the uniformed NKVD (internal police) and taken to reception centers. From there they would be sent to institutions or returned to their parents if the latter could be found. I watched the lads being herded into the *"Agitpunkt"* in the Sverdlovsk station. It seemed to me a hopeful sign that the Russians were not too busy fighting for their present life to forget about the future.

The railroad yards of Sverdlovsk, chief city of the Urals, were a steaming arena of vast movements, far removed from the threat of German bombing. Troop trains were being assembled for the west, supply trains were arriving from the eastern interior of Siberia, and new loads of evacuated machinery and workers were arriving constantly. The yards were jammed with massive Diesel locomotives stamped with the name of Stalin or Djerzhinsky. I was told that the latter, now dead, and once the head of the OGPU, was celebrated for his liquidation of the last war's problem of homeless boys by establishing orphanages all over the Soviet Union.

Giant portraits of Russian leaders were hung inside and outside the massive station building. I didn't notice anyone looking up at them except myself. I had a sense of something missing, but I didn't know what it was. Here Stalin's picture was flanked by huge portraits of white-bearded President Kalinin, swarthy iron-faced Mikoyan, Commissar for Foreign Trade, who introduced American hot dogs and Eskimo pies to Russia, bespectacled Beria, chief of the NKVD, who looked remarkably like our own Secretary of Treasury Morgenthau, and the gaunt-faced Kaganovich, Transportation Commissar, the only Jewish member of Stalin's cabinet or Politburo.

Hungry and depressed after a week's lack of hot food, we were again taken in hand by our savior, Colonel Fedrovi. He telephoned the big public restaurant in the center of the Ural city and ordered a hot meal. Pale and dirty, we boarded a bus that took us up the hilly main street. Sverdlovsk, the queen city of the Urals, was a startling study in contrasts. Old Russia and modern Russia existed side by side. Gray, unpainted log cabins, half sinking into the snow, stood directly alongside massive new skyscraper factories whose great windows reflected the cold Siberian sun. There was no transitional architecture; either the buildings bore the mark of czarist centuries or the stamp of Stalin's latest five-year-plan. The Asiatic cabins were decorated with pleasantly carved trellis-work over the doors and windows, an example of old Russian handicraft. The pink, red, or yellow plaster of the new factories and apartment houses stood out against the snow. They were of the modern daylight type, with great areas of glass. In one corner the ancient city still maintained its great unpeeled log stockade that surrounded hundreds of one-story log cabins. The only way I could see of passing through the pointed log wall was through the heavy wooden gates that opened from the inside, a century-old protection against the raiding Mongol tribesmen from the east. This unchanged corner of the big factory city looked to me exactly like pictures of American stockades built by the Pilgrims. Trolley cars and buses moved quickly through the streets, clanging and honking. We passed the small wooden house where the last of the Romanov czars had met his fate. A plaque commemorated the incident.

There was a line of refugees and factory workers a quarter of a mile long standing in the snow outside the big public restaurant as we filed into a special banquet room, as distinguished guests. We were served a memorable meal. There were fresh caviar and chopped onions, fine Swiss-type cheese, a steaming yellow soup with bits of pickle and tender meat in it. Then came beef Stroganoff, a chopped, roasted beef, swimming in a creamy sauce of hot sour cream. With this were plates of hash-browned potatoes, crowned with squares of fresh, melting butter. Baked pickles were served as a side dish. We drank two kinds of sweet wine, port and Madeira, followed by stewed fruit and tall glasses of sweetened half-coffee, half-milk. After our eternal rations of cold corned beef, bread, and tea this was indeed a meal. We walked back to the train greatly heartened and later cheerfully decided to go without supper in order to conserve what food we had left.

Our train pulled out for Cheliabinsk, the next big factory city of Asia. As we moved slowly through the night, we saw the mining cities of the Urals on every side turning out the ore for tanks and guns so that Russia might live. There could be no slackening now that the Germans had begun their great plan of surrounding Moscow; the snow-filled darkness was lurid with the sparks of blast furnaces.

Still warmed by the fine meal, Colonel Fedrovi produced a small bottle of vodka. It was scarcely enough for all of us, so the colonel introduced what he said was an old Russian custom. He filled every third glass with water and explained that after two or three drinks you couldn't tell the difference.

The great wooden station at Cheliabinsk was decorated with the customary pictures of Stalin and the members of the Politburo. Inside were great posters depicting Russian soldiers pinning the Beast of Berlin to the snow with a bayonet. I suddenly remembered what I was missing. It was advertisements. There is no commercial advertising in Russia — no pictures of toothpaste, cigarettes, chewing gum, autos; only the huge portraits of the leaders, the ever present statue of Lenin pointing to the future, the war posters, and the red banner slogans that ended in exclamation points. The Government advertises itself, its leadership, and its plans. It dominates the land. And there were no pictures of beautiful girls to tell us how they kept those pearly teeth and that schoolgirl complexion.

We had hopes of getting a plane to fly us across the Urals again to Kuibyshev on the Volga. Flying conditions were bad, however. The station commandant told us that one Soviet Douglas transport had cracked up crossing the Urals the previous week. Colonel Fedrovi finally induced him to hitch our car to one of the rapidly moving troop trains for which we had been constantly making way. Our food supply was now running very low. The situation would be serious if we were on the train another full week.

A yard engine poked us across the tracks past scores of big idle locomotives and hundreds of empty box cars, many of them bearing the marks of Kiev, Odessa, Minsk, and Kharkov. There were hundreds of cars stamped with the Latin lettering of the Baltic States — Estonia, Latvia, Lithuania. The factory people of these newly incorporated Soviet Republics had also been moved to Asia. We could see there could be no shortage of rolling stock in the Soviet Union, if all these engines and cars lay idle even while Russia battled the greatest army in Europe in front of Moscow. These were the trains the Germans hoped to capture by their lightning invasion, but it was obvious that the Russians had been quick enough to save them.

Our car clanked up against the waiting troop train and then we jumped out to see who our new companions were. It was a Cossack cavalry regiment. The doors of the cars were open and strapping western Siberian troopers dangled their legs outside. They looked extremely cheerful. It was an encouraging sight.

The Cossack major was typical of his men, broad, hard, and vital. His wind-tanned face was scarred from ear to chin, a memento of the Civil War. I asked him about the situation at the front. He responded lustily and said with bravado: "The Germans will get no farther." I admired his long curved sword and he eagerly unsheathed it for me to examine. With pride he said it had been in his family for three generations. His grandfather had worn it at Sevastopol.

His men wore the blue scarves or "bashliks" which proclaimed them Orenburg Cossacks from the Urals. I had seen Spahis in France and Guardsmen in England, but I decided that these Cossacks were the glamour boys of the war. They wore their hair in a quiff or curl sticking out from under the black Persian lamb Cossack hats that stuck on the backs of their heads. Under the long, black felt cloak with stiff padded shoulders were Russian blouses with false bandoliers shining from their chests. Their trousers were deep blue with a wide red stripe running down the sides to the black bespurred riding boots.

I asked if they were having a cold trip, but they shook their heads vigorously and pointed to their horses, riding in the same van with them. "They keep us warm." With what I thought I knew of the invincibility of the German tank brigades, I was awed at the cheerful way these men might be going to ride to their death on horseback.

Attached to the troop train, we rushed at unprecedented speed back across the Urals, again passing the ubiquitous trainloads of evacuated machinery waiting to go east on the single-track line. I spotted several more unmapped towns, snuggled in the heavily wooded hills. Floodlit at night for maximum output, they gleamed against the fresh falling snow like spotlighted dance floors.

Before our single candle flickered out to end the nightly rummy game, I caught Walter Kerr examining my brown felt hat thoughtfully. His sheath knife was in his hand. I grabbed the hat away and demanded: "What's up?" "I was just thinking what fine felt inner linings I could cut from this hat to put in my boots," he confessed. "You wouldn't want to sell it, would you?" I pointed out that a felt hat was a priceless possession since it didn't look as though we were going to be able to buy anything here in the back of the world, but I was open to bargaining. He finally produced a pair of Zeiss binoculars. I was tempted, but considered that as a broadcaster I might have long walks to the radio station during the spring rains when my ski hat would not suffice. "I'll talk it over in the spring," I suggested. Walter reluctantly sheathed his knife and said gruffly: "I'll give you two weeks to make up your mind." When I left Russia a year later I still had my hat, and I also had the binoculars. By the barter system I had traded my flashlight for them.

We reached Ufa on the European side of the Urals at nine a.m., after clocking through the hills at an average speed of 35 to 50 miles an hour, instead of our usual 12 miles a day. To our disappointment, our car was uncoupled from the troop train here and we waved the singing Cossacks good-by.

It was Colonel Hulls's turn to fill the teakettle with hot water from the station supply. When he failed to reappear for a half-hour, we worried, because our engine-driver was tooting wildly in the curious language of Russian railroad engineers. This time it could only be the signal for passengers to climb aboard. As the train jerked out of the station, Hulls reappeared. His face was drawn and we knew something had happened. His arm was in a sling. He explained that he had slipped on the icy platform and broken his wrist. A uniformed member of the NKVD had picked him up and escorted him to a near-by military hospital. Relating how a woman doctor had quickly X-rayed his wrist and set it, he was as amazed as we were to have found such a well-equipped hospital here on the edge of Asia.

We were on the last lap of our long ride toward Kuibyshev, and the weather on the European side of the Urals was cold and clear. I had expected it to be warmer here than in Siberia, but the temperature remained at ten below zero and the sky a pale cheerless blue.

We passed the first collective farms we had yet seen. They were snow-covered huddles of log cabins, banked with dirt against the winter. Some of the roofs were straw-thatched like English cottages. All of them sent up swirls of white smoke from their chimneys. Strangely the smoke rose only about a hundred feet, then mushroomed into a cloud. I thought I could see snow already falling from the new-formed cloud. At sunset the reflection from the northern ice-glare relieved the bleakness of the snowy Russian countryside by tinting the wooded hills with gold. Framed by the car window, the scene reminded me strongly of a Grant Wood painting.

We passed over a long steel bridge thrown across a deep ravine. A few hundred yards from the steel bridge lay a brand-new wooden bridge, half concealed in the wood. It was an alternate bridge in case the steel span was bombed. In no other warring country had I seen such foresight. I knew there must be some highly developed organization behind this preparedness, some unseen factor that made this limited network of single-track railroads function as competently as it did. I remembered that I had not seen a wreck or any evidence of a derailment. There must be some hidden strength which few of us in America and England were aware of, else we never could have predicted Soviet Russia's speedy collapse.

Great crowds of refugees were sleeping in the railroad station at Ufa, and the tracks were banked for miles with snow-covered machinery from the western factories. Here the railroad branched off to Magnitogorsk, the Siberian city of steel and iron, to Bukhara on the Persian frontier, to golden Samarkand and the Tomb of Tamerlane, and to Tashkent on the Afghanistan border. Those were the forbidden frontier areas, which no foreigner had visited in years. Behind us stretched the vastness of Russia, curving around half the world, with its cities ancient as time. In front of us was European Russia and Moscow, where the most gigantic armies in history were locked in a battle that would decide the fate of Europe.

Kuibyshev was the next station and we settled our accounts with Colonel Hulls, who had bought our tickets from his supply of Russian money. Our trip had cost us only 200 rubles' fare, because traveling on the third-class "hard" is the cheapest form of travel in Russia. If we get the expected diplomatic rate of exchange, set up since the war, of 12 rubles to the dollar, our fare would be only $16.66 — pretty cheap for a 2,000-mile train ride, from the Arctic Circle to Asia and the Volga.

As we neared our destination, we suffered a series of minor misfortunes. Eddy Gilmore had put his medicine supply in the suitcase traveling in the sealed car from Archangel, so he asked me for some of my aspirin, with which I was treating a three-week-old cold. In shaking out the pills, I unfortunately dropped the bottle on the dirty car floor and spent the better part of a half-hour picking up the pills and dusting them off. Dirty as they were, I knew they were irreplaceable, and I salvaged every one.

We held a small party during the afternoon to celebrate the approaching end of the long trip. Ralph Parker produced a bottle of rum that he had been hoarding for a future Christmas celebration. We discovered a small bottle of vodka in Colonel Hulls's kit and, with the aid of some Worcestershire sauce left over from our food supplies, we managed some fair cocktails. They were a success. The Royal Air Force officer who was making the trip with us felt the effects immediately and decided to go to bed in the middle of the afternoon. He put on thin cotton pajamas and fell asleep uncovered, with a ten-below-zero breeze blowing through the broken train window. He awoke with chills and fever. Colonel Hulls was furious over our break in discipline and worried over the condition of a man for whom he felt responsible. With British dignity he said nothing about his bottle of vodka disappearing. Despite his broken wrist he left the train at the next siding to fill the kettle with boiling water to make tea for the sick man. As the colonel offered me a steaming hot cup, the train lurched, sending the scalding tea over his bandaged arm. I can testify that the British are not always unemotional.

At the next stop Eric McGloughlin and Ralph Parker went for a cooling walk in the snow. They whistled and sang as they wandered down the dark tracks. Ten minutes later Parker came back and announced that he had become separated from Mac. We decided to organize a search party for him before he missed the train, when he walked in. His face was covered with blood and he looked half-stunned. Several teeth were missing and his lower lip was gashed. We got him into his bunk and he explained that he'd fallen down a locomotive greasing pit in the center of the tracks. He had only saved himself from disappearing below by clawing at the icy edge. Pointing at his missing teeth, he remarked: "They were only pivot teeth anyway." We reminded him callously that a Russian dentist was certain to put some stainless steel teeth in their place, because, from what we had seen, it seemed to be a national fashion.

A long line of hospital trains passed, coming east from the Moscow front. They were all-steel Pullman types, far more modern than the rickety wooden car we traveled in. It was another indication that all the best in civilian life in the Soviet Union was going to the men in the Army. I remembered a red slogan across one of the stations; it had quoted Lenin, saying: "Everything for the Front."

As one hospital train halted alongside us, I peered in to see the shaven heads of Red Army men lying in steel berths. The corridors of the train were spotlessly clean. Several less badly wounded men stood at the car door, gray-faced. They wore their uniforms and gray cotton bedroom slippers. All the doctors and orderlies were women. I looked a little ruefully at the thick mattresses in the hospital train. Mine, thin at the start, had now been pounded into a stony wafer. I awoke every morning with a sore back.

That night a stranger came into our car. It was an old peasant woman, carrying the inevitable brown knapsack on her back. She crept in from the cold and fell asleep on the floor alongside my bunk. The *provodnik* put her off when he discovered her, but she seemed to harbor no hard feelings against him. I gave her a hunk of bread.

At the next siding I got off to stretch my legs and walked past a line of green wooden freight cars with bars across the windows. These were the famous prison vans in which exiles had ridden for centuries to Siberia. Two young women peered from out the barred windows and, seeing us, made frantic signals. I waited expectantly until they pulled down the window and, smiling, offered me a piece of candy. Before I could take it, a sentry armed with rifle and bayonet walked over and gestured significantly with his rifle. I walked away and the prisoners seemed disappointed. I thought they looked a lot warmer and happier than some of the people on the outside in the cold. The sentry himself was covered from head to foot in a greatcoat of unclipped sheepskin, but from the scowl on his face I knew he would have traded a lot for a few minutes of warmth inside a train. The powerful girls who patrolled the tracks, however, tightening the tie-plates against metal shrinkage due to the cold, were inured to the piercing wind. Their expressions never changed, whether they munched a piece of bread or pulled on huge iron wrenches. Their look of stolid patience seemed to be frozen on their faces.

I noticed another side of the Russian character as a crowd of peasant women said good-by to three young Red Army men bound for the front. The mother of one of the boys wept bitterly as she kissed her son. The lad tried hard to keep his features composed and turned quickly away as the train started. Weeping and wailing uninhibitedly, his mother ran after it, and her cries started a wave of hysteria among all the older peasants on the platform. They who had seen war ravish this bloodstained land only twenty years ago knew what war meant.

The next stop was Kuibyshev. We packed hurriedly and excitedly, giving the *provodnik* the odds and ends of food we had left over. We had eaten our way through sixteen pound cans of corned beef, four cans of herring, three half-pound tins of cocoa, six cans of condensed milk, five pounds of sugar, four pounds of tea, four pounds of butter, seven pounds of jam, four pounds of cheese, one pound of salt, three bottles of Worcestershire sauce, and nine loaves of bread on the seventeen-day train ride.

November 22   ✍ We were met at the Kuibyshev station by Philip Jordan, of the London *News Chron-
icle,* and Colonel Greer, the British military attaché. They
were impressively dressed in handsome ulsters, fur gloves,
and tall astrakhan hats. I suddenly became very conscious
of my weather-beaten dirty clothes and my unbathed state.
But they were very reassuring and told us how glad they
were that we had finally reached Kuibyshev. They had heard
of our arrival in Archangel and had been worried since we
had been overdue for two weeks. They piled us into cars,
took care of our luggage, and cheered us up generally.

We drove to the Grand Hotel, and as we entered the warm,
lighted lobby, with two enormous vases at least six feet tall
standing in the corner, I realized that we had reached civilization at last. The hotel manager apologized for our rooms
and said that we had to live two-to-the-room for a while, but
when I saw my new abode, with real beds, clean sheets, thick
mattresses, electric lights, and comfortable chairs, it looked
like a palace to me. Russia, I thought, was not so bad after
all.

We walked into the dining-room, where a crowd of correspondents fairly stampeded to welcome us. They had been
evacuated from Moscow a month before. The sight of us
meant more to some of them than just old and new friends.
It meant in some cases that their relief had come and that
they could go home to America. Cyrus Sulzberger of the
New York Times, whom I'd last seen in Washington, was
overjoyed to see Ralph Parker. He could now take leave to
marry the lovely Greek girl he had left behind in Ankara.
Henry Cassidy, an old friend from Paris, was overjoyed
at the sight of big, capable Eddy Gilmore. Henry was under
the delusion that he would now be immediately permitted to
go back to America. I asked for Denis McAvoy, who had
been pinch-hitting for CBS until I arrived, but he had already left weeks ago. I shook hands with the other correspondents, Arch Steele of the *Chicago Daily News,* Morris
Lovell of Reuter's, full-bearded A. T. Cholerton of the London *Daily Telegraph,* dean of all Russian correspondents,
Robert Magidoff of NBC, Henry Shapiro and Meyer Han-

dler of the United Press. They told us that Ambassador Steinhardt and the new Soviet Ambassador to Washington, Maxim Litvinov, had flown out to Egypt the previous week with Alice-Leone Moats and Quentin Reynolds.

The hotel dining-room was packed, the food was hot and good. An eight-piece orchestra played loudly in one corner of the small room. As I munched the hot meal, I listened to the plaintive stories of the other correspondents about the miserable living conditions here in Kuibyshev. I was truly surprised by their complaints. Then I realized that after Archangel and the seventeen days on the train I had already become accustomed to the hardships of Russia and to me Kuibyshev and the Grand Hotel were a great step upward in man's conquest of nature. The other correspondents had experienced reverse circumstances. They felt that Kuibyshev was primitive after the comforts of Moscow, but I was happy in the knowledge that I wasn't going to live the winter in a snowbound, unheated log cabin.

Next morning I awoke rested from my comfortable bed, cheerfully got out my Russian textbook, and strolled over to the telephone to order breakfast. I made myself as clear as possible to the telephone operator, but all I got in return was a flood of words. I tried again with the same result. Then after waiting half an hour without any appearance of breakfast, I walked downstairs to order it in the restaurant. After days of going through precisely the same maneuver over the telephone, I discovered that my phone was not connected to the hotel, but that I was vainly ordering breakfast from the city operator.

I walked over to the American Embassy to say hello. All the members were glum. The country town of Kuibyshev was for them also a great step down after Moscow. And it didn't look as though there would be any Moscow very soon. The news from the front was bad, too. The Germans had mounted another new offensive against the capital on November 16 and they were gaining rapidly in their plan of encirclement. They had already crossed the Moscow Volga canal at Klin, some thirty-five miles from the city, and advance forces were actually behind the city. The Nazis had announced to the world that they could see the towers of

Moscow through field glasses. Daily telephone calls to the secretaries remaining behind in the Moscow Embassy as neutrals in charge of United States property, brought us disturbing word of ceaseless air raids and the nearing thunder of heavy artillery.

The hot food and warmth of the Grand Hotel, however, left me little to desire, with the exception of a bath. The Grand possessed a public washroom with cold running water, but no bathtub had ever been installed in the pre-Revolutionary hotel because Russian guests were expected to avail themselves of the city's public steam baths. Fearful that my only suit might be stolen at the baths, I restricted myself to daily sponges out of a teakettle of hot water provided by the chambermaids.

Evidence that the Soviet organization was still standing up despite the historic battle before Moscow came in the extra facilities that appeared in the dining-room for the comfort of the diplomatic corps: cutlery that had seen service in the now empty Savoy Hotel in Moscow, plates from the Intourist Hotel, Kiev, and silk handkerchiefs thrown over the table lamps stamped "Metropole Hotel, Moscow." The old flat-footed local waiters were replaced by some extremely shapely blondes and brunettes to soothe the jaundiced eyes of the refugee diplomats.

At the press office I discovered that several cables from New York awaited my arrival in Kuibyshev. They were from Paul White, CBS news director. One asked if I needed any money, the other was a schedule of broadcasting times. Both were two weeks old. I immediately asked for a thousand dollars to be transferred to the American Embassy through the State Department. By this means correspondents could secure the newly established diplomatic rate of exchange of twelve rubles to the dollar. This brought the cost of meals down from about twelve dollars a day to six.

Kuibyshev was a refugee boom town. Its population was swollen by a half-million refugees from Moscow. The sidewalks were eternally crowded and many of the pedestrians looked decidedly different from those I'd seen in Archangel. Mixed with the sheepskin-coated peasants were thousands of workers and intellectuals wearing ordinary European clothes. There were even a number of smartly dressed girls from the ballet and the evacuated institutions. Kuibyshev was a city of memories for Russians. I saw people bump into each other on the crowded streets and then hug each other vigorously. Evacuated from different parts of the country, they were meeting for the first time in years.

But the correspondents were extremely despondent. One of the world's decisive battles was thundering six hundred miles away and the only news we could get was what came over the Russian radio. The Moscow newspapers were flown to Kuibyshev irregularly, and by the time we received them they were at least three days old. One of my first moves was to hire a secretary-translator to read the Russian newspapers to me. I was introduced to Lily, a plump, strawberry blonde in her late forties, who had long experience as a translator for foreigners. Lily's only fault was her unabashed giggle. We newcomers had grown tired of seeing each other in the two and a half months it took us to get to Kuibyshev, and great was our disappointment when the other correspondents sourly corrected our misconception that the Soviet Union would provide us with young and lovely secretaries to spy on us. In fact, my shipboard agreement with Walter Kerr that he would go out with my secretary and I with his was completely shattered when Walter hired the only other available translator, Oscar, a sixty-year-old World War veteran.

Cable communications between Kuibyshev and New York were disrupted by the siege of Moscow. Each time I was sent a new schedule of broadcasting times from New York, they arrived a week too late. Transmission across the 4,500 war-torn miles between the Volga and the Hudson Rivers was delayed from three to eighteen days even at urgent rates. I finally sent a cable to Paul White suggesting that he furnish me with a time schedule at least two weeks in advance. He readily complied, and Robert Magidoff of NBC escorted me through a half-mile of ice-glazed streets to the Kuibyshev radio station.

It was an imposing five-story white concrete building erected during the second five-year plan. Across the street were the gray, unpainted wooden cottages of old Russia.

The hilly street ended in the bleak, mile-wide ribbon of the frozen Volga. There was a wasteland of wild rolling hills on the other side of the great Bow of Samarra, where the Volga made its great bend.

Magidoff introduced me to the director of the Kuibyshev Radio, Mr. Mendelsohn, a smooth, efficient, and non-committal Russian who spoke excellent English. He had been an exchange student at Columbia University. With pride he showed me through the newly equipped studios. No one could have failed to be impressed by the way this emergency station had been set up in the short time since its personnel had been transferred from Moscow. The walls of the large studio rooms had been sound-proofed with huge rugs from Bokhara and Turkestan. The colorful wall drapes gave the studios an unusual flavor of the East, and they were more luxuriously appointed than any of the emergency air-raid shelters I had broadcast from in Paris and London. They lacked only one thing, clocks that worked.

I shook hands with the Anglo-American announcers. The most interesting was a former New York schoolteacher, Miss Burrows, a kindly gray-haired Negress. Born in Harlem, she spoke Russian with a decided American accent and addressed even me as "comrade." The other announcers were also American women, from Massachusetts and California. Although they were married to Russians, they were still young enough not to have forgotten their American slang.

My first broadcast was made at four o-clock in the morning, for the time difference between New York and this city in the back of the world was nine hours. Miss Burrows began the broadcast of Soviet war news to America and England with the traditional words: "Workers of all lands, unite!" Then she read a few news items, looked at a small pocket watch, and announced to the world that "by my watch it is thirteen minutes to four o'clock. Mr. Lesueur will make his scheduled report at ten minutes to four, Kuibyshev time. Calling CBS, New York. Calling America."

Later I received cables from New York asking that I check on the correct time in Kuibyshev, for it seemed that Miss Burrows's watch was invariably thirty seconds too fast or thirty seconds too slow. Thus whenever my voice was "intelligible" in America, I was picked up in the midst of my report or else I ended before my scheduled time. Nevertheless, I held a great advantage over the newspaper correspondents because I had direct transmission.

I would write the broadcast in the early evening, make the three-mile walk back and forth to the censorship office through the snow, drop off a copy at the radio station for their scrutiny, and return to the hotel to go to sleep. The radio station phoned me at three in the morning. Hastily re-dressing, I would start out for the studio, my sheepskin collar pulled over my face against the stinging snow. It was a mile round trip across the icy streets. A pair of skis would have come in handy, but I couldn't buy any; all were going to the Red Army. Kuibyshev was just coming to life as I walked home each morning after the broadcast. I could see lights blinking in the little wooden houses as workers got up to begin the morning shift at the factories. All through the night the yellow gleam from the windows of the factories lighted the glistening snow-covered streets. The new provisional capital of Soviet Russia was working twenty-four hours a day.

Despite the mountainous piles of snow in the middle of the streets, I didn't dare walk on the sidewalks. The labor gangs digging a new sewerage system for the boom town had left numberless unguarded holes in the pavement. I dreaded falling into one and not being discovered until daylight, frozen to death. The temperature was sinking as winter came on. The big thermometer outside the door of the Grand Hotel hovered at twenty-five degrees below zero as I scrutinized it each morning before going back to bed.

November 23　　　　　　　　Kuibyshev has reached the saturation point in the number of refugees that can be fed and quartered. I'm told that no more refugees are permitted to leave the train here. They must now proceed across the Urals into Siberia. My chambermaid tells me that during the time of famine in the 1920's trains sped past Kuibyshev to the Urals without stopping, for fear of being raided or contaminated by the typhus-stricken residents of the Volga plain. Starving men, she said, would often fire wildly at the trains in desperate protest, as they hurtled remorselessly by.

The new provisional capital is a melting-pot of people from the captured West and besieged Moscow — peasants, factory workers, correspondents and diplomats from the far corners of the earth, gathered into a country town that once was the terminus of the ancient caravan routes from China and India. High-powered automobiles honk their impatient way past shaggy camels pulling sleds along the snow-piled streets. The Rolls-Royce of British Ambassador Sir Stafford Cripps skids across the unpaved streets; the black Packard limousine of Japanese Ambassador Tatekawa spins its wheels while slant-eyed Tatar peasants reluctantly prod their Siberian ponies out of the way. Everything is white with snow and the streets are continually blocked by stalled trucks, whose drivers build fires under the engines to thaw out the frozen crankcase oil.

November 24 ⚑ In the midst of the depressing front dispatches I received some bad news, too. My suitcase is "missing in action." The sealed freight car in which we loaded our diplomatic mail and our extra bags has finally arrived in Kuibyshev, but the seal has been broken and the car was rifled. Nothing is missing from the diplomatic mail, I am told by the British Embassy, but my suitcase and those of Ralph Parker and Eddy Gilmore have disappeared. This means that I have just one suit, the one I am wearing, for the rest of my stay in Russia. My typewriter paper, carbons, extra underwear, soap, socks, and other priceless possessions have disappeared with the bag.

We immediately wrote a letter to Solomon Lozovsky at the Soviet Foreign Office, informing him of our loss and our position regarding clothes. We are sure he will do something about this, because thefts from foreigners don't pass unnoticed in the Soviet Union.

November 25   📭 I visited the Kuibyshev City Soviet. The secretary of the Kuibyshev Council was thirty-three years old, a dark-haired, strong-jawed Estonian and member of the Communist Party. He worked until far into the night. As a matter of fact, my interview was arranged with him for ten o'clock at night, his first free time. He said that Kuibyshev was facing the great problem of expansion. Housing had to be arranged for the evacuated workers from other cities; water-mains had to be laid to these houses, together with a sewerage system. He said it would be a great task to dig these now that the earth was frozen, but it would be done. And the work was going on. The Government had given him 11,000,000 rubles for improvements to Kuibyshev, but he said the Town Council was meeting almost constantly to cope with many new problems. I asked whether there was a food shortage and questioned him about the bread lines outside the bakeries each day. He shook his head regretfully and said that it was because of bad organization. He added: "I must do something about that right away." He told me that the bakeries had had trouble getting fuel for their ovens this week.

I asked him if any work was being done on the projected dam across the Volga, at the Bow of Samarra. He told me that this had been shelved until after the war, but it would be the greatest dam in the world and eventually would produce more power than Boulder and Grand Coulee Dams put together. I must have looked amazed. But he continued: "First we must make Kuibyshev livable." Drawn and weary-looking, he explained his greatest task was to find houses for the refugee workers, for the embassies, and for their large staffs, and to get them food. Besides that, he was working on the setting up of the refugee factories and trying to get power lines extended to them.

The telephone jingled constantly as I talked to this harried man, so I finally bade him good-night. It was well after midnight when we drank our last cup of tea and I left him to battle with his problems.

The next day I noticed that the Kuibyshev local newspaper, the *Volga Commune*, had delivered a scathing attack on the Town Council. It accused the Kuibyshev Soviet of lack of foresight because of its meager facilities to meet the great evacuation problem. It declared that there was no reason why the digging of sewers should go on in winter when it should have been completed the previous summer. There was no reason why the streets of Kuibyshev should have remained unpaved. The city Soviet should have demanded money from Moscow for the paving a long time ago. Nor should they have been so woefully short of street-cleaning equipment that the streets of Kuibyshev were mountains of snow and rivers of ice. It was my first sight of the Soviet policy of self-criticism.

Life in Kuibyshev was very dull. There was no opportunity for us to meet any Russians since they seemed to be reluctant to enter the hotel, where few but foreigners were quartered. Besides, a militiaman, posted at the door, refused entry to any casual visitor. The residents of the Grand Hotel were a motley lot — Soviet diplomats, American and British correspondents, Japanese correspondents, and Polish officers. The members of the Mongolian Military Mission, from the Mongolian People's Republic also stayed there, with their bouncing black-eyed children, who ran screaming and unhindered up and down the corridors. They wore little native costumes of long blue embroidered kimonos.

Although Kuibyshev was a thousand miles from the sea, it had the atmosphere of a port. From time immemorial the Volga had been the chief means of transportation for the fifty million people dwelling on its banks. When Kuibyshev was Samarra, it had been the giant city of the Volga region. The old trading town had a great past. Now as the provisional capital it possessed a walking League of Nations, with its diplomatic missions from thirteen states as well as from the many autonomous Soviet Republics.

I was now beginning to feel that the Grand Hotel, which had housed prominent traders for a hundred years, was not too aptly named although there were fifty-five rooms in it. I certainly missed a bath, and the public washroom and lavatory accommodations were primitive. But the Russians were doing their best to make the diplomats and correspondents happy. The jazz orchestra played nightly in the restaurant.

The room was far too small to accommodate all the noise, and virtually no one danced. There was an acute shortage of women.

The one break in the day's routine of translating the Russian newspapers, reading the communiqués, and listening to the radio was a visit to the diplomatic store. Only foreigners were provided with passes to enter. Here I was able to supplement my diet of cabbage soup, stewed beef, and rice with a few eggs, apples, and candy. Here, too, we could buy vodka and sweet Russian wine and champagne. At another shop we could buy cotton socks, thin-soled shoes, coats, and boots at prices which made the foreign correspondents hesitate to present the items on their expense accounts.

But even while the Germans were still straining, inching forward in a desperate effort to enter Moscow, conditions improved at Kuibyshev. The efforts of the Kuibyshev Town Council could be seen and felt. All night long, labor gangs from the prison camps near by broke the icebound ground with crowbars and laid their lines for sewerage and water. Work was started on a tremendous air-raid shelter, as deep underground as a subway. The engineers who had built the Moscow subway arrived to superintend its construction.

November 26　　　　　　　　　✍ Walter Kerr, Janet Weaver, of Intercontinent News, and I got a break today. We were invited to a Red Air Force training field. I'm sure the American military attachés would have liked to accompany us. We started early in the morning and bumped across the icy rutted roads, crowded with sleds drawn by short-necked Siberian ponies under their high yokelike harness, or *duga*, and lines of snow-powdered camels hitched two by two, pulling high-wheeled wagons. We skidded past them in our modern car, a large sedan called a Zis, the Russian version of a 1936 Buick. They are powerful cars, used mainly by high Soviet executives. Like the German Mercedes, they are employed as military staff cars.

We reached the heavily guarded barbed-wire gate to the airfield and presented our passes to the sentry, bundled from top to toe in a huge sheepskin-lined coat. The wool on the inside of the coat was unsheared and at least three inches long. Only the sentry's eyes and nose could be seen. I began to wish I had a similar coat as we walked around the snow-packed field, looking at small Russian fighter planes parked at dispersal pits. The pits were really like open-roofed igloos. The planes rested deep in the center, their wings flush with the ground. The snow walls made a good windbreak for the mechanics.

A group of husky young pilots were standing near one of the planes and the colonel in charge of the field led us over to them. They reminded me of American and English pilots, young, clear-eyed, rangy fellows who grinned sheepishly as they stood answering our questions in the posture of loose-muscled, completely relaxed athletes. Their ages ranged from nineteen to twenty-three. They were pilots in training and they had seen no combat work yet. I wondered why they had not been rushed up to the Moscow front, where the invincible German armor was at that moment battering its way to within twenty-five miles of the Soviet capital. I surmised that the Red Air Force must be far from exhausted if these pilots in the last stage of advanced training, flying regular fighter planes, were not being thrown into the battle.

The planes were I–17s, small Messerschmitt-like fighters, mounting two machine guns, fired by a button on the stick, and a cannon shooting through the propeller hub, discharged by pressing a foot pedal on the floor. They were much smaller than the P–40, Hurricane, or Spitfire and, unlike any other pursuit planes in the world, they were fitted with skis. The Russians had designed their landing gear so that the wheels retracted straight up into the fusilage, whereas the wheels of American, British, and German planes all fold inwards, making it impossible to fit skis. One of the youngsters pointed at the skis on his plane and explained that they were so highly polished that they needed no grease, but if the snow was wet, they were difficult to use because it was hard to gain flying speed off the snow. There was a little sub-ski on the tail. The blue-eyed, tow-haired pilot said that it was necessary to make a three-point landing instead of a wheel landing such as our American pilots normally do on good fields. He told us, however, that the use of skis made it possible to land almost anywhere there was a clearing, so emergency fields could be utilized right up against the front lines.

In talking to some of the pilots, I could see that, just as in every air force, there were two types of young men — the serious-thinking, quiet, disciplined type and the quick-thinking, glib, nervously active lads. Several of the pilots were Komsomols, or Young Communists, and these answered our questions with the poise and fluency of trained speakers, apparently as part of their training as organizers. They were quite unlike the average American or English pilot, who generally reaches only for the nearest words.

I asked how it was possible to start an airplane engine in the steel-cold wind that blew across the airfield. One of the boys smiled and explained that it was done by pre-heating the oil. He said that before American P–40s could be used at the Russian front, special petcocks had to be built in so that the oil could quickly be drained out of the crankcase, put into a heater, and poured back smoking hot at take-off time. He pointed to a small white camouflaged boiler at the side of the field where oil was being heated.

The colonel asked: "Would you like to see them take off?" We nodded, a bell clanged, and the boys ran to their planes, mechanics tugged at the propellers, and without a hitch the cold engines roared into life. The three planes taxied into the wind, throwing up great clouds of snow in our faces from the propeller slipstream. They were air-borne within thirty seconds.

I was particularly interested in the Red Air Force clothing because my feet, encased in Royal Air Force flying boots, now felt like lumps of ice. I thought the Red Air Force possessed the world's champion boots. They were of long fur, inside and out, heavy Eskimo dog fur sewn together decoratively so that one side of the boot was black and the other side brown or white. When pulled up, the fur leggings covered the pilot's knees. The lower part of the boot was of good-grade Russian leather, while the sole was a heavy layer of pure felt. They were built for temperatures many degrees below zero, and the felt sole conducted almost no cold from the metal flooring of a plane. The rest of the Red Air Force outfit consisted of a regulation helmet and goggles with a flying overall put on over a regular Red Army type uniform. A heavy fur-lined vest was worn underneath. The gloves, of mitten types, had split palms so the pilot could get his fingers out when necessary. Each pilot carried a .38-caliber revolver.

Just when we thought we could stand the cold no longer, we were escorted down into a dugout. It was a classroom. A group of mechanics were attending a blackboard lecture. It was very much like the lectures conducted on airfields the world over, except that here the husky shaven-headed lads were sitting below the surface of the ground, while the bitter wind whirled the snowdrifts five feet overhead. We commented that it must be difficult to service a plane in this subzero weather. The instructor agreed, but added: "Of course, but it's only late fall now."

As we left the field, we were introduced to the commander, a full colonel, a husky, professional-looking officer with a twinkle in his gray eyes. He wore the gold star of a Hero of the Soviet Union. I asked him how he had won it. He smiled and said: "Not in this war."

He had fought against the Japanese at Khalkhin-Gol in 1939. Describing the campaign, he said that on May 11, 1939 the Japanese troops unexpectedly attacked the frontier guards of the Autonomous Mongolian People's Republic. This was a few miles east of the River Khalkhin-Gol. Under Japanese pressure the frontier guards withdrew until Mongolian Soviet troops came up to help them. They pushed the Japanese back in a ten-day battle and then the Japs brought up reinforcements. They again launched an offensive on May 28, bringing up further reinforcements.

"During the next three weeks I saw plenty of action," the Red Air Force colonel reflected. "In July," he said, "Lieutenant-General Kamatsu Bara brought up two infantry divisions, six cavalry regiments, a mechanized brigade, and heavy artillery and again began a push, trying to take the Soviet Mongolian troops from the rear in a flank attack. We countered with tanks and drove the Japanese back. They dug in, building concrete pillboxes and wooden bunkers. We decided that the Red Army would have to surround and destroy the entrenched enemy." He described the operation, which was directed by then Major-General Georgi Zhukov, who was now commanding the central front. "For eight days the Red Army offensive lasted," he continued, "and we knocked out two Japanese divisions and 146 Japanese planes. It was the second time we had beaten the Japanese inside of two years."

Thinking of the Mongolian Military Mission back at the Grand Hotel, I knew now why they got such courtesy from Soviet authorities. The Red Air Force Colonel said proudly: "I brought down thirteen Japanese planes myself. Eleven were I–97 fighters and two were Savoia-Marchetti-types of Italian design. . . . I was only a youngster then."

His story impressed me. The only knowledge I had before of the "undeclared wars" between Japan and Russia was from small items in the American newspapers about frontier clashes. Later I checked the information in the Lenin Library in Moscow. In the spring of 1938 the first "test war" took place. The Japs had declared that a strip of Soviet territory near Lake Khassan was part of Japanese Manchukuo. This was only a comparatively short distance from Russia's Pacific port of Vladivostok. The Japanese had picked the spot where the borders of the USSR, Manchukuo and Korea converge.

A violent clash took place on July 29, 1938. The Japanese surprised the Soviets and captured important points in their first lunge. Under orders not to invade Japanese territory, the Red Army had a difficult task to face. They could not outflank the entrenched Japanese. But using all types of modern arms except cavalry, the Russians forced a complete Japanese retreat on August 11, 1938. Hundreds of minor border clashes between patrols followed until the Japanese attacked the autonomous Mongolian People's Republic the following year.

Apparently the Soviet Union, unwilling to be dragged into a large-scale war at a time when its greatest enemy, Hitler, was rattling his sword in the west, had contented itself with giving the Japanese a lesson.

November 28   ✍ Accompanied by a censor,
I got a chance to interview a Red Army artillery expert
today. Quiet and confident, with smooth gray hair that
matched his eyes, he looked more like a professor than a
militarist to me. He explained that Germans had pushed
their armored divisions to within twenty-five miles north
and west of Moscow. The Nazis had concentrated the greatest number of their armored divisions on two sides of the
capital, in huge pincers from Kalinin to Tula, with the pivot
on the Napoleon road, the Moscow-Smolensk highway. With
a steely glitter in his gray eyes, the colonel said that the
Germans were attemping to draw off the Soviet forces to the
center of the Moscow suburbs by concentrating a large number of infantry divisions at Mozhaisk. His confidence puzzled me, but somehow I figured that if he could sit there
smoking a cigarette, there must be a good reason. He told
me that the Germans were trying every trick in their bag.
At Tula the Germans attempted a brilliant psychological attack. At dusk they gathered their forces for an all-out smash
at the Red Army defense, and simultaneously every German vehicle, tank, armored car, truck, motorcycle, and even
airplane, turned on its headlights and searchlights, completely shattering the blackout and presenting the awesome
spectacle of lights shining from every point on the hilly,
wooded horizon. Carried away by his description of the attack, the artillery expert said that the only thing that saved
Tula at that moment was Russia's secret weapon, the great
cannon Katusha. He said he took refuge behind a tree as the
earth shook with the repeated reverberations of the secret
Soviet weapon. The German attack faltered and the headlights went out. The Red Army itself delivered a counter-
blow when complete darkness had fallen, and Tula was
saved.

He merely smiled non-committally when I asked him
what "Katusha" really was. From the information I was
able to gather from foreign military sources, refugees, and
even my chambermaid, Katusha was indeed highly secret.
It was said to be operated only by the most trusted troops
of the Red Army, uniformed members of the NKVD, Rus-

sia's secret police. I gathered that Katusha was mounted on a truck, backed into position, and fired by an electric push-button on the dashboard. The truck then turned around and fled in a hurry so that the weapon would not fall into German hands. Each truck, it was explained to me, was equipped with a special detonating device to blow Katusha into junk in the event of an emergency. The secret of its success apparently lay in its multiple explosions. According to these descriptions, each shell burst and scattered small pieces which also exploded, shattering everything within a large area.

I heard the Germans had dropped leaflets over the Russian lines warning the Soviet High Command that if they continued to use Katusha, the Germans would resort to poison gas.

My own theory was that Katusha was a huge rocket mortar whose projectile burst, scattering other smaller explosive rockets. One Red Army man who had never been allowed near the secret weapon told me that it was impossible to mistake the noise of Katusha. It was like a thunderclap. "Trees," he said, "are blown about by the concussion." The weapon was invented by Kostikov, a celebrated Soviet military engineer. Other Russian military men admitted that the Germans might have captured several Katushas which were not destroyed in time. Later I heard that the Germans had attempted to imitate the Soviet secret weapon with a six-barreled mortar that supplied multiple continuous explosions by throwing a huge weight of shells into the air almost simultaneously.

November 29 Lily excitedly rushed into my room this morning shouting that Rostov had been retaken. It was the first good news I had heard since I arrived in Russia. Marshal Timoshenko had sliced into the right flank of Field Marshal von Runstedt's southern group. Five "invincible" German panzer and motorized divisions under General von Kleist had fled from the Sea of Azov port in a hurry.

A few days later the American and British Military Missions were especially heartened to learn that the Germans had been thrown back from their easternmost position in Russia, the city of Tikhvin, near Leningrad. Here General von Schmidt had aimed a spearhead at Vologda, the junction through which my train had passed a month before. But disregarding these blows on the flanks of his gigantic invasion forces, Hitler had reinforced his center drive against Moscow. Fifty-one of his crack Nazi divisions were actively engaged at Moscow, threatening the destruction of the nerve center of the Soviet rail system.

November 30   The United Press received an urgent cable from London asking for confirmation of a rumor that was sweeping England like wildfire to the effect that Marshal Timoshenko was none other than "Timothy Jenkins," son of a Welsh miner who had emigrated to Russia. Actually Marshal Semion Konstantinovich Timoshenko was born in 1896 to Bessarabian parents and had been a farmhand until he was mobilized at twenty into a czarist cavalry division.

I was asked to step into the office of the director of the Anglo-American radio department during the afternoon, where I was spoken to politely but firmly by Mr. Mendelsohn for departing from several words in my typed and censored broadcast. He said he knew they were merely minor changes (one was from the word "very" to "much"), but added: "The girls who read your copy as you talk are bound to report these errors and they positively must not happen again."

I read in the papers today that the British tanks which our convoy brought to Archangel have already been in action and some of them may be smashed up by now. I didn't feel so good either.

December 2   My cold was five weeks old today. I didn't think I'd ever get rid of it. The Soviet doctor told me I must have more rest, but until I could get another room, I continued to get home from the broadcast at five o'clock in the morning and awaken at eight o'clock, when Gilmore's secretary would come in to read him the morning communiqués. I was compelled to stop broadcasting and go to bed, for my cough was making it impossible for me to talk. My secretary-translator, Lily, had found me a doctor. He was a Russian assigned to take care of the diplomatic colony. Before the war he had been personal physician to the old Shah of Persia. He was middle-aged and kindly, and his remedies were old-fashioned. He advised me to drink hot milk with butter and honey and he provided me with mustard plasters. He had no aspirin, since his supplies had not yet reached him from Moscow, so I delved into the supply I had recovered from the train floor.

Lily bought me milk and honey at the special store set up for diplomats and correspondents, and she also secured a prize — an electric stove. She said she told the hotel management that I might die without one.

December 4   Got up out of bed to meet some Russian girls, Galya and Rita, both eighteen years old. Galya, a shapely, full-breasted Brünnehilde, was apparently of the Volga German strain, with long blond hair reaching to her waist. Rita was a small, plump block-buster, pure Russian with very fair skin and honey-colored hair. She had a slight Tatar tilt to her blue eyes.

I was surprised to find that neither of these strong, husky girls worked. They lived with their families, wangled their way into the hotel each night, and waited for someone to dance with them. They seemed too young to be under-cover workers for the secret police. Still coughing, I walked Galya home through the snow, only to find that she lived on the other side of town. She guaranteed to teach me Russian.

On my return to the hotel, the cloakroom attendant gestured wildly at my nose. I discovered that the tip of it had gone completely white with frostbite. He pulled a small jar of goose grease from behind the counter and told me to rub it in gently. The time-honored Russian remedy worked. My nose looked normal next morning.

December 5 ✒ Henry Shapiro took me to
see my first sample of Soviet culture in the Bolshoi Theater,
atop an icebound hill on Kuibyshev Square. It was a handsome theater, about as large as the auditorium of a Mid-
western college. Unfortunately, we arrived a little late and
no amount of pleading would get the usherettes to open the
doors while the first part of the opera was being sung. It
was a pocket edition of *Aïda,* interspersed with variety
dancing and solo singing.

The audience was variously composed of intellectuals
and factory workers. No one looked very dapper, because
Kuibyshev was certainly a one-suit, one-dress city. Few
refugees had been lucky enough to bring more than a limited
amount of clothes when they left Moscow or the conquered
west. The orchestra members were as poorly provided. Some
wore leather windbreakers. Others wore striped morning
suits. Some violinists wore tuxedos. But the music was first-
rate. The cast of *Aïda* had no costumes, nor were there any
settings. There hadn't been time to move stage sets from
Moscow, in the face of more important traffic. The hundred
or so people in the cast, including a large women's chorus,
were bearing up in spite of the fact that they all lived together in an overcrowded dormitory. Despite some notice-
able coughs, they all looked fairly healthy. Although they
were dressed in street clothes, their characters were transformed once they began to sing in Russian. They were trans-
figured refugees singing to a refugee audience. I forgot that
there were no stage sets. Some of the music was by Tchaikovsky and Rimsky-Korsakov, and as I looked at the program I realized that for the first time in my life I was seeing
their names as they really should look: Чайковский and
Римский-Корсаков.

During the frequent intermissions we joined the prome-
naders in the lobby. I became acquainted with the Russian
custom of walking two by two in a circular line around the
lobby, greeting friends as they passed, and talking to companions. Almost everybody, including the girls, was smoking. Their cigarettes were Russian "papirosi," with a long,
empty cardboard tip.

December 6   ✍ Took a walk down to the banks of the broad, frozen Volga. The other bank is known as the Giguli Hills. Hundreds of years ago these hills were hide-outs for the Volga robbers who preyed on rich traders of Samarra. According to the story my old chambermaid told me, the Volga robbers often seized the traders as they marched with their caravans, slit their throats, and hanged their bodies on gallows set on rafts that drifted down the great Bow of Samarra, as a warning to any punitive expedition that might be sent from the city.

Down at the riverside some floating houseboats were frozen fast in the ice near shore. Husky stevedores were loading them. Through the frosty air I could hear them chant: *"Ras, dva, tri* (One, two, three)" to the ancient tune of the Volga boatmen. Some of the modern boatmen, however, were toting 7.62-mm. ammunition on their backs.

General Sikorski arrived in Russia this week to sign a declaration of friendship and mutual assistance with Joseph Stalin. This is his first visit to Russia since the Polish National Council opened diplomatic relations with the Kremlin on July 30, 1941, five weeks after Germany invaded Russia. Sikorski is reported eager to settle boundaries now. Until shortly after the German invasion of Russia, well over 250,000 Polish soldiers and civilians had been in concentration camps all over Russia, from the White Sea to Kamchatka. In the last few months many of them have been released, and they are training in uniforms with a few arms supplied by the Soviet Government. They live under canvas for lack of other accommodation, but according to the Soviet newsreels, they seem to be surviving the winter pretty well. A number of pretty Polish girls have chosen to join the Polish Army in Russia as nurses. I spoke to a Russian cameraman who had been sent to their encampment at Buzuluk. He didn't have much to say about the Polish soldiers, but he was in raptures over the Polish girls. In fact, the greater part of the newsreel was devoted to close-ups of one or two of the Polish nurses.

General Sikorski, whom the French treated rather

brusquely during the Battle of France, when they paid small attention to his description of German blitz tactics, was invited by Stalin to the Kremlin. We were all intensely interested in his trip because no eyewitness reports had come out of the capital since the evacuation and the start of the second German offensive against Moscow on November 16. On the return of Sikorski to Kuibyshev, I questioned the members of his party about the meeting with Stalin. They told me the noise of artillery rattled the windows of the Kremlin during their visit. Stalin looked tired and gray-faced but confident. They thought his placidity denoted a man who had his nerves completely under control.

Apparently Russia is not in such a tight spot as some think. Joseph Stalin prefers to let the Russo-German boundary dispute wait until after the war. It looks as though the dispute cannot be settled now to the satisfaction of both governments.

The inevitable banquet left nothing to be desired. My informant was particularly impressed by the awe with which the Russian waiters approached Stalin, as though he were a sacred object. He wore his usual plain beige uniform tucked into high black boots. Unlike his pictures, his mustache is getting gray and his hair grizzled; he has a small bald patch. Stalin must be a small man because Sikorski, who is not tall, claims that he is taller.

I learned that there had been some embarrassment over the discussion of the disposition of Polish Jews. In the conference with Stalin the Poles unfortunately used the word *"zhidi"* for Jew, a word which is banned in the Soviet Union as derogatory to the Jewish people. In the Soviet Union only the word *"ivrai"* is permissible, and the Poles had forgotten this. It appeared from the discussion that Stalin was willing to permit the Polish war prisoners to leave Russia to join the British Middle East forces; but Polish Jews were to be regarded as Soviet citizens. Stalin said he favoured "a strong Poland" after the war.

My Polish informants were deeply intrigued by Stalin's mysterious exits and entrances in the Kremlin. They said that after parting from him at the banquet hall, they motored to another building at the other end of the walled citadel.

When they arrived, they were surprised to find Stalin already there to greet them. They said he seemed pleased at their mystification, but said nothing in explanation. They realized that the Kremlin had underground passageways connecting its buildings.

December 7–8   With my broadcast written and censored, I set my alarm for three o'clock. Then I got into bed for a nap before the long, cold hike to the studio. Eddy Gilmore and I were asleep when the phone rang at half past one. Eddy answered it. I could hear him say: "The Japs bombed Pearl Harbor." Then he stumbled back through the dark to bed. For a few moments we lay silent. Then in one voice we both said: "Pearl Harbor! Why, that's America!"

Throwing our fur coats over our pajamas, we ran up and down the corridor, knocking on the doors of the other correspondents' rooms to tell the news. Excitedly, we all gathered in Henry Cassidy's room. Henry felt that the time had come for him to get out of its hiding-place the bottle of Scotch he was saving for Christmas. Everyone talked at once and all of us made plans to leave Russia immediately for the Far East. Although we knew Russia would keep on fighting even if Moscow were taken, nevertheless her armies would be split up if the Germans captured the Soviet capital.

Leaving the discussion, I went down to the restaurant, where a few Poles were still dancing with their Russian girls. As I neared the dining-room, I was surprised to hear the band in the midst of a Russian version of *Anchors Aweigh,* a song they had learned only in the last two weeks. It seemed a good omen. Still clad in my pajamas and fur coat, I made the announcement from the floor that America was at war with Japan. The Poles stopped dancing and the band put down its instruments. The waitresses and cooks came out of the kitchen to join the discussion. Their eyes sparkled at the thought that America would soon be an ally of Russia.

All night long we American and British correspondents talked over the great event. One of the boys recalled that his Russian secretary had said to him a week before: "The

Japanese are acting mighty funny." She was referring to the Japanese correspondents who lived at the hotel with us. They had always done a lot of drinking, but she had never seen them get drunk every night, as they had been doing for the past week. Somebody recalled that a drunken Japanese correspondent had walked over to Captain Olson, of the Aid-to-Russia Mission, one night and asked him what he thought of the strained situation in the Far East. When Olson said he knew nothing about any strain, the Jap had laughed drunkenly and gone back to join his table of Jap newspapermen.

I made a quick tour by telephone of the embassies in Kuibyshev and discovered they all had the news and were deep in discussion now at three o'clock in the morning. Quickly writing a new broadcast, I ran up to the radio station and read the new version to the censorship office by phone. It was an unprecedented cutting of red tape. The broadcast was not heard in the United States, I learned later, but I felt much better for having let off some steam.

The city was in darkness as I walked home in the stinging cold, but the lights of the many embassies threw an amber gleam on the snow as the diplomats pondered the world-shaking event.

Three of the correspondents planned to leave Russia immediately.

December 8 dawned bright and cold, and although we had heard rumors that the Germans were taking a beating in their drive on Moscow, we were completely engrossed in the new situation, in which we found ourselves belligerents for the first time. Almost all of us had observed the struggles as spectators for more than two years. Meyer Handler, Walter Kerr, Henry Cassidy, and I had all been together in Paris during the fall of France. Arch Steele had been covering the Sino-Japanese War since its beginning. Eddy Gilmore and I had worked together during the London blitz. But we had only been spectators. Now it was our war.

We came in for some light kidding by some of the British officers next day at lunch for having criticized Britain so outspokenly in the last two years and being caught flat-footed ourselves at Pearl Harbor. But two days later some of the smiles were wiped off when we heard the news over the British radio that the *Prince of Wales* and the *Repulse* had been sunk.

I was lunching with General Mason MacFarlane and Admiral Myles, the Chiefs of the British Military Mission to Russia, and with Major Victor Cazlett, British liaison officer to General Sikorski of Poland, when a correspondent strode excitedly into the restaurant and announced loudly that the *Prince of Wales* and the *Repulse* had been sunk. Looks of extreme displeasure crossed the faces of my British hosts and they demanded of me: "Who is that man?"

I explained that he was an American reporter, and an accurate one, but I decided it was always a mistake to be a bearer of bad tidings. The British military men left the table without finishing their lunch and hurried back to their Embassy.

During the next few days we wondered what had happened to the Japanese correspondents who had been living on the same floor of the hotel with us. They had disappeared. They had decided to stay in the safety of their own Embassy until the first shock of their Government's treachery passed. At the little three-story house of the American Embassy, U. S. Minister Walter Thurston advised us merely to look through the Japanese from now on without seeing them. He told us that he had not received an official notification that we were at war with Japan until the afternoon of December 11. The great battle in front of Moscow had delayed the message for three days although it had been sent triple priority and uncoded on December 8 from Washington. It was simply a circular to all foreign legations and embassies instructing them to notify the governments to which they were attached of the Congressional vote and the declaration of war. It was just signed "Hull."

I sent a cable to Paul White telling him that I was able to leave Russia by plane for Teheran, Persia, and rushed around getting my exit permit and Iranian visa while I awaited the reply. It came saying: "We fully covered Far East stop Burdett already in Teheran."

Every morning I said good-by to Walter Kerr, who was leaving on the next plane out of Russia for the Far East. He gave me some of his meager equipment, including an extra bottle of aspirin and a pair of ski pants. For three days straight he returned each morning from the airport, explaining that he and Sulzberger and Steele had succeeded in getting to the airport through the snowdrifts, but visibility was too low for the plane to take off for Persia. The third morning he said sheepishly that this time his Intourist car had been unable to get through the snowdrifts to the airport, but the plane had taken off. It was the last one that would leave Kuibyshev for a month.

December 12 ⊯ But the world had another surprise for us. Tonight as I sat in the press room of the Foreign Office, the teletype machine connected to Moscow began to click out the end of Hitler's dream. A glowing communiqué announced that the great German plan to surround Moscow could now finally be declared crushed and the armies of Germany were in full retreat in the snow. The Russians had won the Battle of Moscow.

There was plenty of time to think on the lonely walk back through the dead streets from the Kuibyshev radio station. That night I wondered if the Japanese would have dared strike at Pearl Harbor if they had known that their Axis partners on the other side of the world were really doomed to failure only twenty-five miles from Moscow.

December 13 ⊯ This morning I was called into the censor's office, where Mr. Palgunov, the press chief, stared at me through his thick-lensed spectacles and asked in good French: "Would you like to go to Moscow?"

"You know the answer to that," I said. "I didn't travel forty days and forty nights to get to Russia just to stay in Kuibyshev."

Palgunov smiled and said: "You will assume all responsibility on the plane?"

"What time do we leave?" I replied.

"Be at the airport at nine o'clock tomorrow morning. But dress warmly." I didn't bother to go to bed after getting home from the broadcast at four o'clock to pack.

December 14   ✠ Promptly at nine o'clock we reached the Kuibyshev airport after pushing Intourist cars through the deepest drifts. A Soviet Douglas bomber, in full winter war-paint, with white wings and a blazing red star under each wing, stood with motors running. A stiff wind blowing across the airport brought the temperature down to 26 degrees below zero. One of the Russian crew helping us with our bags grinned and said: "Soon it will be winter."

Boards had been placed on each side of the warplane to accommodate passengers instead of bombs. Two women secretary-translators accompanied the correspondents. We huddled together for warmth. As the unheated plane soared above the vast frozen forests and clearings of the Volga region, I climbed up into the machine-gun lookout post in the roof.

We were following the course of the Volga and flying about five hundred feet above numberless little isolated farm settlements. These were the "populated points" of the Soviet communiqués, completely isolated from each other and the world by the drifting snow. Snowbound Russia looked very much like Western America in the depth of winter, except that each huddle of snowbound houses surrounded an imposing tulip-domed Byzantine church. The graceful onion-shaped spires, gold and white, rose lustrously against the great white vastness. From horizon to horizon Russia had changed very little in appearance from the old czarist days, but I knew that most of those churches were now museums or clubs.

Although the Red Air Force crew had thrown some heavy tarpaulins over the floor of the plane, I made the mistake of pulling the canvas over my legs instead of putting my feet on top of it. Contact with the frozen metal flooring soon made my leather-incased feet feel like ice blocks. I was wearing Royal Air Force flying boots, but they were not designed for flying over Russia. I longed for the felt-soled fur boots the Russian crew was wearing.

Unable to stand the agony of our frozen feet, we took turns getting up and stomping up and down in the tail of the plane. It was like a solemn, funereal march of overdressed zombies.

The extreme cold and the bumpiness of the tree-hopping flight produced the usual result among some of the correspondents and the two women secretaries. I felt queazy myself. But it wasn't messy. Everything froze instantly.

Over the outskirts of Moscow our plane skimmed the tree-tops to ensure recognition of the red star on the wings. Although the invaders had been driven back from the outskirts of the city, we could see that many gun positions even in the rear of the capital were still being manned in case of a sudden reverse. Barbed wire was stretched across the Moscow-Volga Canal on posts driven through the ice. Huge, snow-filled tank traps, dug by Moscow's housewives, protected the capital's flanks. Artillery positions were cleared and waiting on the top of hilly vantage points. I was relieved when we passed safely over the long, white barrels of Soviet anti-aircraft positions. I'd heard that Soviet gunners had a reputation for shooting first and asking questions later.

We circled Moscow Central Airport several times and our pilot answered a recognition rocket from the ground with dripping yellow shells from his signal pistol. Then the bomber bumped across the snow and we stiffly clambered out to thaw in the warm reception room. Kindly airport officials poured hot tea into us.

From the air, Moscow under siege had appeared strikingly modern, far newer than any city I'd seen in the Urals. I saw that the Soviet capital had absorbed its suburbs in the great building boom of the last decade. For the modern multi-storied buildings ran right up to the edge of a forest. I remembered an old history book which related that ancient Moscow was built in a wilderness so that primitive invaders would have a hard time finding it.

We were met outside the airport by Intourist cars and driven to the old pre-revolutionary Metropole Hotel. It was camouflaged so that it looked like a stage set. We entered the gloomy dark lobby and turned in our passports to the hotel management, according to the Russian custom of having a complete record of everyone who stops at a public hotel. Then I was shown to a room. I was elated to find that it had a bathroom attached. My first move was to strip and take a hot bath — my first full-length soak in two months.

Dressing hurriedly before it got too dark, I trotted, half ran, toward near-by Red Square. Dusk was falling as I saw the red walls of the Kremlin for the first time, and the great Byzantine Cathedral of St. Basil at the other end of the square. Its nine fantastic snow-covered domes reached toward the sky like a scene out of the *Arabian Nights*. Red Square was almost deserted. A stiff wind whirled the snow around a line of crude sleds loaded with fodder and pulled by snow-encrusted Siberian horses. Their silent, sheepskin-coated drivers hunched their shoulders against the knife edge of the wind. In the gathering dusk I walked over to an enormous block of square red marble. It was the famous mausoleum where Lenin's mummified body has been kept since his death. A flock of black rooks came cawing over the Kremlin walls, like wind-blown scraps of charred paper. I felt as though I were walking through the pages of a storybook. So that was the Kremlin. From Tatars to Napoleon, invaders had sacked it, fires had gutted it. And just a few days before, another invader had been beaten back from its gates. Here it stood, triumphant. I trudged through the snow down to the broad boulevard that ran alongside the Moscow River. It was frozen silent.

The Red Kremlin walls were almost unscarred by bombs, although here and there I could see that the century-old bricks were flaked by bomb fragments. A silent sentry, rifle in hand, looked down at me from an ancient loophole in the crenelated walls. I felt that the danger of the convoy trip and the hardships of the long train ride were worth this glimpse of the seat of the power that had halted Hitler.

The streets were almost deserted as the darkness grew deeper, and I carefully retraced my steps back to the hotel. As a complete stranger to Moscow, I had no desire to get lost. Armed patrols of Red Army men began to gather at every corner. They knew that only a fortnight ago German parachutists had landed on the near-by Sparrow Hills, where Napoleon had looked down for the first time on Moscow, his helpless prey.

Back at the hotel, I found the correspondents sitting down to a hot meal. For the old-timers who had been in Moscow at the start of the war, it had no such thrill as for us newcomers who had been struggling to get to the capital for two months; so when I announced that I was going to do a broadcast that night, a chorus of groans went up. Most of the boys thought they deserved at least one evening's rest after the grueling plane ride, but I explained there was no rest for a broadcaster so long as he was scheduled to speak at a prearranged time, and I had been scheduled for this night. So the typewriters clacked and next day America was informed that Moscow was still there after two months of siege.

My attempt at broadcasting was a nightmare. Radio Moscow had promised to send a car for me with a night pass so I would not be arrested for violation of the midnight curfew. The car came late and I wondered if I'd get to the studio on time. My worries were well founded. The armed patrols which I had seen on the street corners at dusk had multiplied. Every two hundred or three hundred yards my car was stopped, grim-faced Red Army men threw open the door, poked a loaded rifle tipped with a shining bayonet inside, flashed a light in my face, and demanded my night pass and my passport. Their trigger fingers seemed very nervous to me. Apparently parachutists and spies had been caught wandering around the city during the siege. *"Commandantski Patrol,"* shouted the sentries in hoarse demanding voices. *"Vasha propusk, pazhalista."* They studied my pass with fierce glances and I learned to my misfortune that the translation of my name into the Russian alphabet on my passport did not match the spelling of my name on the night pass. My hard-boiled woman chauffeur, whose white shawl covered all but her deep voice, talked three or four patrols out of it. But she oversold the next group. They demanded that I leave the car while they checked headquarters by telephone. Getting no satisfaction there, they escorted me through the snow to a near-by hallway. A plain-clothes man stood hunched in the shadows. They addressed him in tones of respect. He gave my papers a cursory glance and then looked me over. With a voice that had the ring of command, he told the patrol to let me proceed. I realized that he was a member of the secret police.

At Moscow Radio I was conducted to a newsroom two floors underground. The broadcasters and writers had the same pale skins and sallow complexions of those who lived in the underground passages of the BBC in London. The man who read my copy for suitability for broadcasting over the official Moscow Radio might have been a censor in London. He was a slender, sharp-witted Scotsman. I knew that no American slang was going to get by him. He introduced me to the chief announcer of the Anglo-American propaganda broadcasts, a handsome young Harlem Negro who wore an old tweed suit and bright tie with an air which I had not seen before in Russia.

"You from New York?" I asked.

"Yes, sir," he replied. "I was born right on 135th Street. Patterson is my name."

In professional tones he called in CBS New York, and put me on the air on the split second. He was one of the best announcers I'd met in Europe.

I had no trouble going back to the hotel through the same patrols, but they read my papers just as carefully. Next day I got a cable from CBS. It said: "Broadcast unheard in New York."

December 15   I rose early and soaked in a hot bath. I felt I'd need many more before I lost my "gray" feeling. Then I borrowed a guide-book to Moscow and started out to explore the city.

There were few signs of bomb damage. All bomb craters had been filled in and the only fire-gutted buildings I could discover had been carefully boarded up. Compared with London, the Soviet capital was untouched. The streets were not nearly so crowded as those of Kuibyshev and the Ural cities. Only half of Moscow's 3,500,000 were left in the city. The rest had been moved east with the major factories in 1,800 freight cars during October.

The pedestrians were a mixture of city-dressed factory workers and peasants from the country. Many of the peasants had come in during the past month to escape capture by the Germans. Hundreds of these women refugees had been put to work shoveling snow. Safe in Moscow, they looked well fed and cheerful. I was amazed at their vigor as they energetically wielded shovels and scrapers everywhere on the broad, snow-covered streets. None of them ever seemed to stop for rest. I decided that perhaps they worked so hard to keep warm. Later I learned that this capacity for incessant work was natural to these Russian farmwomen.

When I got back to the hotel for lunch, Arch Steele invited me to attend the ballet. All through the terrible weeks that the Wehrmacht and the Red Army had been locked in the momentous battle twenty-five miles distant, the ballet had danced regularly. This was to be the first performance since the siege of Moscow had been broken. We walked up to the old-fashioned and shabby little Filiale Theater on Pushkin Street. Ever since the modern Bolshoi Theater was bombed, the ballet had held forth here.

At the cloakroom we watched a strapping young Red Army girl with a .38-caliber revolver on her hip and a touch of rouge on her lips check her Sam Browne belt. She wore her dark hair in a short "front" bob and her heavy khaki uniform did not hide her excellent figure. There were dozens of Red Army nurses, some of them escorted by officers, others in groups by themselves. They wore the same uniforms as the men. From the muddy appearance of the boots on some soldiers, they might well have fired their last shot at the Germans a half-hour ago and then driven in to see the ballet.

The rest of the audience was composed of pale-looking factory workers on their day off and a high proportion of boys and girls of high-school age. The schools had not opened in Moscow because of the siege. I had never seen the Russian *corps de ballet* before and I don't think I shall ever see them dance again the way they did that afternoon. For weeks the windows of their theater had rattled to the blast of the German siege guns, but today they danced to the victory before Moscow.

The ballet was *The Hunchbacked Horse*, a classic fairy-tale that provided a perfect escape from the war. Dark-haired, slight, and feminine Sulamith Messerer danced the lead. And how she danced! In her graceful dynamic leaps were all the bravado and spirit of a triumphant Russia. The Bolshoi Ballet was dancing for the men and women who had saved Moscow. The audience went wild with delight. The name of Messerer thundered throughout the little theater. Soldiers, officers, men and women, stood up in their seats to shout. The boys and girls rushed down the aisles to the orchestra pit to acclaim the dancers. Every ballerina took countless curtain calls. At the final curtain the audience was almost exhausted with emotion.

Darkness had fallen as Steele and I walked home through the blackout. The ballet had danced for four solid hours.

After supper we went over to the American Embassy. From Llewellyn Thompson and Frederick Reinhardt, the Embassy secretaries who had stayed through the siege, we heard the story of Moscow during its most trying days. They said that for an entire week the militiamen who acted as the traffic police of Moscow had disappeared. No one knew where they had gone, whether they had been removed for their safety or whether they had been sent to the front. The red and green traffic lights of Moscow had still functioned, but there was no one to direct the people any more. High-flying German planes had raided the city with leaflets declaring: "We Germans have no quarrel with the Russian people. We merely seek to rid you of the Jews and Bolsheviks."

A certain amount of restiveness occurred in the absence of the police force, but the Government took a wise measure to control this. Over the loudspeakers set up on every Moscow corner the public was informed that not only were full rations available at the food stores, but they could draw advance rations for the next month. All Moscow quickly responded by joining food lines all over the city. Thus panic was averted although the air-raid sirens moaned ceaselessly night and day. Many of the more nervous packed their bags and were given passes to climb on trains leaving the city. Many others demanded rifles to defend the capital. Naturally, confusion resulted. It was not until Stalin himself broadcast from a microphone set up in the deepest subway station in the city, Mayakovsky Square, during the mass German daylight raid of November 6, that the Muscovites knew they had not been deserted. Stalin was still with them in the Kremlin.

The following week the militiamen returned to duty and the city settled down to the siege. The cannonading grew heavier at the city gates. Barricades were hastily thrown up in the streets. Bus-loads of wounded clogged the hospitals. But the people's confidence never wavered again.

The movies, like the ballet and the annual chess tournament, went on. Soviet organizations managed to take care of the volunteers who wanted to defend their homes. Rifles and ammunition were handed out to long lines of Civil War veterans and factory workers, even to some women. The housewives were organized into sewing groups to make sandbags out of every available bit of cloth. Women and students set about filling the hastily sewn bags with sand.

The American Embassy secretaries had busied themselves counting and listing every piece of American property in the Embassy buildings in case the German invaders smashed their way into the city. They were sure, though, that Moscow would never be declared an open city. They knew that every house and every street would be fought for as bitterly as every populated point that they heard the Germans claim daily over the radio. For two days the city trembled as the artillery fire reached the climactic point. Then it suddenly slackened and the rumble sounded perceptibly farther away. But the State Department representatives had been so close to the scene that I don't think they really knew that the Battle of Moscow had been won until the correspondents arrived in the city. They were very glad to see us.

Back at the hotel the Press Department informed us that we were leaving for the front at dawn.

December 16   We divided into two convoys of white-painted Zis limousines. The auto seats were draped with heavy, colorful Bokhara rugs. I was in a car with a censor and two Red Army officers.

A cutting wind arose with the sun as we drove north along the Leningrad Chaussée. The broad snow-covered highway was filled with hundreds of black-coated workers plodding to the trolley lines even at this hour. Their factories were far out on the city's outskirts. Our cars passed through barricade after barricade. They were huge blockhouses of rough-hewn logs with a narrow, easily closed passageway between. They were in no way as ornate as the solid concrete "dragon's teeth" roadblocks the British had set up the year before on the Dover Road during the Battle of Britain. The Russians had just cut down the near-by trees and joined them together in a series of old-fashioned stockades and wooden forts.

As we bounced north along the heavily ice-rutted Leningrad road, we passed scores of stolidly marching peasant women going back to their homes in newly freed settlements. They had their meager belongings piled high on wooden sleds and dragged them along by ropes. Here and there we saw peasants slowly dragging small sleds with only coffins on them.

We were forced to a skidding stop once to make way for a column of rumbling Soviet tanks, white-painted for camouflage against the snow. Then our two cars again took their place in the endless line of wooden sleds loaded down with yellow fodder and ammunition. Their small, sturdy Siberian horses were driven by expressionless Red Army men whose faces were set against the bitter edge of the wind. They were going north, too, toward the front.

At the first dynamited bridge we turned off the asphalt onto a snowy wood road. A group of Russian sentries scrutinized our passes and then pulled up a crossbar to allow our cars to pass.

We skidded and spun our wheels through a dark pine forest whose towering trees almost hid the light of the day. Here and there we passed a clearing with battered German tanks and cannons standing starkly in the snow. This was the kind of country the Battle of Moscow had raged in. This was the high-water mark of the German advance. We were about twenty-five miles from the city limits of Moscow. The German failure must have been the greatest disappointment for an invading army in history. Hitler's troops could look down the long, straight road that separated them from the Soviet capital. Emergency bridges had been thrown over the tank traps. Dug to a depth of some fifteen feet by the sweat of the mobilized population during the fall, they were now deep with snow. Ice-glazed barbed wire ran across lakes and fields. It was evident that certain areas had been carefully prepared in advance. The defenses were laid out with mathematical precision in the areas in which invading tanks would have to travel to skirt the thick woods. One of the types of anti-tank obstacles in which the Red Army had placed most faith consisted of six-foot lengths of iron rail bolted together in the shape of a gigantic child's jack. No matter which way a tank approached them, they presented a heavy spike. They were difficult to blow up with artillery fire because they had no flat surfaces to catch the blast.

Then we passed the first burnt-out villages. Their charred ruins marred the fresh whiteness of the snow. The only upright objects were the gaunt and blackened chimneys that stood out forlornly. Some of the wrecked foundations still smoked. I watched peasant women who had dragged their sleds of household goods all the way from Moscow, picking about in the wreckage. They had found they had no place to come home to. The older women were weeping silently.

At the roadside was a small graveyard of neatly lettered crosses. We stopped our cars to examine them. The workmanship of the crosses was excellent. The names and ages of the fallen Germans had been carefully burnt in the fresh wood. Many had the outline of an iron cross inscribed below their names. It was remarkable how young the men had been. Their recorded ages averaged from nineteen to twenty-three years. The Soviet colonel who rode with us remarked: "We estimated that 85,000 of those young Germans died in their two offensives against Moscow."

On one side where a number of German and Russian tanks were strewn in an open field, like a junk yard, the surrounding forest was devastated as by a hurricane. There were broken branches everywhere and trees lay tumbled like jackstraws on the ground, evidence of the terrific artillery fire and the death struggles of the tanks. The blackened wreckage of the villages was appalling. Here, too, one or two peasant women poked silently in the ruins of their houses, attempting to salvage what they could. There were only charred, smoking embers.

Our small convoy stopped often to give marching troops the right of way. They were marching just as they had in Napoleon's day, slogging through the snow and bitter cold, on foot. Many of the Russian soldiers wore no steel helmets, only their warm sheepskin hats with thick earlaps. Only a few wore white-painted steel helmets over a lighter peaked hat. I could see that the Red Army reserves were short of this equipment, but the Russians seemed to have no shortage of artillery. Gun after gun wheeled past us, the lighter ones pulled by horses, the heavier by tractors. They had been rushed to the front; no time had been lost to paint them white. Still green-painted as they had come from the factory, they jolted past the white-painted broken German guns, shattered at the roadside, their spiked muzzles splayed out like the petals of a flower.

As we proceeded, the gross rumble of artillery became more insistent. We passed an entire brigade of Red Army men who looked as though they had been marching for days. Their faces were black with fatigue. They were dragging their feet in exhaustion. Several times we saw men stumble as they plodded forward and fall unconscious on the snow. The columns never stopped moving, but I saw fellow soldiers pick up their companions and place them, senseless, on passing sleds loaded with hay. I recalled that many of Napoleon's men had frozen to death on the retreat from Moscow and wondered what would be the fate of these exhausted Red Army men, for they had no blankets. I later learned that during the winter the Red Army carried no blankets, but slept in their heavy greatcoats. When they bivouacked for the night at a village which the Germans had leveled by fire, they quickly dug into the fire-softened earth, next to the foundations, and hollowed dugouts of snow and branches. Throwing a tarpaulin over the top and pulling a stove inside with them, they huddled together for warmth and slept like so many Russian bears.

I was surprised to note that even these columns on forced march were clean-shaven. Our escorting colonel said that

Soviet officers order their men to shave each day for discipline's sake. I asked how they managed it in sub-zero weather. He explained that they heat snow water and work in pairs, the men shaving one another simultaneously.

I watched the living soldiers pass by the dead at the roadside without a glance, and the dead looked scarcely human. They resembled wax mannequins thrown from a show-window, lying about in grotesque, inhuman postures, arms pointing toward the sky, legs frozen as though they were running. Their faces were bloodless, waxy white. The clean, cold air carried no taint of decomposition. But sometimes the wind brought us a whiff of acrid cordite smoke and the soot of a burnt village.

We finally skidded to a halt in the town of Solnetchnogorsk. We were numb from the cold as we stiffly clambered out of the cars and walked over to watch a group of Russian civilians digging a large hole in the frozen ground of the village square. A pile of stiff bodies lay alongside the hole. They were Red Army men who had died to free the city. Solnetchnogorsk, or Sunnyside Hill, had been the first sizable town to be recaptured from the Germans in the astounding winter offensive that saved the capital. It was here that the hitherto invincible blitzkrieg had finally gone into reverse. As we stood shivering in the street, I listened to the Russian officers say: "The city is virtually unharmed, except for a few houses shattered by gunfire. The Germans were surprised in the middle of the night by a Russian outflanking column and they fled, leaving their belongings, and without time for their destruction squads to set fire to the houses."

We were led into a large, one-story frame house, the home of the village druggist. German officers had been quartered here forty-eight hours before. The druggist's wife, Mrs. Garane Bagranov, was a slender, dark, sweet-faced woman, born in Armenia and married to a Russian. She spoke slowly and without emotion.

"Six German medical orderlies were billeted in my house," she said. "They took all the beds, while my daughters and I slept in the kitchen. They didn't molest us because they were afraid of their officers. They went into our drugstore and ransacked it for all the things they could use, like toothbrushes, soap, and perfume. They couldn't read the labels on the drug bottles because they were in Russian, so they threw the bottles on the floor and smashed them. Everything, children's cough medicines, everything. I told them to stop, but they answered: 'We're the bosses here now,' and the breaking of bottles went on. Finally I complained to their officers. They cautioned the men to stop the breakage, but as soon as the officers left the house, the men went back to the drugstore and began smashing things again. They seemed to be mad at the bottles because the labels were in Russian."

Mrs. Bagranov paused and her dark eyes flashed angrily as she thought of the wreckage.

"I ran into the store again," she said, "and told them they must stop. We wouldn't have any medicines left for the winter. But they brushed me aside and went on looking for perfume and broke the bottles they couldn't identify. I went into the street without my coat on and told their officers. Later one of them came in and tacked up a sign. It said that the drugstore was now the property of the German Army. Then the soldiers stopped breaking things.

"After about a week I knew something was happening in front of Moscow. More German soldiers were coming back from the front than were going forward. Then one day the two young Nazi officers I had complained to came into the house and sat at my kitchen table. One of them began to sob. The other rested his head in his hands and began to cry, too. I knew in my heart what had happened. They were retreating from Moscow. Next night while they were asleep, an officer came bursting in the front door spreading the alarm. The Red Army was coming."

Mrs. Bagranov's voice rose with excitement.

"All of them, officers, soldiers, ran around wildly, throwing their things into bags. Their trucks and motorcycles were making a deafening noise outside. Then a few minutes later all was quiet. I opened the door into the dining-room where they slept. They had all gone. We were free again."

The old grandmother, who had stood silent while her daughter spoke, said in a quaver: "They took all our blankets."

I asked the silver-haired "babushka" what the Germans had done to her.

"Nothing," she said. "They just let me starve. But I had some dried bread hidden under my pillow and I lived on that."

The women went back into the kitchen to prepare supper and I leaned against the warm chimney, trying to get the chill of the long drive out of my bones. We would have given a lot for a drink of vodka, but the censor who had the vodka supply said firmly: "In Russia we never drink vodka unless we eat something with it. You must wait."

Shivering, we waited until the table was set with a hot meal. The food had been requisitioned from the Red Army supplies. There was soup, herring, browned beef, and little Russian cakes. The vodka was served in pitchers. All through the night we toasted the Red Army and Hitler's crushing disappointment. I wisely picked out the bed nearest the chimney, and after I lost count of the toasts in vodka, I threw myself on it and fell asleep. When I awakened next morning, I was still dressed, but someone had kindly thrown a quilt over me. It was still dark when I began to stumble toward the kitchen for water. I heard the sound of weeping. I realized that the arrival of the distinguished guests, the foreign corerspondents, in this war-torn village had once more forced the poor old grandmother to suffer almost as much as she had under the Germans. She had been put out to sleep on the ice-cold porch.

At dawn we left to follow the advance of the Red Army. The road wound through forests of dark pines, their boughs sagging under their fluffy white load. Deep in the forest we could see Russian cavalry troops bivouacked for the day. They moved only at night on their raids into the enemy rear. We turned sharply sometimes at strange noises in the somber forests, caused by pine boughs slipping their load of snow. Looking more closely, we could see white-cowled ski soldiers sitting around tiny fires, brewing endless tea and waiting for darkness to fall. They looked like cowled Ku Klux Klansmen in their hide-out.

Here and there the small steppe horses of Russia cropped their fodder noisily in the dark recesses of the woods. The war was hard on horses. All along the roadside their frozen bodies lay in snow-covered blasted chunks. I saw several uncomplaining beasts limping wounded and frightened in the forest. Some of them were lying down in the snow to freeze and die. There was no time to think of wounded horses in this gigantic battle that was deciding the fate of millions of men and women.

Once we passed an entire wood crowded with monstrous lumps of white tanks in hiding, waiting to move up closer to the front under cover of darkness. Some of the Red Army men, woodsmen all, had thrown up neat-looking walls and roofs of rough hewn logs over dugouts as though they planned to stay in this area for a while.

We pushed our car up hills and out of snowdrifts, and once we had to ask the help of a military tractor to get us up the snow-covered side of a steep, ice-glazed slope. German signs were still nailed to the trees, pointing to command posts and field headquarters.

We passed one village in which only half the houses had been burned down. The Red Army men had left the German signs where they stood, as a reminder to themselves and to the inhabitants. It was interesting to note the difference in the German spelling and the Russian for the same towns. In Latin characters the Germans had placed large signs on the sides of peasants' homes, as guides to their own map-readers.

As the sound of artillery grew heavy, we drew up in a clearing in the midst of a heavy forest where, in a wood-cutters' camp, a squad of Russian nurses had set up a casualty clearing station. The buxom, good-natured-looking girls were glad to see us and collected around our cars. They all carried revolvers slung at their hips. We asked the highest-ranking girl, a cool-eyed blonde with her sheepskin hat thrust back over her forehead, if her girls were warmly enough clothed. She smiled. "Warm?" she mocked. Then she began to unbutton her heavy overcoat and conducted our eyes through layer after layer until she suddenly drew her overcoat together again with a loud laugh. From my rather unfavorable position on the wrong side of the car, I could get only a glimpse of what she was wearing — a heavy overcoat, a fur vest, a heavy army shirt, and what appeared to be pink heavy underwear. I wasn't sure. At any rate, we knew now what made the girls look so plump. It was layer after layer of clothing.

The blonde captain of nurses had already been wounded twice, once in 1939 during the three-month Japanese border war and now in this war by the Germans at Lwow.

The nurses were in high spirits over the advance, and when one of the smiling girls learned we were Americans, she jumped on the running board of our car as we started forward and said with fervor: "I always wanted to go to America. Won't you take me with you?" We all wished we could.

The Red Army telegraph linesmen were busy on every side as we moved forward. The Germans in their retreat had sawed down each telegraph pole near its base. Tangled lines were strewn in a jumble all over the roadside. The linesmen, like the bridge-builders, were felling the trees themselves, trimming them, and putting up new poles with remarkable speed.

The countryside was changing now from flat forests with only occasional rises to heavily wooded hills. It grew warmer and began to snow. The thick flakes muffled everything, even the bellow of the guns up ahead. On the opposite side of the road came the wounded on horse-drawn sleds, often with a nurse sitting alongside, holding down the edges of the wind-blown blanket. I remembered what the nurses had said: "To fall down wounded in the snow in this temperature means death within minutes unless you cover the men with blankets." I understood the meaning of some of the boxes mounted on sleds, like small bungalows, that came creaking by. They were hot-boxes with stoves inside. Lucky men had been placed inside these to make the trip from the front line to the casualty clearing station.

Once a brigade of youngsters passed us by. They were no more than nineteen or twenty and I knew this would be only their first action. Their pink, boyish faces were full of wonder as they looked at the wounded going the other way, at the wrecked trucks and German spiked guns and the snow sifting around the stiff bodies at the roadside.

On either side of this road of death were untrodden fields, fenced in by small boards with death's-heads painted on them. They were mined areas as yet uncleared. The officer told us that the Germans were strewing thousands of mines in their retreat, and their method was both simple and deadly. Almost no work was needed because the snow concealed the explosives from sight and the ever falling, impersonal flakes disguised all traces.

Once we passed half a dozen German trucks loaded with rubber boats and tens of paddles. The rivers were long since frozen and it was evident how long the Germans had been held up at this one position, until the rivers of autumn were winter-locked by ice.

We came to the rendezvous where we were to interview General Vlasov, commanding the area. We knew he was simply taking over the last German headquarters as he advanced. But although the sign on the unpainted frame house said plainly "German Divisional Headquarters," there was no one inside. General Vlasov had moved forward again to keep up with the advance of his troops.

A few miles more through the snow-covered forest and we came to a tiny settlement with the unusual name of "Burnt Village." Strangely enough, it was one of the few villages the Germans had not gutted. Here the work of salvaging German war equipment was going on hurriedly. Red Army men were busy gathering up rifles and tommy guns from behind houses and in barns and attics and depositing them in piles on the village square. The Germans had retreated from here within the space of hours.

One happy-looking Red Army man was put-putting through the snow on a captured German motorcycle. When I asked him why it made so much noise, he said gleefully: "All German equipment makes a lot of noise. They think it will scare us."

The Germans had not stopped to bury their dead in this village. Green-gray bodies lay rigid in the snow.

We entered the warmth of an old farmhouse which was now the Soviet Divisional Headquarters. The Germans had vacated it so hurriedly that their excellent maps of the area still remained on the walls. General Vlasov, commander of the Solnetchnogorsk front, was somewhere around but couldn't be found just now, they told us. Instead we were asked by a member of his staff if we would like to see a German prisoner who had just been captured. In a few moments he was led in — a fine-looking soldier.

He was Corporal Albert Koehler of Aachen. He was undaunted, even in the presence of all these Soviet officers and foreign correspondents. We were permitted to question him ourselves. He said bravely that he had been captured going back to rescue prisoners, and the Russian officers nodded agreement. He wore the field-gray double-breasted overcoat that has been standard for the Germans in all their campaigns. It was really not much more than a heavy topcoat. His natty garrison hat was of cotton cloth and his boots the serviceable German jackboots, but they were not suitable for this land of snow and ice. We asked Corporal Koehler if he had been cold.

"No," he replied reluctantly, "not until just recently."

We asked him what equipment he had been issued for winter.

"All of us got a scarf to wear under our hats and a pair of gloves.

Someone inquired why he was fighting against the Russians. Koehler looked surprised and said: "I'm a soldier. I go where I am sent."

"Why are you fighting?"

"To make Germany bigger."

"What do you think of the entrance of America into the war?"

"I heard talk of this on December 14, but we were too busy retreating to discuss it at length."

We thanked Corporal Koehler. He clicked his heels and turned to leave, the very model of a German NCO. One of the intelligence officers whispered to me: "He must be a Hitler Youth."

A violet gloom was falling over the snow as the sun sank behind the wooded hills. Red Army men were busy up and down the streets of the little village, removing engines from the abandoned German trucks, searching through wrecked staff cars for valuable papers; other details were counting

German machine guns, tommy guns, rifles, and bayonets. Mounds of captured war material were growing on the snow. I walked over to examine some of the German trophies, hoping to pick up a tommy gun for myself, but the Russian sentry, although he knew full well that a civilian could be at the front only on special duty, threatened me menacingly with his bayonet. I knew he was under orders to let no one approach the pile.

At another point I watched three Red Army men dismantle the motor from a huge German troop-carrier. The speed with which they worked in the sub-zero temperature amazed me. I studied them as they worked and heard them curse as wrenches slipped on frozen bolts. I had more or less expected to see kindly, patient peasant soldiers going about their work by rote, but these men were as sharp and as full of comment about the difficulties of their job as any mechanics I ever encountered in an American garage. I could see that the cold was just as hard for them to bear as it was for the German troops, in full retreat a few miles away.

Here, I thought, was a small cross-section of the Red Army — hard-looking, muscular, young men who would obviously fight hard for an officer they respected and who had confidence in one whose technical knowledge they trusted. I realized that the idea they were men whom the Russian High Command could afford to use extravagantly was as ill-founded as the legend that Russian soldiers had to have their bayonets welded to their rifles so that they could not ruin them by chopping wood. One of the most impressive sights among the combat troops that still marched through the darkening village was the well-oiled cleanliness of their arms, not an easy accomplishment under these tough conditions. The single-mindedness of these men could not be confused with mere simplicity, I thought. They were elated with the defeat of the Germans at Moscow, but from their talk I gathered that they would have been just as critical of the conduct of the war if they were losing. Their curiosity about the German machines was boundless. They poked about in the inside of tanks and troop-carriers like boys on a treasure-hunt.

I could see that the Red Army was really a melting-pot army like the American Army. It had none of that look of race which belonged to the armies of Britain and France. Here were light-haired Ukranians, dark-skinned Armenians and Georgians, blue-eyed Russians, white-toothed and flashing-eyed Uzbeks, and blond Cossacks from the Don. These were seasoned troops. Their confidence in their own abilities was written on their faces. Their attitude was that the Germans had lost the capacity to surprise or frighten them.

As I watched, the little knots of soldiers suddenly stiffened and I followed their gaze to where two finely dressed officers approached through the snow. They were General Vlasov and General Korol, the Divisional Political Commissar. Dressed in handsomely cut long overcoats that reached the ankles of their white felt boots, they gave the impression of great height, emphasized by their tall gray astrakhan hats. With a smile they approached us, and automatically we walked toward them, followed by a group of obviously admiring Red Army men. The soldiers had no fear of their commanding officers, but seemed drawn to them as an admiring college boy is drawn to a respected professor.

"Zdrastviti tovarishchi (Good day, comrades)," shouted General Vlasov in greeting, and their answer, *"Zdrastviti* General," re-echoed in the snowy street. When it appeared that the general wished to talk to the Americans, the Red Army men withdrew quickly to their work again.

We shook hands with General Vlasov, who looked more like a teacher than a soldier, so tall that his high gray astrakhan hat with the crimson and gold crown made him tower. He wore gold-rimmed spectacles at the tip of his nose. His eyes had a look of bright elation as he told us his men would capture Volokolomsk this very night. "I have sent my ski battalion out to surround the city," he said. "Von Strauss is trying to avoid combat with us. The Germans hold only until they find themselves in danger of being outflanked. Then they'll send their destruction brigades around, armed with gasoline and torches, to fire every house so we'll have no protection when we come in." Pointing to the west where a faint red glow was lighting the sky, he said: "Look, we've already outflanked Volokolomsk."

I asked General Vlasov where he expected the Germans to hold a line for the winter. He replied: "I am not planning my offensive on the basis that the Germans will hold somewhere. I intend to drive them as far as I can."

I persisted in my questioning. "Do you think they'll try to hold at Smolensk?" At the word "Smolensk" General Vlasov looked away and repeated: "Smolensk — that's a different story." I knew then that I must not expect too much of Russia's first winter offensive.

We bundled ourselves into the cars and General Vlasov cautioned us against losing the road and running into a mined area. We thanked him, and our cars spun their wheels on the hard snow.

As the sun went down, the cold became intense. We heard cracks in the forest, sharp as rifle-shots, as the sap froze in the trees. Until eleven o'clock we pushed our car up and down the snowy hills, making room time and again for the forward movement of sleds and marching troops. The night march of the troops, concealed in daylight, had begun.

Finally, we reached our former sleeping-quarters at Solnetchnogorsk. The druggist's wife and her daughters were not surprised at our late arrival. No time was too late for them to prepare a hot supper. The same well-rounded waitress sent down from Moscow was there to serve us. I gazed around the dining-room as I ate. This house on Russia's "Sunnyside Hill" was not so different from homes I had known in Indiana. Above the old shawl-draped piano was a picture I recognized. It was none other than the "Three Little Pigs." I wondered how these Walt Disney characters had got this far east. A guitar hung near the fireplace, and on the mantelpiece was a gilt ikon of St. Nicholas, patron saint of Russia.

With a Russian delight in lavishness, our hostess set the table with all the Red Army provender of the night before, including unopened boxes of candy, one for each of us. As the atmosphere grew more friendly, a correspondent suggested that he and the pretty waitress take a walk outside in the snow to see the stars. The Russian colonel shook his head earnestly and said: "The last three men who took a walk in the moonlight here never came back. They were blown up by mines." We went to bed.

For breakfast we had the traditional Russian meal of "kasha," or brown whole-grain barley, with a piece of butter melting atop it. On the table again were the same large boxes of candy. I didn't realize that to the Russians candy at breakfast was no novelty. They ate it instead of sugar, putting a piece in their mouths while they sipped their hot tea.

I took a last look at the church of Solnetchnogorsk as our cars pulled away. It was from the bell-tower of that gold and blue tulip dome that the Germans first announced they could see, through spy glasses, the towers of Moscow.

We were tired, silent, and thoughtful as our cars rolled back along the four-lane Leningrad Highway, along the brief span of ice-rutted pavement that had stretched immutable and unattainable for the conquerors of western Europe.

December 22 ✒ Adolf Hitler has announced that he will now assume the role of Supreme Commander-in-Chief of the German Army. The Soviet press reports that, in a proclamation that was little short of hysterical, Hitler has fired von Brauchitsch for his colossal failure to take Moscow.

December 23 ✒ There's a mystery man in town. For days Russian and British officials have kept silent about his identity, but today he called us to his suite at the National Hotel for a press conference. It was Anthony Eden, on his first visit to Moscow since 1935. Like the people on the Moscow streets and the correspondents, Mr. Eden was more concerned with keeping warm than he was with stylish dress. He met us in a blue crew-neck sweater, gray flannels tucked into fleece-lined flying boots, and a tieless flannel shirt. He had left his Homburg at home, he said, and borrowed a white fur hat with earlaps from the Navy.

Relaxing in the gilt pre-Revolutionary chair of his Moscow hotel room, Mr. Eden explained that he had made this surprise visit by warship to talk over with Stalin provisional ideas for a post-war Europe. He had also been escorted to the Moscow front by Soviet officers and had interviewed German prisoners. He agreed that *Der Herrenvolk* had not been very well clad for a winter in Russia.

Mr. Eden was very cheerful, much more so than when I had seen him half a year ago in London. He had good reason to be. True, the war in the Pacific was going badly, but the situation had undergone a decided change for Britain within the past six months. From an embattled island, standing alone, waging an unequal battle to hold off the Luftwaffe and struggling to maintain its communications with the Empire, Britain now found itself allied against Fascism with the two greatest world powers, the United States and Soviet Russia. And only a few days ago Russia had demonstrated that she would do much more than give Britain a few months' leeway to fight off an invasion. The Battle of Moscow had shown the world that the German Army was not invincible and that Hitler could no longer hope to rule the world.

Mr. Eden said that the conversations in the Kremlin had fallen into two parts: the immediate conduct of the war, and the organization of the peace. Their objects were the utter defeat of Germany, insurance that Germany would not be able to launch further wars against the world, and a lasting peace for all peoples. As we said good-by, I asked the British Foreign Secretary whether he had discussed the question of a second front with Stalin. Eden replied frankly: "Stalin understands Britain's position. We have just about all we can handle right now between the Pacific and the Atlantic."

He told us we could send the story on the following Sunday, when his cruiser would be safely at sea. I cabled New York to give me a special broadcast Sunday evening, knowing that instantaneous transmission would give me a four- or five-hour beat over my newspaper colleagues, whose stories would clutter the wires for hours.

December 25   ✍ It was my third war Christmas. Paris in 1939, London in 1940, and now Moscow. It was just another day in the Soviet capital. I walked up six-lane Gorki Street, past the lines of women and girls piling the endlessly falling snow at the street corners with the aid of snow-plows mounted on trucks. It was a city scene that might have been placed in Chicago, except that there were no men snow-shoveling. Even the snow-plows were driven by women. The piles of snow had become so huge that a British correspondent who had seen little snow in his native England described them as part of the Moscow defenses.

The real barricades of Moscow confronted us everywhere. They were great lengths of iron rails cemented into the macadam, like rusty asparagus. They stretched from wall to wall between the big apartment houses and completely blocked many of the streets. Sandbags were piled at the sides, bright blots of color against the snow. The housewives of Moscow had sewn them out of every possible material. There were sandbags of faded chintz, of flowered cotton dress material. Although the German threat had been turned back, the barricades were still guarded by impassive sheep-skin-hatted Red Army sentries.

In front of the post office a crowd of passers-by had stopped to examine a colored poster. It was a caricature of Hitler peering hungrily through a telescope at the roof-tops of Moscow from the church tower at Solnetchnogorsk. A huge Red Army man's snowboot loomed up behind him, about to boot Hitler in a vulnerable spot.

Up the street was a huge billboard covering the entire wall of an apartment house. It was the picture of a motherly-looking, beshawled woman pointing down at all pedestrians. While I haltingly translated the caption: "Everyone must defend the Motherland," a shabbily dressed man stopped in front of me, gesticulating violently at the poster and at me. He wanted to know what I, an idle sightseer, was doing to help win the war. Taking the easiest way out, I just said: "I don't understand you." My broken Russian failed to convince him, because many persons in this land of many languages spoke Russian as badly as I did. Finally I told him

I was a foreigner. Immediately his expression changed to one of great respect. He touched his cap, apologized, and walked quickly away.

At the Embassy Christmas buffet that evening, General Faymonville, the Supply Mission Chief, an old-timer in Russia, told me that courtesy to foreigners is ingrained in the humblest peasant. The number of visitors to this back of the world has always been limited. But ever since Peter the Great imported the first celebrated foreigners to his court as architects and musicians, the people of Russia have regarded any foreigner as a rarity and recognized him as a guest of their country. Stealing from a foreigner is very heavily penalized. As a matter of fact, the Soviet Government has set up a special bureau called "Burobin" to take care of the ordinary daily needs of foreign visitors and diplomats. If we had to wait in line for food and clothing the way the ordinary Russian does, all our time would be taken up in mere existence.

December 27   The Press Department suddenly informed us that we were leaving for Kuibyshev on Sunday. I pleaded that I had a broadcast scheduled for that day, but in vain. The Moscow visit was over.

I reluctantly cabled New York to cancel my special broadcast. Since we would be on the train when the Eden communiqué was released, we wrote stories in advance and left them in the Moscow telegraph office. I hastily took another bath before leaving. There was no telling when I'd have one again.

January 1, 1942   The train trip to Kuibyshev was over in three days. We rode on the upholstered "soft" and played poker and Chinese checkers. We invited a heavily decorated Russian colonel who leaned over our shoulders to take a corner at Chinese checkers. He was the type who hated to lose, but he couldn't win a game against us experts. Finally, to stave off another defeat, he began to move his marbles backward into my home base so that I couldn't win either. When I asked curtly: "What are you doing that for?" he exploded and said brusquely: "You did it to me last time!"

Back at the Grand Hotel I unloaded my war trophies before the admiring chambermaids. With satisfaction they hung up the German helmets, and polished the shining brass shell-cases.

We went straight to the New Year's Eve party in the hotel, given by the United States Military Attaché, Colonel Michela. Almost the entire foreign colony was in attendance. There were over one hundred foreigners, but not a single Russian woman. The main dining-room, decorated with tinsel and Christmas trees, was crowded with celebrating Russians. On every landing of the hotel stood two-foot-high statues of the Soviet Santa Claus, known as "Grandfather Frost."

When I walked back from my broadcast at half past four in the morning, all the windows of Kuibyshev were still alight. Phonographs were blaring. I had to by-pass several groups of shouting Russian workers who made their precarious way across the icy streets, falling repeatedly in the snow. The silent Russian militiamen looked on with amusement. The victory at Moscow had provided the gayest Russian New Year's Eve in years. Confidence is everywhere. The army newspaper *Red Star* said editorially today that the Germans can and must be beaten in 1942.

January 3   In Russia a birthday calls for a celebration, and today is the birthday of Natalia René, who has been secretary down the years for a number of correspondents, beginning with Eugene Lyons. The rest of the secretaries gave her a party in Cholerton's room, because it was the largest. One of the correspondents and I were invited, but we came late because we met our new Russian friends, Galya and Rita, in the dining-room. We took them up with us. The look on the faces of the secretaries told all. Natalia remarked as we sat down with our little friends: "This *was* a nice party." Next morning I berated my secretary for being too class-conscious. She said that wasn't the reason at all. She didn't think our new girl friends were very nice.

January 4 ✍ The Soviet Government has just issued a decree of far-reaching importance. Calling attention to the workers' responsibility for increasing supplies to the men in the Red Army, the Supreme Council of the Soviet has ordered an unconditional freezing of the workers to their factories. This includes all refugee workers who were evacuated with their factory machinery out of the reach of the German Army to cities in the Urals and Siberia. Anyone leaving a war factory of his own free will will be considered a deserter. Such persons will be tried by a military tribunal, and if found guilty will be punished by imprisonment for from five to eight years. This ends a situation in which wives working in one factory had the choice of leaving their jobs and joining their husbands working in a factory removed to another city. It sets the seal on those heart-breaking cases of separation of husband and wife and children whose factories have been evacuated to different cities.

Yet this decree is no harder on civilian workers than on those men who have been separated from their families by the Army draft. The Soviet Government says there is no difference between the front and the rear; each must sacrifice equally. For several weeks following this decree the Soviet press gave prominence to cases of men and women factory workers apprehended after leaving their evacuated factories. Emphasis was placed on the severe penalties handed out. These stories in the controlled Soviet press were obvious object lessons to show that desertion from a war factory is as serious as desertion from the Army.

January 6 ✍ Tonight is Christmas Eve according to the old Russian calendar, which is thirteen days behind the Gregorian calendar. The one church open in Kuibyshev was jammed with old women. There were a few old men and only a scattering of young children, brought by their peasant grandmothers. City types of Russian workers were notably absent.

The long-haired priests wore their beautiful gold-embroidered vestments. Hundreds of candles flickered amidst the ikons. Although it was impossible to buy candles in the city shops, the church had a large supply of holy candles which were being passed out among the crowd at a ruble apiece. The system was a simple one. The people in the back passed money to the people in the front, and their change came back to them through the crowd, hand over hand. I spent most of my time passing change back to the people in the rear. The atmosphere was heavy with candle smoke and incense. I was crushed by old peasant women praying in the old Orthodox custom — standing up. I could understand something of what the old beshawled woman next to me was saying: "Guard my son in the Army, O Lord. He is a good boy." It was a scene of Old Russia that might have come from the pages of Chekov. "God is with us! God is with us!" was the chant that resounded through the crowded candlelit aisles.

The English officer accompanying me remarked that the Russian priests were no longer asking God to give Hitler back his sanity, but were now referring to Hitler as the devil. It was plain to him, he commented, that there had been a revival of religion among the peasants in the Soviet Union since the war. He had heard that three more chapels were being reopened in the Kuibyshev area to accommodate the Old Believers.

In the lobby of the church were mewling beggars, the only beggars I had seen in Russia. Several of them were obviously not of sound mind. The Russian peasants crossed themselves before them and dropped kopeks in their outstretched hands, because of the ancient tradition that the insane were touched by God.

Forcing our way out of the densely packed church, we stood in the great throng that jammed the courtyard, to witness the Orthodox Church ceremony of parading the holy ikons outdoors to the people who could not find room to stand inside church. The press of the throng was so great that I had difficulty keeping my footing on the ice.

It was apparent that anyone who wished could attend the services, but there were few worshippers except the old. I asked the Leningrad-born English officer why the Russian cross had two cross-pieces, the lower bar on a slant. "Because Christ was lame," he explained.

January 8   ✐ There's heavy fighting in the Crimea. During the week Red Navy Marines have made a landing on the Kerch Peninsula, taking the Germans by surprise. The transports of the Red Navy streaked across the seventeen-mile Kerch Strait during the night in a heavy storm when no operations seemed possible. Marines and Red Army troops, under General Kozlov, commander of the Caucasus front, jumped off the ships and ploughed through water up to their waists during a gale-driven snowstorm. They stormed the beaches and captured the town of Feodosia. The landing was carried out under the guns of the Black Sea Fleet, and a week later a new commando raid captured the towns of Yalta and Yevpatoria. Converging on Simferopal from three sides while the embattled Sevastopol garrison made powerful sorties at the German rear, the Red Army has succeeded in pinching off the entire Kerch Peninsula. The Crimea is no longer German-controlled.

January 10   ✐ The Red Army announced today that it actually had begun the counter-offensive against the Germans under Moscow on December 7 when General Boldin struck at Guderian's tank divisions outside Tula. Since Japan struck at Pearl Harbor almost at the same hour, December 7, 1941, has certainly become a decisive date in world history.

January 12   ✐ I looked in on a refugee factory in Kuibyshev today. It was part of the great Kaganovich ball-bearing plant which the Western world once feared was going to dump ball-bearings to glut the world market. The factory had been divided into groups of departments when it left Moscow during the early days of the siege as part of the 1,800 freight carloads of factory equipment and workers evacuated from the Soviet capital.

The factory manager, a small, stocky, energetic Communist Party member, wore a plain khaki uniform and boots. He explained it had taken twelve days to move the factory from Moscow to Kuibyshev, and twenty-one days later the plant was polishing its first ball-bearing. The hardest problem had been housing the workers and feeding them. They had been billeted in people's houses in the newly constructed barracks. The feeding problem was met by erecting a central kitchen which sent food to the canteens of a number of factories in the boom city.

The manager said that other parts of the factory had been transferred to Saratov on the Volga, to Sverdlovsk in the Urals, and to Tomsk in far-off Siberia. Of course the principal problem was transportation among the various departments. It was difficult to assemble the finished parts from all these points of the compass, but the factory managers of each plant were doing their best. The manager pointed out that plans for evacuating the factory had been set up well in advance and the process of feeding the parts through the now widely separated departments had been blueprinted months before.

The workers, uprooted from their homes and families, were eighty-five per cent women. They were facing the obvious difficulties of making a new life in a strange town, and I thought some of the younger girls looked homesick. The factory women, hardy, enduring, and muscular, ranged from eighteen years to thirty-five. They still gave a thought to their appearance. I noticed that many of them had visited the beauty shops of Kuibyshev to have their nails painted in the single color available in the Soviet Union — ox-blood red. They wore sweaters over cotton dresses and bright scarves over their hair, or red or white berets.

There was no talk as they worked. I gathered that this was discouraged by the management. Already competitions designed to increase their personal initiative had been started. On the walls in each department of the transplanted factory were posters proclaiming that the workers had taken "a socialist pledge to complete the work quota for the month of January three days ahead of time, besides doing their own quota one hundred per cent and keeping the department clean." The nimble fingers of the workers gave evidence that they were in competition. The proud factory manager told me that this part of the evacuated Moscow ball-bearing plant was in competition with three other portions in other cities and he had reason to think that his factory would come out ahead.

We walked over to the table of a young woman who had won the Red Banner of the Soviet Union. It had been placed on her bench as an award for the previous week's piecework. She could hardly conceal her pride at being the girl singled out for attention by the visitors.

As we left, the factory manager pointed out three or four American machines standing idle. They bore the name "Norman Radius Grinders, Springfield." He explained that they would be used in production, too, as soon as the factory was equipped for two hundred and twenty volts of current.

January 11   Colonel Hulls, British liaison officer with the Polish troops in Russia, our guide and counselor during the seventeen-day train trip from Archangel, invited me to the theater tonight. It was a performance by the Kuibyshev stock company of *Czar Frederick*, the story of how a simple-minded ruler of Russia was superseded by his chief adviser, crafty Boris Godunov. What the presentation lacked in scenery was compensated for by the quality of the acting. The play closed on a pointed scene. The ancient Kremlin garrison sprang to arms at the news that Mongol invaders were at the gates of Moscow.

I noted on the program that the future productions would be confined to historical plays in glorification of the Russian past. There would be no plays this war winter illustrating the Communist system or the struggle of the working class. This was remarkable, judging by the standards of the earlier years of the Soviet theater.

January 13   🦋 If Solomon Lozovsky, the bewhiskered official Soviet spokesman, could put on a feathered broad-brimmed hat and swashbuckling boots, he'd look exactly like one of the Three Musketeers.

Today he held his first press conference since America entered the war. Before going, we discussed the problem of attending along with our enemies the Japanese correspondents. Finally we decided it was diplomatically correct to do so in this neutral country. Eight American correspondents gathered at the long table in the Kuibyshev Foreign Office, opposite Mr. Lozovsky and his pretty blonde translator. The most difficult moment passed when the Japanese and the Americans pretended not to notice one another as we took our seats.

The Tokyo *Nichi-Nichi* correspondent broke the ice by asking the first question: "Is there any change in Soviet-Japanese relations?"

As glibly as usual, Mr. Lozovsky replied: "I can't comment on that question."

There was a palpable atmosphere of strain. Although all the Japanese correspondents spoke Russian, they insisted on asking their questions in Japanese, while another Jap pressman translated their questions into Russian. Mr. Lozovsky replied in his native tongue and his answers were then translated into English by the "sweater girl" secretary seated on his right.

The gist of the press conference was that the Anglo-American correspondents were going back to Moscow, but the Japanese were not. The Domei correspondent demanded the reason for the discrimination. Lozovsky answered smoothly and concisely: "Moscow is the front. The Americans and British are our allies. Only allies can visit the front." Then he added: "I suppose Japan's allies, the German and Italian correspondents, get better facilities on the Tokyo front." The Japs remained silent.

I included Mr. Lozovsky's remarks about the Japanese in the broadcast tonight, but the Soviet censor ran his blue pencil across them without explanation.

January 15   The corps of Anglo-American correspondents is on its way to Moscow again. All the uncertainty attending a train journey in Russia surrounded us. No one knew when the train would leave. I was told to be ready to depart at any time after one o'clock in the afternoon. I hesitated to go down to eat in the hotel restaurant for fear of being left behind, but not until four o'clock in the morning did a telephone message come announcing that I must hurry to the station; the train was leaving. I carted our belongings to the Kuibyshev railroad station and found our car among the hundreds in the yard. It was parked a half-mile from the station, so we trudged along in single file on the ice-bound tracks. The temperature was thirty below.

The Press Department assigned our sleeping-quarters, four men to a compartment. We were assured that the trip would take just three days and we brought enough cold food for seventy-two hours.

These were the weeks of the Christening Frosts, the coldest days of the year, traditionally named for the time when St. Vladimir Christianized Russia by baptizing in the dead of winter. The temperature had sunk so low that the heating arrangements of our car failed to make any headway against the ice-box atmosphere. Everyone slept in his overcoat. Getting up in the morning was an effort because my hair had actually frozen to the pillow.

After three days our train had covered only half the distance to Moscow. Traveling on the single-track line, we waited for hours on sidings to make way for military traffic that fed the Red Army's winter offensive. I cracked my last hard-boiled egg on the third morning and found a layer of ice beneath the shell. To relieve the boredom I decided to shave. Braving the sub-zero lavatory with a mug of hot water drawn from the conductor's samovar, I lathered up. I got one side of my face shaved and then I discovered my shaving brush had frozen solid in the mug.

It was impossible to maintain any energy without hot food, so the censors decided to phone ahead to the next station to have a hot supper ready. Unfortunately we didn't reach the next station until four o'clock in the morning, but that meant nothing to the Russians. They assured us the hot meal would still be there; the Press Department had ordered it. It was only a short walk from the train to the station kitchen, but the temperature had sunk to fifty degrees below zero and several of us had telltale spots of white on our noses from frostbite by the time we reached the kitchen.

Piping hot dishes of browned beef and gravy were awaiting us. These and browned potatoes, salt herring, pickles, and pitchers of vodka slaked our four-o'clock-in-the-morning appetites. The waitresses and the cooks had been on duty since twelve noon, but they served us with unflagging hospitality. Awed at first by their foreign guests, the young waitresses soon became friendly and followed the typical Russian custom of assuming hurt looks because we refused third helpings. Walter Kerr and I lagged behind over a last glass of tea and a talk with the waitresses.

When we emerged from the warm kitchen, we realized we were going to have difficulty identifying our train among the others waiting at the station. Walking up and down the track while the stars flashed like electric lights in the clear night sky, we stopped to see if we could help two little boys and their sister who were crying from the cold. They were moaning: *"Kak holodna, kak holodna* (How cold, how cold)!"* They, too, could not find their car again. All the doors on the trains were barred against them.

We jumped on a train that was already moving, clung to the steps, and banged furiously on the door. A Russian soldier opened it and we found ourselves in the middle of a company of sleeping Red Army men. They slept two to a bunk and some on the floor, wrapped only in their heavy winter overcoats. As the train lurched and bumped, we tramped through car after car of sleeping soldiers. Then, to our delight, we discovered that we were indeed on the same train to which the correspondents' van was hitched. We were welcomed as lost men.

Our train clicked its way across the white plains that stretched from horizon to horizon. At every siding husky track women plodded alongside of the train, feet wrapped in felt boots and burlap, chopping ice from the steel rails. During the day a lemon-colored sun climbed into a frosty blue sky. Its pale beams carried no warmth. As I walked up and down the tracks for exercise, my breath condensed and turned the brown fur of my hat to silvery white. To keep warm I tossed a snowball at two Russian soldiers. The snow was too hard to pack and we threw only hard frozen chunks that were easy to dodge. When we grew tired, one of them confided to me: "I don't like this damp cold. Back home in Siberia it stays at sixty below, but the air is dry like champagne." He thrust his arms out with real feeling. During the snowball fight I had taken off my gloves to avoid wetting them, and the pain of my hands thawing out left me in near agony for an hour.

During the day our engine ran out of wood and we halted for hours at a great pile of cord wood near the track. All the male passengers got out and formed a brigade, passing logs from one to another and finally to a strapping Red Army man who tossed them into the locomotive tender. Next morning I was both cold and stiff.

January 20   Today was the coldest day I have ever known — fifty-two below on the thermometer outside the Metropole Hotel. I watched a flight of snub-nosed Russian pursuit planes drum over Red Square and the Kremlin and wondered how men could stand the fearful cold up there. The sun glistened on the planes' shining skis and I could see the Red Star on the tips of their white wings even though they were well over 5,000 feet up. The air was extremely clear.

On my way to the broadcasting station today I passed a whole regiment of youngsters from fifteen to seventeen. They were marching in military formation, all wearing black uniforms with gilt buttons and high leather boots. They were led by an older uniformed man. These were the trade-school children. Two hundred thousand of these youngsters were called up during the past month from their schools to take a course in factory work.

Moscow is definitely getting its breath back now. Every day the trickles of people on the streets widen into broader streams. Even the cold doesn't keep them indoors. Although the Russians are wearing their impassive winter faces, there is a persuasive cheerfulness in the air. Russia no longer has its back against the wall. It is the Germans who are suffering from dread exposure in the wilderness outside Moscow.

January 21   I spent an hour in the big Moscow department store today. It's called the Mostorg. Although it was forty below outside, I was amazed to find that one of the most crowded counters was the one selling electric fans. The people are buying them now because they won't be able to get them when summer comes. It's apparently a Moscow custom to buy things out of season. There is a good-sized display of bathing trunks, white ducks, and tennis rackets on the first floor, but no tennis balls.

The clothing department is completely empty. There isn't a single article of clothing for sale in it. However, there is a big phonograph and record department and Red Army men on leave and high-school students were busy playing the records on a phonograph before buying them. The red-haired salesgirl, with mascara on her eyelashes, looked exactly like the girl selling records at the five-and-dime store back home. I asked her if she had any phonographs for sale. She looked at me with surprise and said: "*Conyetchna nyet* (Of course not)." The other counters were well supplied with cheap knick-knacks like plastic ash-trays, desk sets, and knife-sharpeners. The same stock was duplicated at almost every counter on all three floors. I bought two neatly made Eversharp-type pencils for twelve rubles each. That would be a dollar each at the diplomatic rate of exchange. I was disappointed to learn, however, that there was no lead available. "Perhaps next month," the salesgirl told me cheerfully.

The cosmetic counter was a surprise. There was a fair assortment left of perfume, powder, and lipstick, but the women customers did not seem to be very much interested. Russian women aged young, I thought. By the time they were housewives and mothers, they had little interest in cosmetics. Nevertheless, the hat department was busy. Well-styled women's colored felt hats were being sold on ration cards.

There were more items available for children than almost anything else — painting sets, checkerboards, dolls, and Christmas-tree ornaments.

Running the Mostorg, I thought, would be a torture for the average American department-store executive. Here was all the space in the world, plenty of labor, and a plethora of customers, but almost no merchandise. There was plenty of money in circulation, too. I watched collective farmers buying handsome hand-painted lacquered cigarette-boxes. These were well worth possessing. They are the work of the handicraft village of Palekh, where an old community of ikon-painters has turned its art to this form of Soviet decoration. The boxes were not cheap. They ranged upwards from two hundred rubles — almost a week's wage for a factory worker. But the collective farmers, with little to spend their rubles on, were snapping them up.

January 22   It is a little warmer today and more people have come outdoors. Apparently some of the refugees have returned now that the Red Army has thrown back the invaders from the gates. The streets are filled with heavy-footed marchers, women wearing black, shapeless overcoats, with unpadded shoulders, which give them a round, dumpy appearance like rag dolls. Their knee-length gray felt boots make their legs look heavy and awkward. I know now why Russians have a reputation for being clumsy-footed. It is because of the layers of clothes and shapeless felt boots they wear to keep warm.

January 25   This is the very depth of the Russian winter. The thermometer outside the Metropole stands at thirty-five degrees below all day.

The Red Army has retaken the city of Mozhaisk, sixty miles away from Moscow, on the Napoleon Road leading to Smolensk, Minsk, and Warsaw. The corps of correspondents has been invited to see the recaptured city. Starting at dawn, our convoy of six cars drove rapidly down the cobbled Smolensk road. After passing the control points on the outskirts of Moscow, not more than a half-hour's drive from the capital, we saw the first signs of war. A huddle of peasants' huts, straddling the highway, had their roofs and walls ripped by high-explosive shells. A little farther along was the high-water mark of battered and abandoned German tanks, their big black and white crosses still visible through shrouds of snow.

The countryside cannot have changed very much since 1812. There are a few more clearings. Man's war against the forests still goes on relentlessly. The woods of spruce and fir encroach like a silent army on the land wrested from them by the plow.

The German stronghold of Mozhaisk had been freed by typical Red Army winter tactics. The main battles had taken place on the outskirts in a series of outflanking moves. Then Russian artillery had pounded the railroad station in front of the city until the Germans were confused over the direction of the main Soviet thrust. The invaders had been compelled to turn their guns around to meet the threat from the northeast, and then General Govorov's main body of troops moved in from the western flank. The Germans had beat a hasty retreat in trucks down the broad Smolensk road, scattering land mines behind them in the deep snow.

Our cars were parked outside the battered railroad station, where hard-working Russian engineers were busy changing the railroad tracks back from the Continental narrow gauge to the Russian wide gauge, a difference of five and one-half inches. It was clear that the Germans had no previous intention of giving up Mozhaisk, because they had arduously changed the width of the tracks to give them a direct supply line straight from Berlin. The parking lot at the station was packed with abandoned vehicles like the outside of a football stadium on the day of a big game. I wandered through them and noted British Bedford trucks captured at Dunkirk, French Renaults from Paris, and Czech Nakladny Autos from Prague. It was a shock to learn that the Germans had dragged this captured equipment all the way across Europe and it give me pleasure to see that the Russians had at last made them give it up.

I saw a familiar bottle sticking out of a snowdrift. I picked it up and read the gold and red label: "Pommery et Greno Champagne. Très Sec. Reims, France." It hurt me to see it. I had spent seven months in Reims when that was the headquarters of the RAF in France in 1939 and 1940. Now the labels had a black inscription printed over them: "Buying and selling forbidden. Reserved for the Wehrmacht." The bottle was empty.

The Russian conducting officers told us that Lieutenant-General Leonid Govorov, whose artillery was responsible for the cracking of this German stronghold, could see us immediately. We walked into his headquarters, a stone building with a carved inscription overhead reading: "1812." Govorov's present headquarters had been standing when Napoleon marched on Moscow. His strong, dark face drawn in tired lines, General Govorov fingered a close-trimmed military mustache nervously as we marched in. Seated alongside him were his Chief of Staff and the Divisional Political Commissar, both tall and distinguished-looking, with smooth, iron-gray hair. They were a Hollywood conception of what high-ranking European military men should look like.

General Govorov spoke clearly and without hesitation and addressed us as though we were in a classroom. He called attention to the defects of German strategy: "Hitler thought he could destroy the Red Army by blitz tactics and failed to take into consideration the resistance of a trained army and an organized state. The German High Command chose to overlook the fact that when the Red Army retreated, it was not crushed." He pointed out that the Germans had lost much of their own will to win when they came up against real resistance and quoted a Russian proverb to the effect that "Fascists are wolves when they meet sheep, but are sheep themselves when they meet wolves."

As an artillery expert, General Govorov naturally placed great emphasis on the superiority in quality and numbers of the Russian artillery. He commented that artillery was Germany's greatest weakness. At the start of the war they were far ahead of the Red Army with their 81-millimeter mortars. But between that and their heavy artillery, they had nothing but light anti-tank guns. The German blitz plan was always to get at close quarters with the enemy and pound him with heavy mortar fire. But the battle with the Red Army showed the Germans the advantage of medium artillery, while the Soviets learned from the Germans that heavy mortars were extremely necessary and put great quantities of these into production after the war started. The Russian soldier was traditionally skillful with a bayonet, he continued, while the Germans did not place much dependence on it, preferring to use their tommy guns in a charge. He could recall no instance where the German soldiers had ever stood up to a bayonet charge, with the Russians yelling their age-old "Oorah!"

The German fighting successes were based on quick mobility and brilliant switching of reinforcements by trucks. General Govorov said that now the Germans recognized the Soviet superiority in artillery and were beginning to bring large quantities of cannon east from their own war factories.

We asked the general where he expected the Germans to hold this winter. He replied that he had no idea, but he would continue to push on as long as he could. General Govorov paused a moment and then said: "The only way tanks can be beaten is with tanks, and the Germans possess a great superiority in this branch of arms." He believed that the Germans had withdrawn their tank divisions for the winter and were re-forming them for new mass attacks in the spring. The Germans, he said, believed chiefly in mass tank attacks, and the only way Russia could overcome the German tank superiority was with the help of her allies.

Eager to impress us with the political significance of the Red Army's fight, General Govorov said that, above all, the Red Army man knows what he is fighting for. Then he turned to his political commissar and said: "Here is the man who tells them."

The commissar rose and said: "The Russian soldier is fighting for his home. Unlike the Germans, he's used to the snow and he's not afraid of the darkness of the woods." He went on to say that he coached the men in what had proved the most successful form of winter attack against the Germans: infiltration through the woods at night, and a bayonet charge just before dawn.

Then General Govorov broke in. He was optimistic, but conscious of the difficulties that lay ahead. During the winter, he said, battles could be only for the roads because the woods and fields had been made impassable by snow. Therefore the Germans had lined the sides of the Napoleon Road with pillboxes of wood and concrete. "We find it possible to cut the roads at times, but it is difficult to hold our positions unless we can knock the Germans out of their roadside pillboxes."

We asked if we could go on toward the front next day and he nodded. Then he concluded: "You must be careful because the snow has not yet been entirely cleared of mines."

Along the village street came a line of German prisoners. They walked past a silent group of Russians who not many days before had been their captives. We followed them into a large frame house, where they formed a squad to be interviewed. They were rather a mild-looking lot, wearing the peculiar downcast expression of prisoners. Their capture had been a psychological blow from which they hadn't yet recovered. The Russian winter, too, had taken the starch out of them. Their uniforms were torn, only nine or ten of them had gloves, and of these some had lost one. They were eager to talk and I gathered that they were glad to be taken from their cold place of confinement to this warm room. Their ages ranged from twenty-six to thirty-six years.

We addressed most of our questions to the brightest-looking man, Corporal August Egger of Augsburg. Shrugging his shoulders, he said the cold was so intense that it had frozen the oil and grease in the German trucks. That was why he couldn't escape when the town was outflanked. Four of the men said sheepishly they had been members of an orchestra in a Berlin dance hall and had been called up only two months ago. They smiled when someone asked if they'd be happier now with violins and saxophones in their hands. I asked if any of them were Hitler Youths. They shook their heads vigorously. "How can we be Hitler Youths? We're too old."

The group was so pathetic and war-worn that we didn't have the heart to question them any further, although they seemed eager enough to answer anything so long as they could stay in that warm room. We walked away and a Soviet sentry ordered them, in German, to line up and march out. I watched them shuffle out of the building looking like Bowery panhandlers in uniform.

In the center of Mozhaisk's town square stood a macabre spectacle. It was a man's legs standing upright on a pedestal. The rest of the statue had been broken off and lay shattered in the snow. When I got closer, I read the inscription on the base: "Lenin."

A single bread store had been opened in Mozhaisk to feed the starving population. They were getting 500 grams, almost a pound, of bread daily.

I walked past the field hospital, where a plump rosy-cheeked nurse smiled at me from the doorway. *"Kak dela* (How's business)?" I called. She replied: "Very good." I asked her what she considered the most difficult problem of nursing. She thought for a while and then said that it was keeping the wounded warm. Next came preventing shock while the men were being dragged or hauled by sled from the woods to the hospital. She gave me the Red Army formula for preventing secondary shock — a slug of vodka with morphine dissolved in it. A winter stimulant she recommended was hot tea with plenty of condensed milk in it.

Walking back along the main street of war-torn Mozhaisk, with its shabby little wood and stone houses, I halted in the debris to pick up some glittering metal in the snow. It was a machine-gun belt. The ingeniousness of man was incongruous in this primitive icy setting. The cunningly fitted black metal webbing of the belt contrasted with the streamlining of the shining brass and steel of the bullets like an ironic bit of costume jewelry. All around were broken bricks and charred wood dirtying the snow. The only thing of beauty that remained in the wake of the invaders was this gleaming necklace of destruction.

The sun was sinking behind the bleak wooded hills as we walked back to the officers' mess for supper. The death-cold wind began to penetrate my heavy sheepskin coat.

The road to the mess hall was lined by Russian sentries, who stooped to squat over smoky yellow fires to warm their hands during their icy vigil. They had poured crankcase oil into the abandoned steel helmets of dead Nazis. The ominous-looking headgear of the soldiers who had trampled over western Europe had become braziers for the Russian peasant boys. It was a heartening sight.

We bedded down for the night in a recaptured schoolhouse where the German staff had lived two days before. The Red Army had sent in a sufficient number of cots with clean mattresses and sheets to put us all up. It was intensely cold, so we sat around a big pot-bellied stove before turning in. An armed guard of Red Army men had been placed outside the door of the schoolhouse to protect us against any German parachutists or stragglers who might still be in the city.

We were awakened at dawn. I had slept soundly under the additional covering of my wool sleeping-bag. I shaved with ice water and then marched to the officers' mess again to breakfast on brown barley kasha, greasy with melted butter, tea and bread. The refilled pitchers of vodka once more confronted us. As we rose, the political commissar poured a full water-glass of vodka and toasted the Red Army. By courtesy we, too, were obliged to drain our tumblers and turn them bottoms-up to show how fully we agreed. It was a bit overpowering. The political commissar was no less affected than we were and before we climbed into our cars, he stood up on a smashed German pillbox guarding the side of the road and pointed out the heights from which the Germans had been driven. He was completely unintelligible.

We drove a few miles farther on, to the famous old city of Borodino, where the main forces of Napoleon's Grande Armée had battled with the Army of czarist Russia. Here Napoleon had issued his famous order of September 7, 1812, as his undefeated Army deployed for battle. "Soldiers, this is the battle you have longed for. Victory now depends on you. It must be ours. It will bring abundance, good winter quarters, and a quick return home. Do as you did at Austerlitz and Friedland, at Vitebsk and Smolensk, and may your conduct today be spoken of with pride by all generations to come. May it be said of you: 'He was at that great battle beneath the walls of Moscow.' "

One hundred and twenty-nine years later a gloating Hitler emulated Napoleon as the Nazi troops reached Borodino. Said Hitler on October 2, 1941: "In a few weeks the three greatest industrial districts of the Bolsheviks will be completely in our hands. At last we have created the prerequisites for the final tremendous blow which, before the onset of winter, will lead to the destruction of the enemy. All preparations, so far as it has been possible to make them effective, have already been completed. This time preparations have been made systematically, step by step, to bring the enemy to a condition in which we are now able to inflict the mortal blow. Today begins the final large and decisive battle of this year." But Hitler proved no Napoleon. Not only had he failed to take Moscow, but his troops no longer even held Borodino and the century-old Napoleon Museum.

Borodino is a little village high on a hill. Between the village and the battlefield the ground is corrugated into deep ravines. A network of barbed wire, tank traps, and anti-tank rails thrust in the ground made it a splendid defensive position. But the Germans fled Borodino without putting up much of a fight.

Just outside the city stood the big, granite monument erected to Russia's General Suvorov, with a huge gray eagle atop it. The Germans had left it unmarred, amidst a shambles of charred and smoking peasants' cottages. But they revenged themselves on the Napoleonic Museum. It was gutted. Set hundreds of yards apart from any habitation, its destruction looked like the work of sheer malice. We parked our cars outside the empty walls of the museum and walked inside. The roof had fallen in and only those exhibits made of iron had survived the gasoline fire laid by the German destruction brigade. We puttered around the ruins and one of us found a corroded bayonet used by the Russian Army more than one hundred years ago. Another picked up an old French stirrup. One of the censors recovered an old cannon ball. I discovered the bolt of an ancient rifle. It was not until I was on my way home late in the afternoon that I recalled that there were no bolts on guns of those days, only flint and steel, so what I had salvaged from the ruins was merely the bolt to the museum door. As we walked around, the steel-sharp wind became more cutting. Several of the boys had long icicles hanging from their noses.

Bumping along the cobbles of the snowy Smolensk road, I could hear the powwow of guns coming nearer on the cold, clear air. Here and there along the roadside lay the stiffened figures of Red Army men, shot through the head. The bodies were piteously barefooted. The dead wouldn't need their felt boots any more. The Russian officer in my car nodded grimly at the frozen bodies and said: "Prisoners. The Germans shot them when they couldn't keep up with the retreat."

We drew up in the little village of Uvarova and heard the Russian batteries pounding away at Gzhatsk, a few miles down the road. The rhythmic thumping of the guns was so loud that we had to converse in shouts. It was as far as we could go. The road ahead had not been cleared of mines. We turned our cars around as the setting sun began to touch the white hillsides with the violet of winter twilight.

A fresh fall of snow was covering up the brown and frozen bodies of dead horses, scattered at the roadside. A group of peasant women were hacking away a stiff hind quarter. The Red Army officer laughed ruefully and said: "It makes good soup." We rumbled past a small clearing where a shattered Nazi tank was sinking into the snow. Near by was a small collection of new birchwood crosses that marked a German graveyard, almost like a garden. I watched a little brown rabbit come hopping out of the woods and make a detour around the black-and-white-crossed tank. It pattered across the untracked snow among the German crosses and scurried into the dark woods beyond. Somehow the rabbit seemed a little footnote to history.

February 1 ✍ To celebrate the breaking
of the Moscow siege, there will be dancing in Moscow for
the first time since the war. We correspondents are fortunate
because the dances are to be held at our hotel. The former
restaurant of the Metropole, with its fountain in the middle,
has been converted into a dance floor. A ten-piece orchestra
plays Russian waltzes and American jazz. Admission is ten
rubles.

When I entered the ballroom the orchestra was just finishing a thumping orchestration of *Sweet Sue*. The floor
was crowded with youngsters, mostly high-school students,
with a sprinkling of young Red Army men. The girls had
all put on their best clothes for the dance and they didn't
look very much different from high-school kids back home.
The young Soviet high-school boys affected very large knots
in their ties, as I remembered doing when I was in high
school fifteen years ago. I was surprised to see that most
of the girls were wearing silk stockings. Since there were
no more silk stockings to be bought in Moscow, these must
have been saved from before the war. Most of the girls
were wearing high-heeled shoes, too.

We correspondents huddled together in a small group,
feeling rather self-conscious. Somebody said: "There is no
use asking any of them to dance with us. They are afraid of
foreigners." We watched several couples jumping around
and unmistakably jitterbugging.

As I wandered around the crowded ballroom, I was
tapped on the shoulder. When I turned around quickly, I
was delighted to see a pretty blonde. She talked to me very
quickly in Russian. I explained to her that I didn't catch
all she said because I was a foreigner and did not understand Russian very well. At the word "foreigner" a shocked
look came over her face and she backed away from me repeating: "Excuse me, excuse me." I waited until the next
number began. Then I walked over to her and said: *"Mozhna*
(May I)?" This time she agreed and I was pleasantly surprised to discover she had a good sense of rhythm, much
better than most European girls. But she remained silent
and at the conclusion of the dance thanked me and fled. I

had broken the ice, however. I wondered if what Cholerton, the dean of Anglo-American correspondents in Moscow, had said was true — that the fear of the Russian people for foreigners had diminished since the war and that the remembrance of the purge in the late 1930's of those who associated with foreigners was fading. After all we were now fighting allies.

I returned to the little huddle of foreigners and we exchanged notes. Several of us had been refused dances, but a couple of correspondents were busy talking to the girls at the other end of the floor. The next dance was too much for me. It was a wild and fast Viennese-type waltz. No American could circle that fast on the floor. The orchestra then struck up its favorite foxtrot, *Sini Plotoshik* (*The Blue Kerchief*). I approached a black-haired, dark-eyed young lady who had been jitterbugging. She readily assented, but was rather disappointed when I proved to be no hepcat. I asked her what she called her hopping dance. She said with some surprise: "Why, that's the Leendy." I couldn't help laughing. I asked her if she had ever heard of Lindbergh. "No," she said; "who is he?"

Later, with an English correspondent, I walked over to two girls sitting at the side of the room. Apparently they had no fear of foreigners and we danced. I asked my partner if she knew the name of the song that had just been played. "It's *Sladki Sue*," she replied, and sang the words in Russian.

When the dance ended at ten thirty, I daringly asked the slender little dark-haired one, Katya, and her companion, the brown-haired, dimpled Ludmilla, if I might walk home with them. I was surprised when they said yes. I waited for them in the cloakroom and watched a number of girls unselfconsciously putting on their pants. These were heavy boys' knickerbockers which they drew on under their skirts and buckled below the knee, for protection against the cold rising from the knee-deep snow.

Through the blackout I walked with the girls and left them at their widely separated apartment houses after asking them for their telephone numbers. It really wasn't much different from America. The big clock in the Kremlin was just chiming the midnight curfew when I got back to the hotel. I immediately reported my success to the other correspondents and the vital news that Moscow girls were no longer afraid of foreigners. Some of the doubting Thomases only half-believed me.

February 5   Moscow is dull and shabby by day. The huge modern utilitarian office buildings aren't very decorative. They are typical of a period in which the Soviet was preoccupied with quickly outgrowing the primitive qualities of old Moscow. The modern apartment houses on Gorki Street are as new and attractive as any in Europe, but since the war their interiors have been neglected. Russia has a special problem with its heavy frosts. In the hallways the plaster is cracking off and there is no one to repair it. Every worker is in either the Army or the war factories.

The Communist Party has suggested that the house committees in each apartment house organize their own repair work for the duration. Since many apartment dwellers are experienced mechanics they will be charged with making repairs in their own apartments after working hours.

On winter moonlit nights Moscow has more glamour than any other city I've ever seen. London is romantic in the blackout when the moon glows on the acres of low medieval roof-tops with their countless chimney-pots, but Moscow, with its immense squares as wide as fields, gives the onlooker a strange feeling of unreality when the winter moon casts its weird blue-green light on the fresh snow.

After curfew Moscow is a deserted city. The snow muffles every footfall. Drifts of white snow pile three feet high against the bases of its tall buildings and make them look as though they were suspended in air. Before your eyes the red walls of the Kremlin rise out of pure space. The dark block of Lenin's tomb seems to float above the snow and the nine fantastic and never-to-be-forgotten domes of St. Basil's Cathedral glisten like an Asiatic stage set. Red Square symbolizes to a foreigner all that is the mystery of Russia.

The Kremlin itself forms a large isosceles triangle with one side fronting on a broad boulevard along the modest River Moskva. Its walls are bolstered with nineteen watchtowers and pierced by five gates. High above all the buildings are the golden domes of "Ivan Veliki," from which the whole city spreads out before a watcher in a mixture of Byzantium A.D. 550 and Detroit 1942.

February 6   ✠ The reason my broadcasts are not getting through to America is that shortly before I go on the air, Moscow Radio's Anglo-American broadcasts are beamed only on England. I have been wasting almost a month walking through the blacked-out, snowbound streets to talk to myself and the censors.

I arranged an appointment with the head of the Radio Committee, Polikarpov, a stocky, muscular-looking man with a shock of blond hair. He wore the customary khaki uniform of a Soviet office executive. He listened to my complaints and said it would take some time to rearrange the broadcasts in order to put my talks on a higher frequency. He explained that it wasn't just a matter of raising the frequency, but of making an entirely new power schedule for the various commissariats which buy time on the Soviet radio system. They pay for the time the way a sponsor does in America.

It seems that Tass, the Soviet News Agency, uses the radio at the time when I should like to broadcast, in order to transmit its news at dictation speed for the provincial newspapers scattered throughout the vast Soviet Union. The Commissariat of Forests and Fisheries and the Commissariat of Railroads also use the Soviet radio to broadcast orders and schedules to their outposts in Siberia, the far north, and the Soviet Maritime Province. Their schedules will have to be rearranged in order to give me additional time, which will be charged against the account of the Soviet Information Bureau. Meantime there is no use in my trying to be heard in New York until the change is made.

Three days later Mr. Polikarpov phoned me and said that he had made arrangements for the various commissariats to change their broadcasting schedules. Unfortunately, I had some bad news for him. The United States had just gone on war saving time. My broadcasting time will now be an hour ahead. The schedules will have to be rearranged all over again. Mr. Polikarpov was speechless.

I had difficulty getting him on the phone during the next week. He was invariably in conference. Finally I had no choice but to write a long letter to the Vice-Commissar of the Foreign Office, Solomon Lozovsky. Although the fact had never been publicized, Lozovsky was known to be the Russian wit who played the radio role of the "Red Invader" at the start of the Russo-German War. With his wise-cracks in German, he had interrupted German domestic news broadcasts until the Nazi announcers were frantic. His method had been simple. A powerful Soviet transmitter had been taken off the air and beamed on the same frequency as the Deutschlandsender. When the Nazi announcer paused for breath, or at the end of a paragraph, Lozovsky butted in. For as long as he continued, the bewhiskered old Bolshevik was the anonymous hero of international radio.

My secretary took him my letter explaining the importance of the Columbia broadcasts, and she told me he had read it with interest. He was going to turn it over to Scherbakov, head of the Soviet Information Bureau and intimate of Stalin by virtue of his position on the powerful Politburo.

The letter was highly effective. The head of the Radio Committee quickly reached me by phone and immediately arranged an appointment. When I came to his office he was lighting one cigarette after another in chain-smoker style. Surprised, I asked him why he had started smoking, because the last time I conferred with him he had told me that he was forbidden to touch cigarettes because of his heart. Polikarpov answered ruefully: "Until you are heard in America, I am smoking against the doctor's orders."

Within a few days he informed me that my broadcasts would henceforth not only be beamed directly on New York from Moscow, but would be fed to the Soviet radio stations in the Far East and beamed on San Francisco. I was delighted to get a cable after my next broadcast informing me that my words were being heard clearly on the West

Coast. Columbia's engineers were reversing the network for my allotted three and a half minutes twice a day.

February 8   🐦 Today I talked to two young men who have just escaped from the captured Ukraine. For months they were members of a partisan band that walked and fought its way across the Ukraine. They've had a few weeks' rest in Moscow now, but there's a look in their eyes that shows they have seen much hardship.

"We were among the last to leave Kiev," said the slender, dark-haired youngster who had been working in the big Kiev movie studios. He was about twenty-four. "We could hear the Germans coughing, they were so close."

"Did many people get out?" I asked.

He nodded. "Only about thirty per cent of the population was left behind," he said, "and they formed a volunteer army to hold back the Germans until the regular troops could withdraw."

His companion in the retreat, a well-built movie technician, pointed at the map on the wall of my room. "We joined a band of partisans and made our way right across the Ukraine by foot to the Red Army lines. We traveled by night and we hid during the day in forests and in peasants' huts," he said running his hand through his curly blond hair. "Not one peasant ever betrayed us," he added proudly.

Then his face fell and he said: "I got sick once while we were crossing the steppes and my comrades built a fire to give me some warm food. But we never did that again. That fire cost two of my friends their lives. The Germans spotted us. We fought until nightfall with our rifles and one trench mortar, and after dark we fled. All the collective farms we saw in the Ukraine had large signs in the village streets proclaiming that the German Army was dissolving the system of collective farms on January 1, 1942."

The dark-haired lad interrupted: "The Germans call them 'socialized farms' now. And they held man-hunts to search out any persons who had been members of a Soviet organization. They even killed anyone they discovered making preparations to pack and leave when they entered a village. The peasants who hid us and fed us told us that the German Army had held new elections to appoint a farm manager." He shook his head. "What a farce those elections were! The only ones who remained to vote were old men and women. Every decent Soviet man had fled. True, there were some Red Army deserters. We saw them. And a few old kulaks who had formerly owned land offered their services to the German Army. The elections were under the auspices of the German Army. Anyone who disapproved of the German candidate was told to raise a hand. No one dared." The dark-eyed boy was silent for a moment. Then he said: "The Germans are trying to lure Ukrainians with religion. They broadcast choir music from the radio stations at Kharkov, Kiev, and Odessa. They have even started an ikon factory going in Kiev."

"One night," broke in the blond partisan, "German officers recognized us as we sheltered in a village, pretending to be collective farmers. They seized us and threw us into an enclosure surrounded by barbed wire. There were many wounded Red Army men in the prison cage. No one tended them. Once a day they threw us some frozen potatoes. At night the women of the village would creep up to shove bread to us through the barbed wire. When the German sentries found them, they shot at our poor women. At dawn, during a blizzard, we escaped. In the next village we found the members of our band. We hid in a cellar with them for three days while the Germans searched for us."

"Then we started out again," said the dark-haired one. "In some villages we saw new signs ordering all Jews to wear white arm-bands. Nobody was paying any attention to the order. One day we ran completely out of food. We were afraid to enter the village because a small squad of Germans was there. So we decided to attack it. We posted our men on all sides and fired our rifles and shouted. The Germans thought they were surrounded, so they fled. They came back next day and took three of our men prisoner. But they escaped. They told us that a German squad was leading them off to the woods to execute them when they made a break for it. Two of them were wounded, but the German soldiers were afraid to follow them into the forest."

The dark-eyed youngster showed his white teeth in a smile and said: "I suppose they told their officers that they finished our comrades off. We left our wounded at the next village and the peasants hid them. Our women never betrayed us, even though they knew the Germans would shoot them for harboring patriots. We saw some German officers conducting their business with the Ukrainians through the help of German interpreters, who were only about fourteen years old. That shows that the Germans had long been planning their attack on Russia."

The partisan shook his head with a puzzled expression. "You know," he said, "those boys spoke perfect Ukrainian. They must have been trained since childhood in special schools. How methodical those Germans are!" he added with wonderment in his voice.

"What are you two going to do now that you're safe?" I asked.

Their eyes lit up with pleasure.

"We're going down to Alma-Ata near the Sinkiang border," said the athletic blond. "That's the Soviet Hollywood now, and we're going to collaborate on a picture about partisans in the Ukraine."

Before they left, the two partisans asked me eagerly what America thought of Soviet Russia. I told them frankly that during the period when the Soviet Union had a non-aggression pact with Germany, America had distrusted Russia. The young men were silent and glum. "But now that America sees the fight you're putting up against Hitler, we're proud to have you as allies," I added tactfully.

They shook my hand earnestly and said: "We're glad, too."

February 10   How many Communists are there in Russia? No figures are available since the last party congress before the war, but a drive is now on to increase the membership in the stringently restricted ranks. Most believe that the party comprises between a million and a half and two million members, or less than ten per cent of the population of 193,000,000. On every side I hear that the heaviest losses in the Red Army are among the Communists, for they are expected to be examples to the rest of the men.

Now the Soviet Union is making a drive to increase party memberships within the ranks of the Red Army. In order to encourage soldiers to join the party, the entrance requirements have been relaxed for the war. Instead of needing a recommendation from party members who have known him for three years, a soldier can now be recommended by persons who have known him for but a year.

Another important change that will make entrance into the party easier for a soldier is that instead of remaining a candidate for a year, as in peace-time, he now must wait only three months to take his examination in Marxist philosophy and Soviet principles.

The expansion of the party within the Army is based on the belief that the best criterion of a man's worthiness and devotion to Soviet Russia is the way he fights for his country. Only the best fighters are being invited to join. The men who will run Russia in the years to come are those who are now fighting for their State.

February 12   With the Germans receding from Moscow, the food situation is better. The lines in front of the food stores and public canteens have grown shorter, though it may be that more people are staying home because of the cold.

The gustiness of these people is impressive. They push their way into the trolleys and subways with much effort, but no quarreling. They work in stone-cold factories and go home to their unlit apartments at night as though these hardships were a part of the law of nature itself. I hear no complaints. As they tramp through the streets, the patient and enduring peasant women wear expressions that are sweet and placid. The men, on the other hand, often wear a habitual frown. Yet I feel an elemental vitality when I mix in the crowds. Their actions seem crude and compelling compared with those of the Americans and English, but in this seems to lie their strength. I can't help feel-

ing that if the Soviet Government allowed the opening of
night clubs, saloons, and burlesque houses instead of har-
nessing these people to the economic machine, Moscow
would be the lustiest city in the world, a sort of giant old-
Western frontier town. But under the pressure of the war
Moscow is certainly puritanical.

February 15   Every month the house
managers in each apartment house re-register the tenants
for their monthly ration cards. Prominent publicity has
been given the case of the secretary of one house manager
who turned over to him the receipts for the new ration cards
she said she had distributed. The secret police discovered
that she had falsely signed the receipts and they really
belonged to people who had been evacuated from Moscow
during the October siege. Her mother was accused of getting
food-stuffs on the cards and reselling them in the public
market.

The girl was tried by a military court and, according
to the law of August 7, 1932, accused of the theft of State
property. Her sentence was death and confiscation of all
her property by the State. The house manager was sentenced to ten years.

The newspapers are also giving prominence to a series of
prosecutions against house managers who permitted the looting of apartments whose tenants were evacuated to the
east. There has been a great deal of this looting during the
three months of siege and it is hard to pin the blame because
many persons gave those who remained behind permission
to remove anything in case the Germans broke into the city.
Now that the Germans have failed, some of the former tenants have regretted their decisions. At any rate, a number
of stiff jail sentences have been handed out to those guilty
of breaking into evacuated apartments.

February 17   I was awakened this morning at seven o'clock by a terrific clatter on the square outside the hotel. In the half-light of dawn I saw with amaze-

ment what appeared to be Hitler's dream coming true — a long line of big black tanks and troop-carriers built to hold thirty-five men at a time, churning in convoy along the snowy streets, their crooked crosses plainly visible. The lines of workers marching to the factories stood agape at the sight. It took me a few moments to realize that they were all driven by Red Army men. It was captured German war material headed for a Moscow factory to be refitted with Soviet guns and turned into fighting machines for the Red Army.

February 20   I am beginning to be aware of the vast Soviet organization fabric behind the home front. The Komsomol, or Young Communist League, is a powerful factor. The boys and girls who are members of this organization are not members of the Communist Party, but they do a great deal of work among the public as junior organizers, morale-strengtheners, and instillers of the Communist spirit and are models for the rest of Russian youth.

I went to the headquarters of the Komsomols to talk to the secretary of the league. Olga Petrovna Mishakova. I was escorted by some very polite young Komsomolkas into a comfortably furnished office. Behind the desk sat an uncommonly handsome young woman. Her ash-blond hair hung in curls around a well-shaped head. Her friendly smile displayed strong, white teeth. She seemed a perfect example of Nordic womanhood, and I thought that if she had been born in Germany, she might well have been a model for German Aryan *Mädchen.*

I asked her what were the eligible ages for joining the Komsomol. She told me from sixteen up to twenty-four. Bluntly I asked Miss Mishakova how old she was. She shook her head, smiled, and said: "I don't have to answer that."

"What are the ideals of the Komsomol?" I asked. "To mold the boys and girls of the future," she replied. She emphasized that athletics was one of the main platforms of the Komsomols. She herself went skiing every day in the winter from six o'clock in the morning until eight o'clock, before coming to the office.

"What hours do you keep?"

"I go home when I'm through."

It was eight o'clock at night when we talked and one of her secretaries brought in a dish of cookies, tangerines, and hot tea. Mishakova offered me a cigarette.

I wanted to know if it was true that the Soviet Union did not allow the circulation of fashion books among the women because it was felt there was no place for women's ornamentation in the struggle to build up the country. Mishakova laughed and said: "Of course not," and took a Soviet pattern book from a drawer. The street clothing shown in its sketches looked to me exactly like American models. Mishakova then said "Do you think that I would dress as simply as I do now if it weren't for the war?" I thought she looked very attractive in her dark skirt and light-blue sweater, high-heeled pumps, and silk stockings, but she explained that every girl in the Soviet Union would dress as smartly as she could if war had not reduced civilian supplies. "We have plenty of fashion books, but now there is no material for a woman to make clothes of," she said regretfully. I asked if the Soviet girls made their own clothes. She shook her blond curls. "Before the war Soviet women were beginning to buy most of their clothes at the department stores because they were all working and didn't have time to make their own."

I inquired about the strength of the Komsomol since the war. She indicated that it had grown tremendously in the past year. There were 12,000,000 dues-paying members of the Communist Youth before the war, and now there were not less than 14,000,000. She said that so many young soldiers in the Army had made application to join that her office was overwhelmed with the mail. She explained the difference between the Communist Party and the Communist Youth. Members of the Komsomol had less responsibility, and joining did not necessarily mean future membership in the party. "Of course," she continued, "regulations of the Communist Party are much more stringent than in the Komsomol."

She pointed out that many of the nurses in the Red Army

were members of the Komsomol, so I asked how the Germans treated Komsomol prisoners. Mishakova pursed her lips and said: "Of course, they are more brutal toward us.

"The Komsomol has no limits to its membership," she went on. "It outnumbers the party by at least ten times and there are no limits to what its growth may be. The party, on the other hand, is kept within a certain size to ensure positive leadership." Mishakova added that religious believers were accepted within the ranks of the Komsomol although they were barred from the Communist Party.

"The duty of the Komsomol," she said, "is to be in the vanguard in the factories and the Army, too." Even members of partisan detachments in the German rear were joining up, she told me, and getting their applications through the German lines to Moscow. She said proudly: "Only this week I accepted twenty applications from partisans fighting deep in the Ukraine." I asked her about the duties of a Komsomol who is a member of a partisan detachment fighting in the German rear. Mishakova smiled and said mysteriously: "I can't tell you that until the war is over." She added that half the membership of the Moscow Komsomol had gone to the front, and four out of five Komsomols in Leningrad were defending the city in the front line. Those who lived in regions away from the front were busy organizing the Voskreseniki, or Sunday workers, who toil on their day off and give their wages to the Government defense fund. The work of the Komsomols was particularly important on the collective farms, she pointed out. "On the farms there are no party cells, only the district party organization."

It seemed to me that the Komsomol was a centrally directed combination of the Junior League, AWVS, YMCA, YWCA, CDVO, and Young Folks' Leagues.

"In the Army," Mishakova continued, "the task of Komsomol members is to help the officers and to be a model for the rest of the soldiers. Like the Communist Party, the Komsomol has its organization within the Red Army regiments."

During the war, she said, the Komsomol was advocating

a sports program for young people, especially encouraging everyone in the Soviet Union to learn how to ski in case he was called upon to take his place in the Red Army. Miss Mishakova told me she herself was also increasing the study of literature in the schools and was stressing the works of Schiller, Goethe, Upton Sinclair, Jack London, H. G. Wells, Theodore Dreiser, Shakespeare, Chekov, and Tolstoy.

As I paused to think of a new question, Miss Mishakova asked if she might direct a question to me. I agreed and she asked me what forms of organization we had for the young people in America. I explained the Boy Scout and Girl Scout movement. She nodded her head: "Yes, we call this the Pioneer Movement in Russia. They work with youngsters up to the age of fourteen." I remarked that in America there were also other organizations that young people might join, like the Y's, 4-H clubs, and church societies, and a great number of our young people went away to camp each year and received some training in citizenship there. Mishakova nodded vigorously and said: "The Soviet Union is doing the same thing in its camps for the Pioneers."

I inquired about the next task of the Komsomol. She explained it would be the training of the women of Russia in the use of modern firearms.

"Does that mean that the Government expects that women will have to march alongside their sons and brothers?"

"Not necessarily, but no one can foresee how long this war will last. The drain in human life is becoming so great that a time may come when women will take to the field to defend their country."

According to the plans she outlined, all over the Soviet Union training schools would be established in the spring, and the young Komsomolkas would be encouraged to learn the use of rifles, tommy guns, and mortars.

Next day I asked my secretary-translator if she thought it would be a good idea for me to send some flowers from the little shop on Gorki Street to Mishakova to show my appreciation of her long talk with me. Indignantly my secretary replied that Mishakova would be insulted. "A woman in the Soviet Union," she said, "expects to be treated just like a man when she does a man's job. You wouldn't send a gift to a man you had interviewed, would you?" she demanded.

February 22   Last night as I walked through the blackout to the studio, it was so dark with the moon down that the beam of my flashlight seemed to make the surrounding gloom even more impenetrable. At two o'clock in the morning the Moscow sky was suddenly lit up by the pale, flickering colors of the northern lights. I decided to mention this in my broadcast today, but the censor refused to pass it. He said: "No northern lights have ever been visible in Moscow because Moscow is not far enough north." Despite all my arguments, he had only one answer: "You wouldn't want to broadcast false information, would you?" This all seemed to have no bearing on the war or Soviet politics, but he was adamant.

February 23   The members of the British squadron of RAF pilots who were stationed in the far north, in the Karelian Isthmus, to defend Murmansk against German bombers, are returning to England. The Soviet Union has decided to award the best fliers with the Order of Lenin.

This has caused some confusion at the British Military Mission because they must make a reciprocal award to Soviet pilots who are presently on a mission in England. But the comparable award to the Order of Lenin would be the Distinguished Service Order, and the British, who are extremely scrupulous about awards, are disturbed. They thought there had been an understanding that the Soviet Government would award the RAF pilots the Order of the Red Star, which is comparable to the Distinguished Flying Cross, but apparently the Soviet Government decided to go one better. Because of tradition, however, the British are still determined to reciprocate by awarding only the Distinguished Flying Cross to the Soviet pilots in England.

February 25 ⚑ Every Soviet officer and NCO wears an extremely large wrist-watch. They look like ordinary pocket watches with straps fitted to them. Because of the necessity of training millions of new reserves this winter, now that Russia has granted time to replenish its Army from the war factories, there is a shortage of wrist-watches for the new Army.

With the Red Army's emphasis on artillery barrages, split-second timing has become a matter of life and death for the combat troops. One of the most successful tactics now used in the winter woods is timed infiltration. White-cowled ski units are sent through the woods, ten or fifteen at a time, moving along separate paths. Thus the German scouts are unable to spot a large body of men working around their flanks. Each of these small groups is given a rendezvous at an appointed time and place on the other side of the forest to form for attack. Any inaccuracy in time in reaching the rendezvous will ruin the whole operation, besides exposing the Red Army men to their own artillery fire, which opens up at the appointed minute.

The Red Army also seems to be more concerned with maps than the British or French. Every officer I see carries a large leather map-case hanging from his Sam Browne belt. It has celluloid windows for quick reading and a luminous-dialed compass strapped to the top of the map-case.

I bought one of these compasses at the Mostorg department store this morning and admired its stout construction and accuracy. It was one of the few things of good quality obtainable in the department store. All of the commodities manufactured for civilians look like cheap gimcracks alongside it. The only conclusion that I can draw is that Soviet factories and workers can turn out goods of high quality when they are ordered to do so.

February 27 ⚑ My long-deferred request to see one of the batteries of anti-aircraft guns that encircle Moscow has been granted.

We bundled ourselves into cars at nine o'clock in the morning and passed through the control points on the edge of Moscow, then turned down the snow-covered Smolensk Highway. A Russian officer escorted us in the leading car. When he finally stopped at a bare spot in the road where no houses were visible and there was only a bleak snow-covered rise on one side, I though his car had broken down. Instead he jumped out and said: "We have arrived."

Then he led us up a snowy path on the south side of the hill and disappeared into the blackness of a tunnel. I followed him into the darkness, half-blinded by the glare of the sun on the snow outside. I could only feel my way through the tunnel until I reached the sickly yellow light of an overhanging electric bulb. I was inside a wood-lined tunnel that ended in large, warm underground barracks. The Russian colonel turned around and asked: "How do you like it?" He was pleased with our amazement.

The entire hill had been hollowed out into extremely comfortable galleries, like the hide-out of movie serial "outlaws." Red Army men were sitting at tables, reading and playing chess, while some of them rested on bunks in an adjoining room. The rooms were sunk ten feet into the ground, but narrow panes of glass near the ceiling let in the daylight. Electric lights with current from a small generator supplied the rest of the illumination. This was one of the anti-aircraft batteries which I had heard bellowing on the outskirts of Moscow long before the guns on the roofs of Moscow buildings went into action.

The commanding officer, a strapping, pleasant-faced colonel, explained that this battery was in the center of the ring of the great circle of fire that protected the Soviet capital. It was their duty to try to break up the formations of German bombers before they reached the city. I asked him what his men did when there was no air activity. He said: "Of course, we always keep a lookout on duty, but there is a lot of spare time on our hands, so the political commissar here" — and he beckoned to a tall, slender young officer — "has arranged for correspondence courses for the men, and some of them are studying to be engineers. Others are studying languages and some just read."

I asked the political commissar what books the men liked best. He replied: "Oh, the best Soviet authors, but you may be interested to know that one of our men has become quite an expert on Shakespeare since the war. He has read *Hamlet* many times." Because there is no "H" sound in Russian, the commissar pronounced it *Gamlet,* in the same way all Russians spoke of "Gitler" and Harry Hopkins as "Garry Gopkins."

We asked a few more questions while we thawed out in the warm room and admired the rough hand-hewn furniture that the men had constructed in their spare time. Finally the commander said: "Enough of this. Let's eat." There was the usual bountiful spread in the officers' mess room — all the regular rations of the Red Army, plus carafes of vodka and boxes of candy. We began the meal with raw salt herring that prepared our thirst for the toasts to come. The vodka had been kept chilled outdoors and was so cold it went down almost tastelessly, without the usual burning sensation. After eight or nine toasts everybody, including the officers, was feeling fine.

We rose from the table and staggered to the next room, where lines of chairs had been set up. The battery had decided to put on an amateur performance. First came a scene depicting the life of the Germans on the other side of the front, some thirty miles away. The chief character was dressed in a very natty blue German parachutist's uniform with yellow buttonholes. The commander explained to us proudly that this was the actual uniform of a parachutist who had been captured near by. Three of the boys formed a small orchestra with two accordions and a saxophone. Afterward the men danced. It was amazing to see these Russians, who looked so clumsy-footed in their heavy felt boots, performing dizzy gyrations in their camp slippers. At the climax of the dance some of the men sitting in back of me were carried away by the frenzy of the music and leaped from their chairs and whirled like dervishes in the famous Russian kazatzka. The commander could no longer control himself either, and throwing off blouse and pistol, he jumped into the center of the floor and went through an uninhibited performance. The room was in an uproar of boot-thumping, cheering, shouting, and accordion music.

Suddenly in the midst of it all a bell clanged madly — the signal for an air raid. The men grabbed their coats almost as though it were part of the dance and fled through the long, black tunnel that led to the outer world. In less than thirty seconds the room was deserted. Even the commander had left without a word of explanation. Pop-eyed, we grabbed our coats and hats, too, and rushed out of the cave. Crowding my way through the black tunnel, I blinked my eyes at the glare of snow and sunlight outside and struggled up the slippery path to the top of the hill.

All I could see at first were the thin, white pipestems of guns sticking up through the snow. As I came closer, I saw that the gun crews were already in position around 3.7-millimeter anti-aircraft artillery set in open igloos that broke the wind. In the platinum-blue bowl of the sky there was nothing visible. Then the guns spoke, and miles off to the west the white blobs of anti-aircraft fire drifted in the blue. Three bee-like dots were humming toward Moscow. In the distance other anti-aircraft took up the challenge and soon the high-flying planes were surrounded by smudges of black and white bursts. The Nazi warplanes proceeded unwaveringly on their course, then suddenly turned at a right angle and climbed until they were out of sight. The guns stopped firing and, cold and shivering, we made our way back into the warmth of the underground galleries. The commander said with a laugh: "Those were reconnaissance planes. Fritz does this once a day. It gives us practice."

We had two or three drinks of vodka for the road, and the commander and his commissar were in a pleasant state of mellowness. Some of the Red Army men supported one or two of the correspondents to the cars. The colonel and the commissar got in the same car with me and pretty Janet Weaver, the Georgia-born American Girl reporter for Intercontinent News. The commander complimented us on our ability to speak Russian and, feeling that his commissar was being left out of the conversation, he reached over and grabbed the commissar's hat off his head and said laughingly: "You see, he has no horns."

We invited all of the officers of the battery to dine with us in Moscow that night and attend the dance in the Metropole Hotel. The commander said he would be delighted to go, but he couldn't leave his battery. No doubt several of his officers could find the time.

After a snooze in my room, I wandered onto the dance floor at nine o'clock to look for my friends and suddenly recognized several of the officers with whom we had spent such a pleasant day. One of them was wearing his dress uniform with its coat-tails buttoned in back. His head was shaven in the ancient military tradition, and if he had worn a monocle in his eye, he would have looked exactly like a German Junker. He was standing alone without a partner. I watched him step over to several girls to ask for a dance, but they refused. I suggested to my own dancing partner that she do me a favor and dance with the young officer. She looked over at him and said: "No, thank you." I asked her why not. "I just don't like his looks," she said.

Several officers of the American Military Mission whirled past me on the floor, dancing with one girl after another. I could see that the Russian fear of foreigners was wearing off rapidly.

Later I joined the shaven-headed officer and his orderly in the correspondents' private dining-room and finished out the evening over a bottle of wine. I asked what he usually did when he came back on leave to the city. He said: "I go to the movies or to a party with some of the boys." Then he added: "You know, this is not my home town. I am from Kiev, so I don't know many people here."

"What about girls?" I asked. "What do your men do, coming to a strange city on leave after three or four months at the front. Are there any brothels in Moscow? "

He looked up at me in surprise and said: "Of course not. There are none anywhere in the Soviet Union."

"What do your men do, then?"

He smiled and said: "They just walk down the street and wink!"

March 1   ✔ Moscow looks reborn each morning. She wears a bright new face of whitest snow like a woman with her make-up on to start the day. Every early pedestrian has to break a new path because the fresh fall has gone untracked during the long hours of curfew.

I have what the American colony calls a "Moscow throat," a low-grade infection which keeps hanging on. Almost every person in the city seems to be hacking and sneezing, but there are no reports of an epidemic here. However, the hard-working press attaché of the Polish Embassy is down with typhus back in Kuibyshev.

The Moscow subways have now been posted with bulletins warning the population to guard against typhus. One of them has been hung near the big portrait of the 1812 retreat of Napoleon in the Revolution Square station. There's always a knot of subway travellers in front of it, studying the scene with satisfaction. Napoleon is something of a hero in Moscow. There are many plaster busts of him scattered throughout the commission stores. My secretary doesn't think there will ever be that feeling toward Hitler because of his gigantic failure.

She tells me the thing to take for my cough is what she calls "streptocide," one of the new sulfa drugs. I gather that before the war everyone in Moscow swallowed sulfa drugs as though they were aspirin. Now it's all going to the Red Army, and the drugstores are out of it. I asked Captain John Waldron, the young American Army doctor attached to the Supply Mission, for his advice. He doesn't recommend sulfanilamide for my case and has given me some of his meager store of aspirin.

March 2   ✔ The Government issued a new decree today. It allows the hardest-working collective farms to increase their sowing areas during the war. The Government has now given collective farms the right to utilize the unused land of adjoining collective farms, despite the fact that the land of each collective farm is owned by its farmers in perpetuity. The collectives farming the land belonging to other farms will have to pay the State tax for their use of the land.

March 3 ✍ Russian social life has some unfamiliar customs. If a toast is offered to you by a woman, or if it is an extremely important toast, such as to the Red Army or Stalin, it is considered bad form not to drain your glass "do adna," or "bottoms up."

It is extremely bad form to whistle. It is done only when giving the "raspberry" at a bad stage performance.

It is considered poor taste to reveal your suspenders in public, with your coat thrown over your arm. I teased my secretary about this custom, saying that it was regrettable that a man couldn't show his suspenders in this "worker's paradise." She asked me if the same convention was the general rule in America. I was forced to admit it was.

When forming a line at a bus stop, it is customary to ask the person at the end of the line if he or she is last. If he says yes, you take your place immediately behind him. The Soviets don't bother with the French system of taking a numbered ticket from a street-corner box to denote their place at a bus stop.

The militiamen who act as traffic policemen are very polite, but strict. No jaywalking is allowed in Moscow. In the first weeks I was here the rules seemed to be relaxed, but now that the sound of gunfire has retreated west from the capital, the militiamen are becoming less tolerant. Jaywalkers who cross outside the lines are hailed by a whistle and a blue-uniformed militiaman fines them up to thirty rubles right on the spot. They get a receipt for their fine.

I wondered why all the militiamen seemed to be of such small stature and now I learn there is a theory that they are picked for smallness to avoid the effect produced by the czarist police. At any rate, a tall militiaman certainly is conspicuous in Moscow and every one that I have seen so far seems to be under average height.

Party members once used the familiar form of "ti," or

"thou," when addressing other members of the Communist Party, but this personal relationship seems to be outmoded now.

As in England, I see girls walking through the hotel with streaked hair, dark at the roots. The numberless Soviet beauty parlors are running out of henna and other hair-dyes. In the hotel barber shop I sit for hours awaiting my turn. Once I was just about to step into a chair when a young tank officer, wearing the gold star of a Hero of the Soviet Union, walked into the shop. He shouldered his way past me, and the girl barber smiled ingratiatingly to him. As a Hero of the Soviet Union he got precedence over everyone else. In the barber shops some of the men have their whole heads lathered and the barbers go over their craniums with a sharp razor, leaving them entirely bald. This is an old Army custom to avoid lice. Yesterday I watched an Army colonel having his head shaved while a young high-school student, wearing a tie with an extremely large knot, was having his long, straight locks set in waves with a wave-setting fluid. I seemed to be the only one who thought it peculiar.

March 4   There is a tow-headed little boy named Vassily living on my floor. He always wears a little embroidered "Tatar" cap on the back of his head. His father is evidently a Soviet official, for in addition to us foreigners none but prominent Russians are permitted to live in the hotel. He told me he is a "Timur" — a member of a children's organization of that name.

Vassily tells me that sometimes he helps shop for a family whose father is at the front. He says he waits long hours in line for the mother, who works in a factory. He has a proud twinkle in his eye as he tells me of his deeds and I don't really think he does all he can for the war effort, since he goes to the movies every day. When I ask him what is worth seeing, he always gives me a very excited report. The war movies are right down his alley. They are a combination of an American Western and a war film in which the hero, a Red Army tankman or Red Air Force pilot, is having a pretty hard time of it, but holds out until reinforcements arrive. The schools haven't opened in Moscow this year, so Vassily has plenty of time on his hands.

Whenever I ask little Vassily what he ate that day, he always answers me with true Russian pride: *"Mnoga, conyetchna* (Plenty, of course)." He looks thin but healthy.

The other day he sold me a hand fishing-line with a little sinker and hook. It was brand-new and marked eight rubles. I finally brought him down to four rubles and then gave him back the fishing-line. As he pocketed the four rubles, he pulled out a wad of paper money that would have choked a horse. Money is no problem for him and he doesn't bother, like children in almost every country, to search along the sidewalks for metal kopek pieces. He could buy very little with them.

One day as a troop of cavalry trotted through the street in front of the hotel, Walter Kerr and I asked Vassily what he was going to be when he grew up — a cavalryman or a pilot. He looked at us with great seriousness and said: "They put guys like us in the infantry."

March 7   A new exhibition at the Museum of the Red Army opened today. I took a trolley up to the Park of the Red Army, past the huge star-shaped Theater of the Red Army, the largest in the Soviet Union, crossed in front of the Red Army House, a modern hotel for men in the services, and entered the low two-story building of the museum. I introduced myself to the colonel who had arranged the exhibit and he was glad to show me around.

The exhibit of the trophies commemorating Hitler's gigantic failure was highly realistic. Monstrous German Skoda tanks and French Panhards, muddy with battle, sprawled across the floors. Both tanks had iron crosses painted above the black and white Nazi crosses, indicating that every man of their dead crews had been decorated.

In the center of the floor stood a German staff car, a camouflaged Mercedes. The colonel remarked: "We left that the way it was abandoned." The dome light of the car was lit, and inside you could see a huge map of Moscow and the suburbs spread over the rear seat. A German tommy gun rested in one corner, and binoculars, tins of canned food, and cigarette butts littered the floor.

Alongside was a great collection of captured machine guns — Polish, Czech, French, Rumanian, Finnish, Hungarian, and German. The colonel pointed out an old American Marlin. It had been manufactured before the last war, and the colonel thought that it might have been picked up in a museum in Poland and, since it still worked, the Germans had thrown it into the great battle.

I was interested in a strange-looking machine that resembled a Buck Rogers weapon. It had six stovepipe-like barrels set in a circle. "That," said the colonel, "is the new six-barreled mortar."

The largest group of spectators was gathered in front of a showcase that held a pair of ersatz German snowboots. The smiling Russians were hypnotized by their gigantic size. Their own light and comfortable felt boots were pure sheep's wool. These were the most enormous boots they had ever seen. They conjured up memories of the seven-league boots of fairy-tales. Designed to be worn over the German jackboots by sentries who were compelled to suffer the rigors of the Russian winter, the German version of the Russian "Valenki" weighed nine pounds each and had hobnailed wooden soles three inches thick. It was clear that the German who wore them never had a chance to run away.

Near by was a showcase containing thousands of bright new iron crosses. These had been abandoned at Kalinin, ninety miles from Moscow, after being brought all the way from Berlin to be awarded at the German victory parade in Moscow.

Another glass case held the pictures of hundreds of young German soldiers. They had been snapped in the photo studios of the Reich, and the boys had posed in their best uniforms. They had been nice-looking youngsters then, far different from the wolf-faced prisoners I had seen. Across the aisle was a collection of European money found on the dead. I felt an odd pang at the sight of thousands of francs in brightly colored French money. Mixed in with it was Czech and Polish paper money brought in by these conquerers transferred to their death on the Eastern Front.

I pointed out to the Russian colonel that the parachute draped on the wall, labeled "Luftwaffe," was not actually German. Its round shroud-cords pointed to the fact that it had once belonged to an RAF airman who had bailed out over the Reich. It had come a long way.

My guide was as much puzzled as I was over his exhibit of ancient blue and gold-braided English and French uniforms which the Germans had looted from some European museum and lugged with them all the way to the suburbs of Moscow. He could only conjecture that perhaps the Germans had planned to establish a museum of their own in the Soviet capital, starting with these uniforms of 1812.

An entire room had been devoted to an exhibition of Soviet propaganda leaflets and newspapers dropped and shot over the German lines. Among the most impressive samples were some excellent phony copies of the *Völkischer Beobachter*. The Russian product had exactly the same format as the German original, but the news was decidedly different. The methods of distributing the leaflets were on display. There were small mortars to make high lofting shots for close propaganda work, and rockets to be used when the wind was right. The third method was a huge plywood airplane bomb that would hold upward of ten thousand leaflets. Its small explosive charge was designed to burst it at a suitable altitude. I decided it ought to be called the "Scherbakov cocktail," after the chief of the Soviet Information Bureau. All the leaflets were provided with small coupons which, if presented to a Russian soldier, would allow the bearer to become a prisoner safe from harm. In another case were hundreds of soiled leaflets that surrendering Nazis had turned in during the winter. One anxious German soldier, unable to find a leaflet, had torn a picture of Stalin from a child's schoolbook and used that as his pass to a Russian prison camp.

Outside in the snowy park was a long shed. Inside were parked eighteen different types of German mechanized equipment, from coffin-shaped amphibious tanks to huge thirty-five-seater troop-carriers. The colonel said reflectively: "The Germans must have a lot of trouble servicing all their different types of armored vehicles. They have no less than seventy, counting all they captured throughout western Europe." He explained that the Red Army has only twenty-eight standard types, outside of American and British models.

In front of me was a tremendous steel ball. It looked to me very much like Beebe's bathysphere. It had a loophole cut in its six-inch-thick steel and it was pockmarked with dents from machine-gun bullets. "That was a pillbox from the Finnish Mannerheim Line," said the colonel. Then he pulled aside a snow-covered tarpaulin shrouding a 150-millimeter cannon. "This," he said, "we took from the Japanese in 1939 in the Battle at Khalkin-Gol." I examined it closely and prepared to describe it fully. That night when a description of it appeared in my broadcast, the censor blue-penciled it. "Lesueur," he remarked, "you are reporting the Russo-German War and not an incident that has nothing to do with the present situation."

March 10 ◄ The eight a.m. broadcast for New York comes at two in the afternoon in Moscow. I sometimes stop in at the commission shops on my way home from the radio station. They are a very important feature of Moscow life. Numbers of them are scattered all over the city. They are a kind of combination of pawnshop and "thrift" store and they never lack for customers.

Here you can buy second-hand clothes, ranging from pure silk pajamas from Mongolia fit for a mandarin, to curious ivory knives fashioned in the Soviet Arctic from walrus tusks. There are brocades from the East, damasks from Syria, ivory boxes from Samarkand, silk rugs from Turkomen, carpets from Bokhara, print frocks bought in Paris and America before the war, old Russian prints, modern oils, and buttons. (No one ever throws away a button in Russia if it is of original design. They are put on new coats and dresses or sold back to the commission shops.) Here are wonderful figurines that once graced a boyar's home in czarist days and black persian-lamb coats discarded by a ballerina. On the shelves are ikons, cameras, watches, paintings, second-hand shirts, ancient opera hats, and modern Soviet costume jewelry.

Some commission shops specialize in certain items. Some are better known for their bric-a-brac and paintings than others; some have old Russian pre-Revolutionary dishes as their main stock. There is a certain amount of pre-Revolutionary jewelry to be bought, but it was being picked up fast, with so much excess purchasing power among the public. Since the manufacture of men's and women's clothes stopped with the war, when all factories were turned over to war production, the commission shops are the only resort of the Moscow woman who wants to refurnish her wardrobe. The commission shops of Moscow satisfy woman's eternal passion for window shopping.

The people who frequent the stores are a cross-section of Russia. There are collective farmers in their peasant dress who have just come in from the country for the day. There are slender, pale-faced factory workers on their day off, well-dressed writers and artists, Red Army officers and their girls shopping for rings, and Red Army privates visiting Moscow for the first time in their lives, still carrying their rifles and the small soot-blackened pots in which they cook their soup at the front.

The mechanics of the commission stores are simple. If you have something you want to sell, you may deposit it at the shop and set a price on it. It will be displayed, and when it is sold, you will be notified. The money is paid over to you in cash after the store takes its commission. The other source of the commission stores' stocks is the *"skupkas,"* established on every other side street of Moscow. Here you may bring in your goods for appraisal and take your money then and there. Your former possession is distributed to a commission shop, which fixes its own price. Since all is Government-controlled, the prices in the commission stores fluctuate arbitrarily by Government order.

The oddest thing I ever saw in a Moscow commission store was an old set of hickory-shafted golf clubs made in Scotland for the old-fashioned gutty ball. I wondered if anyone would ever buy them, since there are no golf courses in

Soviet Russia. The game is considered "bourgeois," I guess. There would certainly be plenty of room for golf links in Russia.

The normal daily turnover of stock in the shops is remarkable. Many times I priced an article one day only to note its disappearance on the next. That is, all except the famous solid-gold cigarette-case. This is the talk of Moscow. It rests among the watches in the showcase of a shabby little shop on Petrovka. Its price is beyond the reach of any ordinary citizen in the Soviet Union, but it is a symbol of what a Soviet citizen could buy if he could only work hard enough. Its tag reads 40,450 rubles. At the ordinary exchange rate of five rubles to a dollar, it would cost an American more than $8,000. There was always a crowd staring at it whenever I entered the store. It was as out of reach for them as the Hope Diamond.

One day I watched three Red Army privates examining it. They were in Moscow on leave from the front and they wore their soiled uniforms and wound stripes proudly. All of them had drunk a reasonable amount of vodka, and the anxious eyes of the woman behind the counter never left the precious gold cigarette-case as they fingered it with their war-soiled hands. Its gleaming polished surface was getting sadly begrimed with greasy fingerprints as one of the privates carefully measured it alongside his long Russian cigarette. Then he handed it back and said in the tone of a man making a casual decision: "No good. It's too small for my kind of smokes." When I left Moscow it had not been sold. I don't think it ever will be.

March 15   The first boxing matches of the war were held in Moscow today. They took place in the Trade Union Hall, the Noblemen's Club before the Revolution and now used for pep rallies by the Komsomol and for lectures on international affairs. I paid nineteen rubles for a ticket and was besieged outside the door by high-school boys trying to buy it from me. The building is one of the handsomest in Moscow, with white columns on the outside and a spacious interior decorated in red and gold, its broad corridors hung with Revolutionary scenes and oil paintings of Lenin and Stalin.

The auditorium was crowded. The fights started at three in the afternoon, so the audience was composed of students, Red Army officers on leave, out with their girl friends, and factory workers on their day off. As in American college matches, no smoking was allowed, applause was discouraged during the bouts, and the referee left the ring when the bell clanged.

Some of the best Soviet boxers were on display. They didn't give me the idea that they were competing for prizes or honors; certainly there was none of that "killer instinct" that goes with our "Golden Gloves." I realized that since true professionalism would be a form of capitalism, these Soviet ringmen were really professional amateurs supported by the State. The best of them gave exhibitions throughout the Soviet Union.

The boys were young, tall, and slender, far removed from preconceptions of Russians as squat, hairy, and short-legged.

The star exhibition was between the heavyweight champion of Russia, Nikolai Korolev, and the champion of the new Soviet Republic of Latvia. The big blond champion had just returned from a winter of fighting as a partisan near Moscow and he was slow and distinctly out of condition. He was an old favorite with the audience, but the applause that greeted him failed to overawe the tall and rangy Latvian, who nevertheless, heavily outweighed, lost the four-round bout on points to Korolev.

I was surprised at the audience. I had never seen such a polite gathering. The spectators were unusually quiet, as though they regarded boxing as a form of "culture." Boxing apparently does not spring from the Russian spirit like dancing. The audience seemed to find little expression of itself in the fights. Many times I had felt more audience excitement and heard more applause and shouting at the ballet.

I approached the heavyweight champion after the fight. and found that, like most big men with physical self-confidence, he was good-natured and smiled easily.

"What is your ambition as a fighter?" I asked.

I was almost bowled over by his reply. Without hesitation Korolev answered: "I'd like to fight Joe Louis."

Taking in my look of surprise, the big blond fighter explained. "Of course," he said, "I know I wouldn't have a chance with him. I'd just like to fight him for the experience. We Soviet fighters don't get the training that Americans do," he went on. "That's everything. Look at me," he said, pinching the fat on his ribs. "I'm not in condition." Then he brightened. "If we ever meet when the second front is started, I'd certainly be grateful if Joe Louis would give me a lesson."

March 17　　　　　　　　　I finished writing my broadcast early and went downstairs to the dance tonight. It took me some time before I found Katya and Ludmilla in the crowd. They agreed to come up to my room to smoke a cigarette, but it took a lot of coaxing.

"Are you Komsomolkas?" I asked them.

"Certainly," said Katya proudly. "Would you like to see my card?" It was a small red pasteboard with her name and picture on it. There were spaces stamped to indicate that she had paid her dues in the organization.

"I used to be a member, too," said dimpled Ludmilla with a pout, "but I dropped out because there were too many responsibilities. I guess they don't want 'Hooligankas,' " she added with a laugh.

I offered them some tangerines which I had bought in the diplomatic store. They were the first tangerines the girls had seen since the war, but they politely declined. I had been told that Russians considered it bad manners to accept gifts too readily, so I coaxed them and they then ate the fruit avidly.

"My sister-in-law has a special ration card entitling her to five oranges a month for her baby," said Ludmilla, "but she's never been able to get the oranges at the stores."

I showed the girls some of the Soviet leaflets the Press Department had distributed among the correspondents. Their fancy was taken by the big sepia print that was dropped over the German lines at Christmas time.

It bore a large picture of a lovely Christmas tree glowing with tinsel and candles. On one side sat a kindly German grandmother, her knitting in her lap; in the other chair sat a plump German housewife, two small children playing at her knee while she read a letter from the front. The only caption on the propaganda picture was a single ruthless sentence in German. It said simply: *"You'll* never see home again."

I walked the two girls home before going to the radio station. Like all Russians they loved to sing. I was learning enough Russian to understand the words. They weren't much different from the jazz I had grown up with: "I don't know from nothing, there's nothing I can do, all I really know is that I love you."

I didn't know them well enough to be flattered.

When I got home from the broadcast at three o'clock in the morning I jotted down some of the Russian words I was learning that sounded familiar in English.

Hooligan and *Hooliganka* meant just what they do in English except, of course, that *Hooliganka* is the feminine gender.

The traditional shout of the charging Russian soldier, *oorah,* was nothing but our *Hurrah.*

I had heard the Russian word *magoo* before. It means: "I can." Therefore the phrase "The Great Magoo" could only mean "The Great I Can."

The Russian word for brains or intelligence is *oomny* and therefore I thought the name of an American cartoon character, "the Great Oom," was easily traced.

I remembered that in New York's garment center the Russian word *schlapa* is commonly used instead of the English word *hat.*

Everywhere in Moscow the English word *stop* is painted along the white street-traffic lines. They say that it was introduced by American engineers. Many technical and military terms have also become interchangeable in both languages, such as *counter-attack, pick-up,* and tens of others.

But I couldn't figure out how the American slang word *hooey* became so generally accepted at home, when in Russian it means the male reproductive organ. Incidentally, the

Slavic talent for cursing would cause an American mule-skinner to blanch. It is based on frequent references to the unfortunate promiscuity of the mother of the target of abuse.

March 20   There's no sign of spring in Russia. Tonight it was so cold and clear that stars seemed to come right down to the old, uneven roof-tops of Moscow.

I was half-way on the snowy walk to the radio station when the sirens sounded. The big guns on the edge of the city began their deep pulsating thunder and soon the drone of the night raiders sounded directly overhead. The guns in Moscow's parks began their challenge.

Until the sirens sounded, there were no pedestrians on the curfew-cleared streets, but as I watched, the doorways began to fill up with shadowy figures. They were the night watchers, the tenants who serve a turn of duty once a week as air-raid wardens.

I hurried along through the snow as the beat of the guns grew louder and the steel shrapnel splinters began to rain down into the wide streets. I had survived all the raids of the London blitz, but I was never so afraid of falling shrapnel before. I longed for the old tin hat Ed Murrow had given me for London wear, which I had left behind as "non-essential." When the drone of the bombers came directly overhead, small cannon from the roofs of buildings I never suspected harbored gun positions began to bark. The noise was deafening but it was one of the most beautiful sights of war. The rapid-firing roof-top guns shot small strings of flaming onions into the night sky. Straight upward climbed the incendiary shells, slowly, like colored beads on a string, red, yellow, and green. I knew they could not hit the planes at this range, but I could imagine that the sight of these flaming onions tearing skyward would be enough to deter a pilot from diving in order to gain more accuracy. Even as I watched, however, I heard an unseen warplane in the skies roar louder and louder as the Nazi pilot dared the Moscow anti-aircraft gunfire. He loosed a string of bombs that "crumped" deafeningly, and their orange flash lit the entire horizon, silhouetting the battlements of the Kremlin against the sky. All around me little cloud puffs of snow rose six inches or more from the towering snow-piles as the earth shook with the concussion of these block-busters. The anti-aircraft guns raised their voices to such a pitch of angry hate that a cold fear began tingling up my spine. The falling shrapnel was so heavy now that overhead trolley wires of Moscow were strumming like guitar strings as the falling steel nicked them.

I flattened myself against the archway of an old museum-church. Two sentries standing across the street walked over to question my suspicious actions. Reassured by my air-raid pass and night pass, we all walked along the streets while shrapnel tinkled on the icy pavement. I had a feeling we ought to take cover fast, but, bound by chains of pride, the two sentries and I sauntered along through the blitz. I don't know how it happened, but suddenly we were all walking faster, almost at a trot. Then we three broke into a run simultaneously, gained the shelter of a hallway in a breathless hurry, looked at each other, and began to laugh.

When the drone of planes passed and the sound of gunfire retreated again to the outskirts of the city, I hurried to the radio station, where, three floors underground, the Soviet announcers and news-writers had not even heard the boom of the guns.

No sooner had I finished my broadcast and started to walk home than the circling Nazi raiders came over again. Moscow guns began their abrupt clamor. I was in no mood for foolhardiness now. When a large piece of shrapnel bounced on the pavement a yard or so away, I picked it up, noted its jagged edges, and felt the thinness of my fur hat. Then I quickly retreated into a hallway. The old woman on guard asked me what time it was. I showed her my watch, but she shook her head and I had to haltingly read the watch for her. I realized that she had been born long before the Soviet Revolution and had never learned to tell time.

March 21   From talks with Soviet military men and foreign observers here I have been able to form a picture of the German invasion of Russia. Soviet experts say that it was apparent that the Germans had hoped for such intensive fifth-column activity in Russia by dissident elements that there would be riots in the Russian rear after the first defeats of the Red Army, followed by a civil war between the Russian collective farmers and workers. As in every country at war, there is no doubt that there are potential fifth-column elements in Soviet Russia, but they are powerless and leaderless owing to the efficient system of internal police. Instead, the German armored forces met such resistance from the Red Army that they had to lend their immediate support to the Nazi infantry. Thus the German tank divisions were forced to neglect their independent functioning, which had led to such great successes in the west. The German plan was for their highly mobilized Army to conquer the vast spaces of Russia and crush the Red Army by superiority in equipment and by the fire power of its highly mobilized armored divisions. Everything had been made mobile — planes, tanks, armored cars, self-propelling guns, motorcycles armed with machine guns, and infantry in trucks.

In one violent surge to the east the German High Command figured they could smash the Russian resistance and reach the Volga, the Urals, and the Caucasus Mountains in a single summer. The main group of the German armies made a deep break toward Moscow with a movement in three phases — one toward Minsk, one toward Smolensk, and the last toward Rostov. The first phase of the war was accomplished very quickly, but the Germans were held up after the first few weeks in their march toward Minsk, and the German High Command began to feel the difference between their walk-through in the west and the depth of the resistance in Russia. At the end of the first month of war the Germans had reached Smolensk, but there they were held up for two months. Their attempt to break deep into the Russian rear was deferred and the central front was fairly well stabilized until October.

Thus by August 1941 the greatest German mistake had become apparent. Their strategic plans for a violent offensive by their mobile storm groups had not worked out. Delays had occurred and the tempo of the offensive was reduced. By September the war had become protracted and the German armies could move only in the south. They were stopped at Leningrad and Tikhvin in the north and at Smolensk in the center. The German plan for a blitz war had failed because of a disproportionate balance between the percentage of motor-mechanized forces making up the vanguard and the slower-moving infantry divisions. Out of 184 German divisions, fully one third were tank and motorized divisions, with only 120 ordinary infantry divisions. This was a gigantic army, but it was still insufficient for operations of such scope across the vast expanses of the Soviet Union. Any delay in the march of the motor-mechanized forces became critical moments. These units were unable to stand still and fortify themselves. Thus these armored spearheads lost their main function as pure offensive forces.

The German infantry itself was beginning to prove itself inferior to the Red Army infantry in that it was undertrained for heavy fighting under field conditions. It had not been trained for the type of warfare that had become necessary. Evidently the German Command thought that all it had to do was score tactical successes with the vanguard of the motor-mechanized troops. So the Germans were forced to retrain their ground infantry in the midst of battle. For their operations in the Low Countries, France, and Poland these troops had been trained only to hold ground behind the masses of tanks and guns. Also, the Germans found that Soviet artillery was superior in range and numbers.

The Germans held a theory that the dive-bomber had replaced heavy artillery in modern blitz warfare and for the most part had equipped their troops with only short-range artillery and mortars. They had definitely underestimated the power of artillery in modern warfare. But the chief mistake of the Germans emerged in the supply problem. They had figured only on supplying their troops for rapid operations and had tried to avoid protracted battles requiring expenditures of large amounts of ammunition and food. They had placed great store on the ability of their troops to live off the land in their rapid progress toward Moscow. Such a quick advance would have simplified the feeding problem, but it had held good only for short distances similar to the campaign in the west, where quick, decisive results had not required replacement of stores. The Germans were forced to divert troops and equipment to furnish a systematic food supply from western Europe to the German forces at a standstill on the eastern front.

A German motor-mechanized group is conditionally composed of 3,000 tanks, 45,000 trucks and autos, nine motorized and infantry divisions, and an air fleet of 500 planes. Daily requirements for such a group are thirty trainloads of fuel and ammunition. So the speed of the German advance was conditioned not only by the delays encountered by the spearhead of motor-mechanized forces, but by the need to organize a supply system in the rear.

During the first phase of the German advance their communication lines were not so extended and supplies could be brought up by truck. In these first weeks the German armies lived off the land and ate up their supplies like grasshoppers, forgetting that winter was coming. Then the Germans began to suffer because their supply lines lay in hostile country and were menaced by partisan warfare.

Another surprise that awaited the German High Command resulted from the fact that their plans for blitz warfare were based on light losses. Their losses in men, tanks, planes, and other equipment passed the mark fixed by the supply chiefs. By September the resources for re-forming the Army had become restricted since all men of the best military ages had already been mobilized for the surprise attack on the Soviet Union.

Hitler made more and more demands from the vassal states, and the reserves entering the Army were qualitatively much lower than the manpower with which he had started. The losses in life, the interruption of supplies, and the wearing out of equipment began to exhaust the motor-mechanized vanguard of the German Army, which was the mainstay of the offensive. The advance was slowed up by the necessity for regrouping battered divisions and the repair of machines.

Even with these difficulties Hitler made the decision to launch a new offensive in October, on the verge of the Russian winter, despite the proof of failure of the essential plan for the campaign. Ordering the capture of Moscow at any cost, he failed to take into consideration that his army was poorly equipped for winter warfare. Concentrating eighty battered divisions on the approaches to Moscow, the Germans made their last advance during the week of November 16. The Red Army, in turn, was bringing up fresh reserves from the rear for a counter-blow. The Germans never dreamed that Russia still possessed a large enough army to strike back, and as soon as the bitter Russian winter began, the German Army lost the initiative within the very sight of Moscow and was on the verge of a catastrophe. Their motor-mechanized forces found themselves unable to operate in winter. Germany could no longer win the war.

March 23　　　　　　　　　　☙ The patience of these people amazes me. If the people of Leningrad are being deprived of food these days, certainly the population of Moscow is not being glutted. Much of the normal supply here is going to feed the freed population in the reconquered villages.

For the last few days there have been no rations in the stores except bread, and the lines in front of the bread shops sometimes extend almost clear around the block. There is no pushing or shoving, although once in a while I see little arguments caused by people leaving the line and coming back many minutes later. It is customary to tell the person behind you to hold your place, but sometimes it is difficult to find the person again, and any attempt to break into the line is resented.

I heard an old Moscow story of the men who possess special passes, because of the importance of their work. This allows them to go to the head of any line without waiting. According to the story, one of them pushed his way up to the head of a line, and when angrily told to wait his turn, he explained that he had a special pass. They indignantly informed him that this was a line of people with special passes.

March 25   ✒ Mr. Palgunov, chief of the Press Department, summoned all the correspondents to his hotel room. He announced solemnly: "You're leaving for Kuibyshev tomorrow afternoon at four o'clock."

It was a bombshell. The Press Department couldn't order us around like that! We hastily called a meeting to protest and then marched back to ask Mr. Palgunov whether this was an order or merely a request for us to go back to Kuibyshev.

He said: "No one can order you to do anything, but you must remember that the headquarters of the diplomatic corps and the press are still in Kuibyshev, and we are asking you to go back."

There didn't seem to be any way out, because if we chose to stay on in Moscow, we would have no means of getting our work censored, and neither the telegraph bureau nor the radio station would accept uncensored copy. We demanded a few days' grace to get our affairs in order, as we had been living in Moscow for two months already, and finally Mr. Palgunov agreed.

March 27   ✒ Istra is a ghost town. All Moscow mourns the passing of this suburb and village which was once filled with hundreds of summer houses, or dachas, where the workers spent their holidays. Whereas all the farms are owned collectively, any person with enough money can build a summer house outside the city and own it outright as private property.

Istra was a pretty place. Now every one of its more than one thousand cottages has been burned to the ground. The Germans left only the little hospital on the hill. Against the fresh greenness of the pine trees, the first sight of the village shocked us all. Only stark and blackened chimneys were standing, like a forest of desolation.

The sprawling, whitewashed Monastery of New Jerusalem, which has stood for centuries, was left in pathetic, gutted ruins by the Germans. It had been one of the most famous church-museums in the Soviet Union. All that was left were empty walls, smoke-blackened by the fire of the German destruction brigades. The Soviets had maintained the gold-domed, thick-turreted old monastery fortress as a museum piece of old Russian culture, famous for its beautiful ikons. The head of the village Soviet showed us around the ruins. Like other Communist Party members, he had fought as a partisan during the German occupation of his village. As he surveyed the ruins of the monastery, he asked if we would like an ikon as a souvenir. He pointed at some battle-scarred examples on the rubble-strewn floor. Taking him at his word, Walter Kerr and I decided to search the dungeons of the monastery cellar. A Soviet sentry saw us disappearing into the blackness and called out a warning against unexploded mines. In the gloom we discerned stacks of pre-Revolutionary ikons piled up in a corner. Most of them were rather battered, but we selected the best. In another room I discovered an ancient moth-eaten soldier's hat of brass and red felt with the czarist double eagle on it. Walter tucked a sixty-pound miniature bronze cannon under his arm.

Loaded down with our souvenirs, we could hardly follow the rest of the party up the hill through the snow to the only building standing in Istra, the hospital. We passed by several peasants, who stared curiously at our strange burdens. I wondered if they thought this was a second invasion of Istra. At the hospital the nurses told us that the hour the Germans discovered they were being flanked, they fled, leaving only a squad to put the torch to the town. It was the most terrible sight any of them had ever witnessed. The snow-crested hills were filled with the hellish glare. When they reached the hospital, the Nazi corporal ordered the nurses to remove the sick and wounded soldiers and civilians out into the snow. The Russian nurses refused. Seeing that the women were adamant, the Germans left. The sound of Russian guns was getting closer.

March 28　　　　　　　　⚑ The new British Ambassador, slender and suave Sir Archibald Clark Kerr, former Ambassador to China, has arrived in Moscow and we correspondents held a dinner for him at the only restaurant available, the "Aragvi," or Caucasian Restaurant, just off Gorki Street. Everyone seemed to be pleasantly well along after repeated toasts — everyone, that is, except the broadcasters, who shouldn't drink before giving tongue at two o'clock in the morning. They were studiously and regretfully sober.

On my return to the hotel, just before the midnight curfew, there was a message directing Gilmore, Parker, and me to call at the headquarters of the NKVD, or, as Americans call them, "the four-letter boys." We walked up through the snow and blackout into a dimly lighted building in the rear of the famous Lubianka Prison. Very few persons know what goes on within those old walls and those few don't talk. A uniformed NKVD man asked for our passes and examined them with great care, even though he had been notified that we were expected. Finally he directed us upstairs, where we entered some well-lighted business offices and were greeted by a young blonde secretary who spoke excellent English. It wasn't so very mysterious, after all. She said cheerfully: "You'll be glad to know that we have recovered the clothing you lost on the train in Archangel."

She opened the door, and neatly piled about the room were heaps of shirts, socks, sweaters, suits, and almost all the odds and ends that had disappeared when our suitcases were looted from the freight car five months before.

We were asked by the uniformed NKVD man to identify our clothes while the English-speaking secretary made a list of the articles we claimed. The secret police had done such a good job that among our scattered possessions I found women's scarves, odd bits of Russian ribbon, which must have been removed from the thieves' homes. Only one of our suitcases was returned to us, the big calfskin bag belonging to Eddy Gilmore. The hinges were broken on both sides. It was obvious the NKVD would have liked to return both Parker's bag and mine, but they had been so mutilated that they were embarrassed to do so. All the shirts and socks had been laundered. Even the suits had been pressed. Virtually all our possessions were there, but I was the most unfortunate because only the vest and coat of my suit of clothes had been recovered. I was still doomed to be a "one-suit" man.

We gathered our long-lost property into our arms and were escorted inside another office, where we met the official who was responsible for its recovery. He shook our hands with the typical bone-crushing Russian grip and asked: "Are you pleased?"

"How did you manage to trace these thieves?" we all inquired.

"It wasn't easy," he replied. "We checked at every railroad station from Archangel and Moscow clear across the Urals until we found one point where a railroad official remembered the car was sealed and another point where it was found the seal was broken. Then we checked all the villages in between until someone was reported wearing European clothes, and then we found the three thieves." He added: "You know, of course, these men were Germans."

"How do you know?" I asked.

"We found letters in German in their possession."

He merely shrugged his shoulders mysteriously when I inquired what had happened to the three thieves, and remarked: "Much of the credit for the recovery of your clothing should go to the railroad police. They did a fine job." That closed the incident.

March 29 ✍ The corps of correspondents left Moscow from the Kazansky Station at four thirty in the afternoon today. There was the usual excitement and confusion among our secretaries and the Intourist girls before we departed. In the station was the ever present crowd of ticket-holders sleeping patiently on the floor awaiting the departure of trains delayed for days. Negley Farson remarked that the confusion over timetables and the scene in a Russian railroad station have never changed. It was like this when he was in Russia before the Revolution.

This promised to be the most comfortable of my train journeys in Russia. We were quartered in the "international cars," with well-upholstered berths. The sun was a brilliant champagne yellow across the snowy wastes of the Volga steppes. Looking out the window, I noticed that the evacuated factory machinery which had lined the sidings everywhere during my previous railroad trips had now been removed. The great industrial migration to the east was completed, but our train was still sidetracked for hours to make way for military traffic headed for the front. Big white-painted tanks and whitewashed field guns went frontward, while long lines of damaged tanks piled on flat cars made their way to the rear with us. Hospital trains hurtled past us. Everything was still white with snow.

April 1 ✦ Looking from the train window, I saw two newly constructed armored trains, massive and jointed with iron scales like prehistoric beasts, painted a gun-metal gray. They resembled a score of wheeled tanks linked together in a long, reptilian chain. One of them was named "Bolshevik of the Urals." The other was "Kaganovich," after the Jewish Commissar for Transport.

As we rolled slowly east, I saw the little peasant cottages in the valleys banked with snow up to their thatched roofs and looking like so many beaver houses in a frozen swamp.

We had each brought along three days' supply of food, including a roast chicken, some hard-boiled eggs, bologna, and bread and apples purchased at the diplomatic store.

March had been the month of the great Russian blizzards, and the snow, held back by the fences along the tracks, towered ominously. One of the thirty-five-foot-high snowdrifts had collapsed across the tracks, and peasant women from miles around had been mobilized to do the digging. They had already worked for two days when our train arrived, but we remained stalled for thirty-six more hours. We went to bed early because the electric lights failed.

April 4 ✦ This is our sixth day on the train, and we have stopped several times alongside great piles of cut logs placed near the tracks. Brigades were formed to pass logs into the tender of our wood-burning engine. Some of us ran short of food, but we managed to buy bread and milk from the peasant women who met the train at the sidings.

Six months ago when I traveled across the Urals, the peasant women were willing to sell their food for rubles. Now they won't accept money, but want soap, tobacco, or some form of goods in barter. I traded a cake of soap for a quart of milk and a dozen pickles.

April 6   ✒ At Kuibyshev. The great spring thaw has begun here. Our cars waded through pools of slushy water on the way to the Kuibyshev airport to meet the new American Ambassador, Admiral William Standley. The flood conditions were so bad that Red Army men were stationed every quarter-mile to halt traffic on one side while the next line of cars and wagons plunged through the deep pools of snow water.

All reporters seem to spend a large part of their lives waiting on cold airfields for celebrities to arrive. Today we waited six hours before a big American Douglas, with the white star of the USAAF on its wings, touched the slushy field.

White-haired Ambassador Standley was the first man out of the plane, and despite his age he jumped down into the slush. We walked over to greet him, but he got in the first words: "Well, boys, what's the news from America?" We confessed that we had heard no news from America for months. The Ambassador smiled and said he had been on a plane so long that he had been out of touch with recent happenings. With him was the new Naval Attaché, Captain Duncan, who grinned at us and said: "Where are those poker-players I read about in Quentin Reynolds's book?" (We mentally noted him down as ready prey, but he surprised us.)

Ambassador Standley's first sight of Kuibyshev could not have been very reassuring. Russia in April is ten per cent rain and ninety per cent slush. We drove back to town past the long lines of prison camps and watched hundreds of prisoners laying a new railroad track, under the watchful eye of armed guards. The prisoners were a depressing sight. I recalled what some Russian friends had told me about their penal system. They regard it as one of the most emancipated in the world, in which a man or woman is not imprisoned for long periods of time, but works off his crime in projects for the State. As we drove back to Kuibyshev we noticed that some of the guards standing watchfully in the towers of the prison camps were women. They wore the usual purposeful look of women workers in the Soviet Union. They didn't regard themselves as women sentries, but just as sentries.

April 8   Admiral Standley called a press conference in the little three-story frame house that is now the American Embassy in Kuibyshev. He said: "Russia will be the decisive front for America in 1942. Japan will get her punishment in 1943." He added that we would not neglect the Pacific, but during the coming year we could do little more than maintain the Pacific Fleet.

We asked him what had actually happened at Pearl Harbor. The Admiral said: "That whole misfortune can really be traced to typical American philosophy." He added: "Our men had been simply unable to imagine Japanese treachery on such a vast scale. We had permitted a spy circle to exist in Hawaii and allowed the Japanese Consulate to send coded messages to Tokyo without attempting to decode them because we were still at peace. That was the American way and that was the sort of way of life we have pledged ourselves to fight for. You might also say," he said with a smile, "that we walked up to the Japanese with a big chip on our shoulder. And, boy, did they knock it off!"

April 10   Today I visited Public School No. 6 in Kuibyshev. It is a typical old school building such as we still have in America — four stories high and seating about a thousand pupils. The school principal, a stocky, intelligent woman, with cropped hair, explained to me that the school's worst problem was overcrowding, now that Kuibyshev had become an evacuée city. Instead of having one session of classes a day, there had to be two. One group of children attended classes from eight in the morning until half past twelve, a second batch from one o'clock to five thirty. The hours from six to midnight were devoted to industrial training of the recently mobilized housewives. The classes had averaged about thirty pupils before the war, but now they had mounted to about forty-five each.

Last year the older pupils, from sixteen to eighteen, worked on the collective farms during summer vacations, but being raw amateurs, they were not of any great help. So this year, the principal told me, one of the new courses was a study of simple agricultural training in the operation of farm machinery, including plows and threshers. The course also included instruction in cow-milking.

I wandered around the corridors and entered the small assembly hall. There was an exhibition of posters. Most of them depicted historical scenes of Russia's great military traditions, following Stalin's speech of November 7, in which he said: "Let the heroic images of our great fore-fathers, Alexander Nevsky, Dmitry Donskoy, Kuzma Minin, Dmitry Pozharsky, Alexander Suvarov, and Mikhail Kutuzov, inspire you in this war!" The schools had naturally followed Stalin's directive. The study of the military victories of the czarist days was certainly a departure in the curriculum of Soviet Russia.

The older boys and girls in the auditorium were tall, well-built youngsters. I asked what they were going to do this summer. They said in chorus they were going to work on the farms.

"Do you want to?" I asked one shy-looking, spectacled boy.

"It is not a question of whether I like it or not," he replied. "But it is interesting and I know I must help."

There was certainly no doubt in their young eyes regarding the ideals of the Soviet Union and no skepticism about their futures. I asked a bright-looking sixteen-year-old what he was going to be after graduation. He said he was going to the Moscow Institute to study civil engineering. I turned to two of the girls. One of them said she was studying to be an agricultural expert, while the other, a husky, laughing blonde, said she was going to join the Red Army as a Cossack nurse. The other children laughed at her ambition, but there was no doubt in her mind that she was going to be just that. She said she was training several hours a week at the Cavalry School in Kuibyshev. The boys told me they were studying physics as applied to the war, practical problems like the digging of trenches, the effect of heat on the expansion of gun barrels, and electricity as applied to explosions of mine fields.

"Otherwise," said an earnest, brown-eyed youngster, "the courses haven't changed much from the previous year." His favorite subject was literature and he asked me eagerly if I had brought any English books with me. He said he had already read Theodore Dreiser, Jack London, and Erskine Caldwell in translation. His great favorite was Theodore Dreiser and he hoped I had brought some of the recent Dreiser books. I said I wasn't sure that Dreiser had written anything lately. His face fell and he said: "That's too bad. He is my favorite author."

The principal led me into several classrooms, where I sat in the back of the room and watched the teachers call on their best pupils, hoping to get the right answers. I recalled my own school days and my teacher's nervousness when visitors came to observe the class.

There were about twenty-five pupils from eight to fourteen in the English class and they kept repeating English phrases that their small, blonde teacher scribbled on the blackboard. She was worried about their pronunciation. So was I. Her accent was even more bothersome. I heard several children repeat the word "Sunday" over and over again. She grew impatient and said: "You must say it with the accent on the last syllable — 'Sun-*day.*' "

Then I walked into the class of eight-year-olds. Many of the little boys had their hair cropped short, but the little girls wore theirs in long braids with hair-ribbons. They looked exactly like my memories of class 3-A, even down to the middy blouses worn by the girls. Their teacher reminded me of the one I had studied under many years ago in Chicago, thin, gray-haired, and sharp-voiced. School-teachers, I am convinced, must look the same the world over.

When I got up to leave, she told the class to stand up and say good-by. They did so in a loud chorus, all except one girl far back in the rear. She was twice as tall as any of the rest and I knew she'd been "left back." She just couldn't bring herself to stand up and show how big she was against all those little ones. As I closed the door behind me, I heard the teacher say: "Valya, you heard me say you were to stand up and say good-by. Why didn't you do it?"

Next came the class in military training, given five hours a week. It was conducted by a sixty-three-year-old man in uniform. The fifteen-to-eighteen-year-old boys and girls were taking apart a sub-machine-gun while the military director explained its workings from a chart. The boys also studied tactics, map-reading, and how to crawl under fire. I watched some of the boys putting together the bolt of a rifle. They did it like veterans of the Foreign Legion. The director told me that the girls had a choice of taking primary nursing or the study of modern firearms.

I asked one of the sixteen-year-old girls: "Why are you studying the workings of a sub-machine-gun?"

"I like it and it's easy," she said. That was that.

The gray-haired military director called to a group of the boys and girls and told them to go to the shooting gallery. I watched three sixteen-year-old girls, dressed in skirts, sweaters, cotton stockings, and low-heeled shoes, throw themselves prone on the mats, tuck their skirts carefully around their knees, and start shooting .22-calibre rifles at small targets seventy-five feet away. They each fired three shots and brought their targets back. Their shooting was remarkably good. One of them offered me a rifle, but I declined. I didn't dare enter that competition.

We walked out into the snowy back yard, where some husky high-school seniors were practicing throwing grenades of the potato-masher type. One of the boys, a big, blond fellow who probably would have been fullback on an American high-school football team, was too good. He threw his grenade clear over the wall and out of the school yard.

Before I left, the Soviet principal was very eager to find out how the school compared with those in America. I told her the children looked almost the same to me, that our studies were not quite so practical, but I myself regretted that I hadn't started the study of a second language as early as her pupils did. I wondered why it was that although Russia was one hundred years behind America in many respects, our schools were scarcely in advance of Russia's.

I asked if I might send the youngest class a questionnaire as a sort of test of their school work. She agreed. I wrote down a series of five questions and she gave them to the gray-haired old lady who taught class 3-A. Later that afternoon the answers were delivered to me by the president of the senior class, with many smiles.

To my question: "Who is Stalin?" most of the children had written: "He is the father and the teacher," exactly as the banners proclaimed in the assembly room, where in white letters on red muslin was a statement that "Stalin is the Father and the Teacher." To the question: "Who is Churchill?" the children usually had answered: "He is the British Ambassador." But for the question: "Who is Roosevelt?" the majority of answers said: "He is a friend of Stalin." To "Why is Russia fighting Germany?" one of the children answered: "Because Hitler jumped over our land." Another said: "Because Hitler is a beast." The last question was: "Why is Japan fighting America?" The answer more often than not was: "Because Hitler told it to."

April 13   ⚑ Today is the anniversary of the Russo-Japanese neutrality pact. *Pravda* said that it was no secret that since the Revolution Japanese-Soviet relations had been submitted to severe trials, including Japanese intervention in the Far East in 1918 and 1922, the occupation of Northern Sakhalin Island and the capture of Manchukuo, followed by the frontier warfare at Lake Hassan and Khalkin-Gol. Said *Pravda:* "It is highly necessary that the Japanese military fascist clique, who are dizzy over their successes in the Pacific, understand that their saber-rattling over a war in the North would be more harmful to Japan than anyone else."

April 15 ✍ There are small patches of ice-free water near the Volga shore and many amateur fishermen are trying their luck. They dip curious Chinese umbrella nets, suspended from a pole, into the stream, pulling them up every five minutes or so. I watch them every day on my way to the radio station, but they are like the tireless fishermen in the Seine in Paris. I have never seen them catch anything.

The waterfront is noisy these days with the hammers and saws of boat repairmen. The Volga rowboats are Eastern in appearance, broad in the beam, with long, slender bows. The little boys and girls have started to discard their winter hats and are wearing little colored embroidered "Tatar" skullcaps. East meets West here in Kuibyshev and the influence of Asia is plainly visible on the streets. Many of the little Russian school girls wear their hair in two long braids down their back, giving them quite a Chinese appearance from the rear. The women, too, wear soft cotton houseslippers, even out in the streets, as in China.

April 16 ✍ Walking down near the Volga today, I met Miss Wu, the pretty press attaché of the Chinese Embassy. She is in Russia on a mission to study Soviet culture and she's very well acquainted with Soviet art and the theater. She speaks Russian very well and has agreed to give me Russian lessons in exchange for English lessons.

I invited her to the performance of Tchaikovsky's *Eugene Onegin,* which was being sung at the Kuibyshev Bolshoi Theater. One of the British tommies attached to the mission sold me his tickets. He calls it: *"Eugene One-Gin."*

The Japanese correspondents have been living at the Grand Hotel since we have been in Moscow. We pass by on the stairs unseeingly. Every night we watch them dining only elbow-length away in the restaurant. Things are going very well for them in the Pacific, so they invariably have a bottle of Scotch standing on the table while they eat. They are the only foreigners who have any Scotch left. On days following victories in the Pacific, the whole Embassy meets for a special banquet in the Grand Hotel. It's beginning to get on our nerves.

Almost every morning, when I enter the public wash-room on the second floor to shave, a Japanese correspondent is parked in front of the only mirror, wielding a straight-edged razor. I often wonder what people in America would think if they knew that by just jostling his elbow I could cut his throat. Unfortunately, it is not open season on Japs in Russia. However, I couldn't resist the temptation of pushing him one morning when he was hogging all the mirror. He gave me a long, cold glance. I stared back innocently.

April 17   ✍ Kuibyshev is a correspond-ent's purgatory. I have grown used to the normal frustra-tion of a reporter's life in Moscow, where virtually the only news sources are the official Soviet newspapers and the only "news beats" are the obscure paragraphs that your trans-lator had spotted and the other translators have missed. A reporter can do almost nothing for himself in the way of getting special stories. For instance, I cannot phone the Commissar of Agriculture or Oil and ask for an appoint-ment. All such requests must be given in writing to the Press Department, which may arrange the appointments in a month's time or ignore them altogether.

But here in Kuibyshev the Moscow newspapers reach us two or three days late by plane although the censorship has arranged for teletype transmission of selected articles. These are typed in a dozen duplicates and handed to the cor-respondents at all hours of the day and night. The result is that all correspondents must maintain a "death watch" on the press office for fear of being "scooped."

I know that Russian executives and Communist Party members have a much better idea than we do about what is going on, because they hear special lectures on foreign af-fairs in their institutions and the "Agitpunkt" clubrooms, from which foreigners are now barred.

Only the other day I heard a second-hand report of a lecture given at the Kuibyshev "Agitpunkt." The gist of it was that the Germans are gathering their forces in the south for a new offensive against the oil of the Caucasus, and the Red Army will cushion the shock and then counter-attack. Furthermore, Hitler is having trouble with the vassal states, especially Hungary. The Communist Party members were reportedly told that Hungary is already putting out peace-feelers to Britain on the basis that its heart is not really with fascist Germany, for they have supplied far fewer divisions on the eastern front than Rumania.

It's impossible to check this report, however, because Communist Party members are wary of conversing with foreigners and dislike being seen in their company.

The strain of the long winter is telling on me as well as on the other correspondents. The complete lack of fresh vegetables, the inertia of seven months' confinement in hotels because walking conditions are so bad in the snow, and the frequent mild attacks of dysentery have made us all irritable and argumentative.

Nevertheless, I recognize in myself a gradual conditioning to life in Russia. I am learning to judge people by their faces and thoughts and not by their outworn clothes. I no longer pay much attention to my own clothes. I allow my suit to go unpressed for weeks, my shoes are as scuffed and worn as a Russian worker's, and it takes so long to get the laundry back that I wear the same shirts for days. I am beginning to appreciate the old Russian saying: "Have a heart and have a soul; all else is passing fashion."

If we are going to spend the summer in Kuibyshev, I am determined to spend the time fishing on the Volga. The sports store down the street is well provided with fishing-tackle and my only expenditures aside from room and board have been for a bamboo rod and line. There are no reels for sale, but I think I can carve one out of a wood block. I once made one when I was about ten.

April 18   ✍ We have had wonderful news today. Tokyo radio says that American warplanes have bombed Tokyo, Yokohama, Kobe, and Nagoya. I picked up the news on the set lent me by the radio station.

The Japanese broadcast said that Tokyo and Yokohama were raided for three hours in broad daylight, and that the seaports of Kobe and Nagoya, sites of the big Kawanishi and Mitsubishi airplane plants, were raided two hours later. The Japanese commentator, speaking musical-comedy English, was at a loss for words to describe his feelings. He said that schools and hospitals in Tokyo were seriously damaged and farming villages strafed with machine guns. Later he added: "I suppose our good friends in Chungking are pleased with these horrors heaped on the heads of our school children. The American planes fled in the direction of China."

Next day all Soviet papers carried the Japanese official account of the raid under a headline much larger than they ever had given to RAF raids on Germany. The blonde room clerk at the Grand called me aside and said that one of the Japanese correspondents had stormed over to her and thrown a copy of *Pravda* in front of her. Pointing to the big black headline, he said furiously: "You people are happy, aren't you, over what happened to our great city!" She said all she could do in reply was to point at the newspapers and say meekly: "But, you see, we are only giving prominence to the account sent out by Tokyo itself."

There was no confirmation from Washington that such a raid had taken place. Actually the Russians treat the Japanese very politely in the hotel, but they find it hard to disguise their feelings. Behind their backs they never refer to the Japanese as "Nipponski," but as "macacos," a particularly odious type of monkey.

I attended the opera with little Miss Wu, who hardly comes up to my waist. She wore a long black silk Chinese evening gown. We joined the promenade in the lobby during the intermission. The entire Japanese Embassy and their ten correspondents were there, and as we came abreast of their group, they guffawed loudly. Miss Wu was highly embarrassed; her tea-rose cheeks flushed a fiery red. In a moment of rage I was tempted to take a poke at their grinning faces, but discretion prevailed. I suspected they were all accomplished jiu-jitsu performers and would pull me apart limb by limb.

I talked the incident over with the other correspondents back at the hotel that night and we agreed that our rising feelings might soon result in an unfortunate diplomatic incident if we are not separated from the Japs.

The news of the bombing of Tokyo has had a surprising effect on the Russians and foreign diplomats here. They radiate satisfaction whenever I mention it. I gathered that our series of defeats in the Pacific had led them to think that America might be content to fight a defensive war merely to win back the Philippines. There's still a feeling that Britain and America are not serious about fighting this war, except as a part-time job. The "phony war" of France is still fresh in the memories of some Russians and diplomats. But our audacious daylight raid on Tokyo has cleared the doubts about America's intentions like a refreshing thunderstorm on a muggy day. The diplomatic representatives of enslaved Europe now know that although we may fight a defensive war against Japan until Hitler is licked, America has no intention of letting the Japs get away with it. We have now thrown down the gauntlet of total war against Japan.

April 19   The hotel is more livable now. A public bathtub has been put in, with a hot-water heater. It is in very great demand. One has to make an appointment for it the night before. [Unfortunately, though, it lasted only a week or so, for the hot-water boiler burnt out and no new one could be found.]

The streets of Kuibyshev are almost clear of snow, homes and offices are being cleaned and the putty on the storm windows is being removed to let out the seven-months-old air.

The Soviet authorities have altered the seating arrangement in the hotel dining-room. There are now three classes of diner: ordinary Russians, who can secure off-ration hotel meals in a small room in the rear; the correspondents' secretaries and the clerks of the various embassies, who eat in the big room adjoining the dance floor; and we correspondents and higher-class diplomats, who have passes entitling us to go into the main dining-room. The system resembles that in Soviet factories and institutions, where rank-and-file workers eat a lower grade of food and executives have a canteen for themselves.

This inequality in food, the most important commodity in Russia today, is reflected even in the comestibles supplied to the foreign embassies. Ambassadors, secretaries, military attachés, and the like are allowed more ounces of food than their clerks. The American Embassy meets the problem by pooling all the food, so that clerks get as much meat at meals as the Ambassador does.

April 20 The Russian winter offensive has petered out because of the thaw. During the winter the Germans have maintained active defense by fighting off the Russians with sharp counter-attacks that have only limited objectives.

Near Kalinin the Germans had erected what they call the "Strauss Line." In its way it was like a miniature Maginot Line. The Germans constructed walled cities by surrounding villages with ice walls fifteen feet high. These were built by pulling up snow, bolstering it with logs, and pouring water over it all, giving the barrier a highly glazed surface, so slippery that the Red Army had to hack steps in the ice in order to surround it. In front of the ice walls were three lines of barbed wide separated by mine fields. Behind the walls were a series of communication trenches dug in the snow, so that any side of the town could be reinforced by men running unseen through the deep snow corridors. In back of the corridors the first line of civilian houses had double walls of logs built in them, the space between filled with dirt. Loopholes were cut in the attics and the musty potato cellars deepened into pillboxes.

In the air the Germans are now using their big bombers at almost ground level, mainly to disrupt Soviet communications near the front. One day they concentrate on a railroad junction; next day they bomb a Soviet airfield.

The thaw has forced operations to cease on both sides. Even the guns are silent because the bogs are impassable for ammunition trucks. The rivers are flooding over their banks, and fields have become marshes of slush.

April 21 ⚑ The Volga broke up at two o'clock this afternoon. There was no roar of crashing ice floes, just a slow, languid movement of mile-long ice pans down the river. I won my bet of a dinner from Walter Kerr, who guessed that it would break up the following week. For five months the Volga has been icebound.

Fifty million people live along the banks of their "Little Mother Volga," and their only means of communication are its broad, brown waters, for railroads are few in the interior of Russia. The Volga people are almost a race in themselves. They settled here in the days before recorded history and many of their descendants have never moved away from the mighty river.

It will still be several weeks before the river is navigable for the huge Diesel-powered oil and grain barges, but many of them have already started up the river from Astrakhan, where the ice broke a week ago. They will have gained about ten days in starting out before the ice is broken in the center and north. Then they'll battle the four-foot-thick ice floes up to the very shadow of the Kremlin, where the oil from sunny Baku goes into the maws of tanks on the Moscow front.

The Volga boatmen still sing their famous song. Many times when I sat in the warm spring sun down at the river edge, I watched these husky stevedores lift the huge crates to the tune of the boatmen's song, but chanting instead: *"Raz, dva, vsali* (One, two, heave)." The tow paths of the old Volga boatmen, or burlaks, can still be seen on both sides of Kuibyshev, where they trudged pulling the great ropes of the barges. Until the middle of the eighteenth century there were well over a half-million Volga boatmen plying their slave-like trade, but gradually they have disappeared. The steam engine was invented and the descendants of the Volga boatmen became the inland seamen of Russia's mother river.

Their story was told to me by Mikhail Petikhov, the little

red-haired chief of the Middle Volga Region. His great-grandfather had been a Volga boatman. So far as he knew, there had never been a time when his ancestors had not lived on the shores of his beloved river.

"Most of the Volga boatmen these days are women," he added with a smile. "In a few days you'll see them loading the barges and chanting the boatmen's song."

April 22   Mr. Lozovsky called a press conference today. There was a tense atmosphere as we took our seats near the Japs. Then Mr. Lozovsky announced that the Anglo-American correspondents would soon go back to Moscow. The Japs were silent.

Mr. Lozovsky is a clever little man who is fond of turning a pointed question back at a correspondent like a boomerang. Jeff Blunden, the Australian correspondent, asked: "What would happen if a British or American warplane made a forced landing near Moscow after bombing Germany?" Mr. Lozovsky shook his gray beard in a laugh and said: "Why should an American or British plane make a forced landing near Moscow? We Russians have plenty of fine airfields to accommodate them."

Then from the other end of the room an American correspondent piped up. "What would happen if an American plane was forced to land on Russian soil after bombing Japan?" Mr. Lozovsky was plainly nonplussed. "There is no point in discussing problematical events," he said firmly.

But the fat was in the fire. Next morning the Soviet newspapers carried a small item to the effect that an American warplane had come down in the Soviet Maritime Province on April 18 and was interned with its crew "in accordance with international law." The crew was quoted as saying they had lost their way after bombing Japan.

Members of the American Embassy were highly embarrassed over the affair. There was a feeling that the Soviet Government believed that the news of the American warplane's forced landing had leaked out from the Embassy to the correspondents. The only American Embassy comment was that the Soviet Government had acted in the only way possible, according to international law. There was an unspoken understanding that if the matter had not been brought up in the presence of the Japs, the five American airmen might have turned up unnoticed in Moscow as newly accredited American Air Corps attachés.

Later we learned that the five American crew members were moved to comfortable quarters not far from Kuibyshev, where they could receive visitors from time to time and get mail and copies of the latest American magazines, books and cigarettes. The Russians had moved the only piano in town into the internees' quarters.

April 23   ✍ The ice break-up has reached the Far Eastern Pacific. The Soviet Union and Japan have initialed a new fisheries pact for another year, replacing the one which lapsed on December 31, 1941. Auctions were held in Vladivostok for the fishing districts whose leases expired in the pact. There were forty-three districts in the auction, ranging from the Sea of Japan to Kamchatka. Soviet authorities leased twenty-nine and the Japanese leased fourteen. Thus the Soviet Commissariat of Fisheries has leased five more fishing areas than they held in 1941, while the Japanese will restrict their activities to five less than they held before the attack on the United States. The Russians exacted a twenty per cent increase in minimum rentals over the price paid by the Japanese the previous year. The Chinese Embassy is the only source that knows anything about these fishing rights. I was told that before the war in the Pacific, Japan's take of fish in these areas went for export only. Japan had been self-sufficient without them. Naturally this fish supply will now go into Japanese domestic consumption. These Chinese sources added that Japan had haggled for a long-term agreement, but the Russians insisted on holding it to a year.

I asked the Press Department for an interview with members of the Commissariat of Fisheries. Several days later I was told that "unfortunately there are no responsible Soviet fishing authorities available to discuss the matter. They are all away on a fishing trip"!

April 24   ✍ The Stalin premiums for
the past year have just been awarded. They were begun in
1939 on Stalin's sixtieth birthday.

One award of 200,000 rubles went to Professor Abris-
kossiv, for his work on pathological anatomy. He is well
known throughout Russia as the man responsible for the
preservation of Lenin's mummified body in the great marble
tomb on Red Square. Since the war no visitors have been
allowed inside, so I have never seen Lenin's body.

Ilyushin, the aircraft-designer, received 150,000 rubles
for his successful Stormovik plane. This was a fighter that
Russia possessed before the war. Too slow for modern combat, the Russians employed their gift for improvisation by
armoring it heavily, providing it with cannon and rocket
shells, and sending it at low level against German tanks.

Kostikov, the military designer, got a similar sum. He
is known to the public as the inventor of "Katusha," the Russian secret weapon.

To Digtariov went 100,000 rubles as the inventor of
the anti-tank rifle, a new weapon put into production after
the war started. It is a simple infantry weapon against German armor, carried by two men on their shoulders. One
man aims and fires the long rifle, while another loads from
a prone position alongside.

The list ended with an unwarlike award to Bagreyev, a
chemist, for inventing a new method of aging champagne in
a short time by electrolysis. I bought some of the Russian
champagne at the diplomatic store and couldn't detect any
difference in the taste from the American-made product.
But it fell far short of the French brands.

April 27   ✍ The mobilization of housewives has brought out a lot of untrained woman-power. All
this week the mobilized housewives have been working to
clean up the railroad line along the Volga, removing empty
ammunition crates, old pieces of machinery, and non-essential odds and ends of war which were tossed aside on the
snow to make way for the military traffic during the winter.

Women of all ages have formed a bucket brigade down the steep bank of the Volga to the river's edge, while others pick up the debris and carry it to the first woman on this human escalator. They pass it hand over hand and deposit it in a neat pile on top of the hundred-foot bank. The women work patiently without much talk, with the same stolidity with which a peasant endures the hardship of nature. Once a day they call a halt to get their ration of brown bread. That's all they get to eat on the job, but they look healthy.

Their children play around the top of the bank as their mothers work and some of the littlest ones take boxes from the piles and throw them down the bank again. A howl goes up from the women, but I never saw a child slapped. They say it's not a custom in Russia.

The thaw left a great deposit of dirty black ice on the streets. On Sunday we saw the "Voskreseniks" spending their day working for the State. Old men, grandmothers, and even little children with play shovels attacked the blackened snow-piles and dumped the memories of a grim winter into the Volga. They had been organized by the Kuibyshev Young Communist League, and hundreds of teen-aged boys and girls worked alongside them, cleaning up the city. Not everyone spent his day off this way. I saw a big line outside the movies.

The spring sun has flooded the streets with youngsters. The braided pigtails of the little girls bounce and slap against their backs as they play hop-scotch on the sidewalks. The boys have a different game. They pile a stack of coins on the pavement and see how many they can knock off by throwing another coin against it. Their pockets fairly jingle with metal kopeks, made of steel and alloys. There are no copper, nickel, or silver coins in circulation in the Soviet Union. They all went into the war effort long before the war.

April 28   Apparently Kuibyshev is undergoing a political spring cleaning. All the former members of the Council of the City have been sent to the front as political workers.

The manager of the Univermag, the big corner department store whose shelves now hold only musical instruments, toys, women's hats and men's caps, children's clothing, and knick-knacks, has also been removed. He was accused of disrupting and sabotaging trade. According to an item in the local paper, the Kuibyshev party committee "had drawn the correct political conclusions" from the actions of Mr. Stoliakov, the store manager. It seems that during the Kuibyshev Fair, when the collective farmers came to town to sell their left-over food supplies, so much needed at this tail end of the winter, the service at the Univermag was so bad that lines formed. Furthermore, the store management did not understand "the correct organization of barter-trade. The Univermag director, Mr. Stoliakov, had disrupted barter-trade at one of the markets." He has been "correspondingly punished."

This must serve as "an object lesson" for the leaders of trade organizations producing for barter-trade. There have been too many cases of farmers exchanging food for barter with townspeople instead of at specially set-up stores. This is in violation of Soviet trade rules.

April 30 ✒ The Soviet press has begun carrying long articles explaining the Anglo-American-Japanese war in the Pacific once a fortnight. The latest article implies that the Japanese holiday in the Far East is over and the military writer left no doubt as to where the sympathies of the Soviet Union lay. He concluded by saying that Japan's problems in this war were now just beginning.

The Red Army has announced that Army regulations governing troops in the field have been drastically revised in connection with the new theories of warfare demonstrated during the German invasion. It is most unusual for an army to change its iron-bound field regulations in the midst of war, and this is an indication that Stalin may entirely reorganize the Army command.

May 1   🏴 May Day is not a holiday for the first time in the history of the Soviet Union. There will be no May Day parade on Red Square. None is needed to bolster morale, but the extra day's work in the factories is a necessity, especially if Stalin's order of the day is to be fulfilled.

Every newspaper in the Soviet Union carries his message in full. His optimistic statement says: "The peoples of all freedom-loving countries look upon the Soviet Union as the force which is capable of delivering the world from the Hitlerite plague. First among these freedom-loving countries stand Britain and the United States of America, to which we are linked by bonds of friendship and alliance and which are affording our country ever increasing military assistance against the German fascist invaders. . . . All the idle talk about the invincibility of the German troops that could be heard at the beginning of the war . . . is now a thing of the past. . . . I order that the whole Red Army make 1942 the year of the final defeat of the German fascist troops and the liberation of the Land of the Soviets from the Hitlerite scoundrels. . . ."

The public buildings of Kuibyshev are decorated with hundreds of red banners planted in groups like huge red flowers. Giant full-face portraits of Stalin and the members of his Cabinet, the Politburo, have been hung on the columns of the Bolshoi Theater, fronting the big public square. On either side are thirty-five-foot-high full-length portraits of Lenin and Stalin. Red banners covered with slogans are everywhere. If England is the land of understatement, this is certainly the country of the exclamation point. Every slogan ends with one.

I found it curious that most of the slogans were stated negatively rather than positively. The big slogan hanging over the Post Office says: "Not a single worker without a war bond!" The one over the Grand Hotel reads: "Not one man must forget his duty!"

Although there is a shortage of cotton goods in the country for civilian wear, there seems to be no shortage of red cheesecloth for the work of internal propaganda. You can

picture May Day in a Soviet city only by imagining yourself waking up and finding the advertising on all the bill-
boards in America replaced by pictures of the President and
his Cabinet.

May 2   We boarded a plane for
Moscow and, as usual, I had only an hour and a half of sleep
after doing my broadcast in Kuibyshev at four o'clock in
the morning. The countryside is a land of lakes. Every
river is overflowing and there are ponds in every hollow.
No military action could be possible under these conditions
of thaw.

We flew over the hilly woodsides of the Volga and below
our plane we could see little Volga villages whose only road
led to the river bank, down to the sole means of transportation for these isolated little settlements. They have been located on the same sandbanks for centuries and every year
the Volga has flooded over them. The peasants retreat to the
hills, and come back when the waters recede.

Here and there I could see from the plane the start of the
spring sowing. Peasant men and women were scattering
grain before the wind as they had for centuries past. The
Volga's left bank is an unbroken, fertile plain, bordered
with trees and edged by sand. The right bank is an uninter-
rupted cliff, worn steep by the river, with little mud-colored
villages clinging to the slopes.

We landed four and a half hours later in Moscow, a city
that spring had magically transformed from the "queen of
the snows." The pavements were clean and dry and the broad
fields of snow were gone for another seven months. I was
invigorated by just walking around the city. One could almost feel the dynamic presence of the Kremlin.

I managed to get the handsomest room in the Metropole.
It had a small glass-enclosed balcony looking out on the
camouflaged expanse of Sverdlov Square. Unlike the heavy
brown furniture of my old room, with its jaundiced yellow
walls, this one was filled with pre-Revolutionary gilt chairs,
an inlaid wooden bed, and a huge silver-mounted desk. The
walls were white, while the ceiling was a deep blue, with a

circle of gold stars. I felt prosperous and expansive in these sumptuous surroundings, with a small foyer and a large bathroom attached. The rent was not high: fifty-five rubles a day (about $4.50).

Out the window I could see the big, modern Moskva Hotel, reserved for Russians, with its four light anti-aircraft batteries on the roof. In the midst of the square was anchored a fine fat silver fish of a barrage balloon.

I called up Katya and met her for dinner in my new room. I scarcely recognized her. Gone were her dark, shapeless winter overcoat and her gray felt boots. For spring she wore a blue checked suit, lisle stockings, and black high-heeled pumps. She was pleased when I commented on her changed appearance. "Everyone in Moscow looks better in the spring and summer," she said proudly. "In winter all we want is to keep warm."

May 3 ⬛ The thaw has driven the Germans out of their flooded trenches. The winter "hedgehogs" of fortified villages no longer control the roads. The Germans are dragging artillery to the dry heights between the fortified villages and are forming almost a complete line of fire along the long 1,500-mile front.

Unlike Napoleon's Grand Army, the Germans have survived the Russian winter. Like a wounded prehistoric beast shaking off the torpidity of winter, Hitler's army, with a clank of iron scales, is dragging itself to the southland, and massing for a desperate lunge at the Caucasus.

Today the Soviet newspapers carried a picture of Marshal Timoshenko awarding decorations to the Red Army troops of the southern front. Moscow's public, accustomed to reading between the lines, has noted the caption on the picture; the city buzzes with the news that Timoshenko's headquarters are now in Voronezh, on the edge of the eastern Ukraine.

This is the first time that I've seen Marshal Timoshenko's name or picture in the Soviet press since I arrived in Russia. Very rarely are any Red Army generals mentioned in the press, much less front commanders. You get the impression here that there is only one man running this war and he lives in the Kremlin.

Rank-and-file heroes of the Red Army are widely publicized; their pictures are on postcards, stamps, and posters, but Soviet generals are almost anonymous unless they have been highly victorious. It is very difficult to get any information about them, their past, their appearance, or their hobbies. Unlike America or Britain, the Soviet Union regards the dossiers of their generals as military secrets. They believe that the enemy should know as little as possible about the man leading the opposing troops. The Germans will have to find out the characteristics that govern his tactics by fighting experience alone.

May 4   ✄ The Red Army is changing its clothes. The quartermaster's corps has been decorated for its brilliant supply work during the winter. Now all winter clothing of the Red Army, including its felt boots, fur hats, quilted jackets and breeches, warm underwear, and fur vests, will be turned in to be mended, disinfected, and stored. The troops at the front, although engaged in battle, are being given summer wear of cotton blouses, breeches, leather boots, and garrison hats. Local Soviet organizations in the rear will arrange with housewives to mend the discarded winter garments. "Every woman in the rear must consider it an honor to mend the clothes of Red Army men who defended the Soviet Union," says *Pravda*.

May 5   ✄ The Press Department escorted us to a German prison camp today. We were told it was a "staging" camp, not a permanent reservation, and most of the prisoners had been taken in the past few weeks. Our caravan of cars turned in a few miles outside Moscow on the Leningrad highway. We got out and splashed through the slush to a thin barbed-wire fence and a long rambling summer house.

I guess I expected to see the German prisoners in chains or at least behind bars, so when I opened the door and forced my way past a group of men standing inside in the dark hallway, I was immensely surprised to find that the men whom I pushed aside were actually the German prisoners. They were quartered in five or six small, bare rooms with cots, but could wander around the rest of the house at will and talk to each other. On the cots were clean sheets and thin gray blankets. Some of the prisoners spent all their time lying down and did not even get up when we entered the room.

The Germans were an assorted lot, some tall and husky and some thin and slight. Only one or two of them had the physique and arrogant bearing of those I had seen captured in France two years ago.

I picked out the huskiest and toughest-looking of the lot, who stood sullenly against the wall and stared at us. His name was Karol Bluml. He was thirty years old and an NCO. He explained that he had been leading a squad on patrol when he was surrounded by a superior force of Red Army men at Rzhev. "So," he said quietly, "I was taken prisoner."

He had no sooner finished the sentence when I heard a grunt from a tall, lanky German lying on a cot, with a blanket over him. He turned to me and said in good English: "He wasn't taken prisoner. He surrendered with sixteen of our men."

The tough-looking NCO turned around quickly. "You're wrong about that. I was surrounded. I had to give in. We would have been wiped out," he said heatedly.

The German on the bed lifted his pale, sick face and said: "I assure you, gentlemen, he surrendered."

The abashed NCO lapsed into sullen silence.

We walked into the next room. Another correspondent turned to me and said loudly: "Why don't they show us a Hitler Youth? I'd like to see one of the rats."

Before I could answer, a pink-cheeked youngster standing near by said quietly: "I am a Hitler Youth."

We both did a slow double take and gaped at the fresh-faced youngster. Perhaps we both expected to see a steely-looking automaton in the green-gray uniform.

He told us his name was Helmuth Hoffmann, born twenty-two years ago in Stuttgart. "I used to be a newpaperman myself," he confessed with a grin. "The *Württemberg Economizer*." He said he had been in the war ever since the Germans stepped across the Russian frontiers and had never had a day of leave. Helmuth spoke freely and seemed to have confidence in us Americans. He told me he had written lots of letters home to his mother, but so far as he knew, none of them had ever arrived and he knew they must have been stopped by his officers, who censored all letters.

In the retreat from the outskirts of Moscow he had suffered frost-bitten feet and could no longer walk. Sorrowfully he related: "I crawled into a cellar, and while my company retreated after losing all their transport, I was forced to await the arrival of the Red Army."

"Were you frightened?" I asked.

He nodded. "I certainly was," he said without embarrassment. "But several months before, I had found a leaflet dropped by the Russians which contained a pass saying that with this I could go through the Red Army lines and become a prisoner without being harmed. I always kept that in my pocket where no one could see it because I thought perhaps some day I might need it, and now the time had come."

"What did you think would happen to you without it?"

"I thought I would be killed," he said seriously.

"Who tells you that — your officers?"

"Sure; they think so, too."

Hoffmann said that the greatest shock in his life came when he scrambled out of his cellar hiding-place and walked toward the nearest Russian sentry, searching his pocket for his Russian leaflet. "You know," he said dramatically, "I had carried that leaflet in my pocket for two months, and then at the crucial moment I discovered I had lost it, and I was very frightened."

"Well, you're safe now," I pointed out.

He nodded in pleased agreement.

"How about the Germans? Do you take prisoners?" I inquired.

"Sure," he said. "Generally we do, except during December, when we got orders to shoot all prisoners during the first fourteen days of the retreat. That was a divisional order, and afterward it was rescinded."

Hoffmann had now become the editor of the camp paper and he pointed to it on the wall. It was carefully drawn in crayon and contained news from the front and a few local items about camp characters. The news, of course, was supplied by the Russians.

I wandered into another room. A group of prisoners clicked their heels as I entered. They were poor physical specimens and they explained that they had been working in a factory until two months ago, when their class had been called up.

"Who does the work now?" I asked.

One of them said: "Women, I suppose, or French prisoners."

"Were there French prisoners in your factory?"

"Oh yes, a great many of them."

"Do they work well?"

"Some do, some don't," he said with a shrug.

I turned to another little fellow and pointed to his felt boots, which were obviously of Russian origin. "Where did you get those?"

"A Russian soldier gave them to me." He looked so blue-eyed and innocent that it was hard not to believe him.

"Has Hitler ever been in Russia?"

The little fellow in the torn uniform answered hesitantly: "Yes. Hitler came to visit us at Kaluga during the winter."

"What did he say?"

"That we must shorten our lines for the winter in order to attack again in the spring."

"Do you think the Germans will attack again?"

"Of course," said the blue-eyed German peasant instantly.

"What is the Nazi party system like in the German Army?"

"There is no party system in our Army," he answered with pride.

It looked to me as though it was the German peasants and workers who sought the land of the Russian peasants and workers, and that Fascism was only a new system that supplied them with the tanks and guns with which to try to get it. Pessimistically I reflected that there would always be wars between different European coalitions so long as countries were denied equal access to the world's resources.

From every side I got the same answer to my questions. "We are fighting to make Germany bigger." "We retreated to shorten our lines." I asked every prisoner I spoke to if they had any trouble from the Russian partisans. They said blankly that they had never come across any. I asked one German if he knew what a partisan really was. "*Ja wohl*," he said; "a partisan is a man who defends his home."

The Russian camp commandant suggested that we speak to the most intelligent prisoner in the group, a fine-looking, tall young officer. He was in the medical corps. His English was almost unaccented and he explained that he had spent years studying in London. He was Ulrich Kuhl, twenty-seven years old, and a graduate of the Jena University. He told us that conditions at the front had been bad during the winter. The main casualties came from frostbite and skin diseases caused by scratching lice. He indicated that the German Army was using an ointment of ten per cent ichthyol mixed with vaseline for frostbite and he thought fully thirty-five per cent of his casualties were a result of the terrible cold.

"Will the Germans be back this spring?"

He was quite certain they would. He added: "But we'll need a rest. Many of our men are tired and we suffer from a lack of clothing."

Like all the rest of them, he wore his uniform turned inside out to expose the seams so that lice-hunting would be easy.

I walked over to the library provided for the Germans and saw a table full of Russian propaganda booklets and leaflets and a bookcase containing not only the translations of Marx's *Das Kapital* and Lenin's works in German, but copies of banned German books, especially Goethe. There were also several copies of Jack London's *The Iron Heel* and a number of Heine's works.

There was no doubt that the bulk of the German prisoners

were simple lads, but firm believers in German invincibility and their Führer. I figured it would take a lot to knock this out of their heads.

One of the Russian guards (and there weren't many of them) introduced me to an attractive young Russian girl. He explained that she was a translator for the German prisoners. I could see that the German prisoners felt no malice toward her.

"Do they give you any trouble?" I asked.

"No," she replied smilingly; "they're quiet now."

I glanced into the last room as I left. Two young Nazi airmen in sky-blue uniforms stood stiffly erect beside their cots, their chins sunk on their chests, in deepest melancholy. We were met at the door by a small knot of prisoners who badgered us for cigarettes. I talked to one simple peasant boy in the group. He didn't seem very bright, but his experiences had been among the most remarkable of this war. He related that his division had been stationed at Le Havre on the English Channel when it was suddenly ordered to entrain for the eastern front. He said that ten days later they reached a railhead and his division tramped through the snow up to the Smolensk highway. He went into action three days later and was taken prisoner within forty-eight hours. In three weeks he was in Moscow, having completed Hitler's dream. He had marched from the French coast to Moscow in twenty-one days. I watched him go out the door, pick up a double-bladed ax, and walk casually past the Russian sentry to the woodpile. It looked to me as though he could have split the sentry's skull with the ax and escaped. Then I realized that no prisoner could cover the miles of slushy wasteland between him and the German lines without food and shelter. They were glad to be fed and in a warm place.

At the radio station that night I told a Red Army officer about my talks with the German prisoners, especially the fact that none of them had encountered Russian partisans.

"How were the Germans dressed?" he asked.

"As usual," I answered, "in thin overcoats and leather boots — very few snowboots."

"There's the answer," he said. "Those were front-line

troops. I can tell by their clothes. You see, the German garrisons in the rear are warmly dressed, with clothes stolen from the peasants. And those are the Germans who have trouble with the partisans, for there are very few partisans operating near the front lines."

May 6 🚩 All war factories in Russia are on an "incentive" basis. I visited a Moscow clothing factory today. It was making uniforms for the Red Army. Everything was done by piece-work. All but one per cent of the workers were women, and they did a twelve-hour daily shift, with one hour for lunch and one free day a week.

The factory manager, a forceful young Communist Party member, told me proudly that his workers had fulfilled their April quota by 115 per cent and his factory led in the competition of all clothing factories in the Soviet Union. He said that the leading department of the factory had not only won the Red Banner for the month, but all three hundred and fifty women had attended a theater party *en masse* as their reward.

He escorted us to the factory dining-room and said he had a surprise. We would share the additional prize that had gone to the members of the winning department. It was a fresh salad of lettuce and tomatoes, raised in the hothouse of the factory farm. They were the first fresh vegetables I had tasted in seven months of meat and rice. It was almost a new taste sensation.

Later we were escorted to the day nursery. Seventy per cent of the women workers were married and many brought their youngest children to the nursery each morning and took them home at night. It was divided into three rooms, the first for infants, another for toddlers and the third for children up to eight. A little serious pigtailed girl was playing a music box as we entered and a small group was dancing solemnly around her.

Nurses in fresh white uniforms circulated among the children. The pale but healthy-looking toddlers were seated on tiny chairs in a kindergarten class. Their nurse told them to stand up as we entered, and they said seriously:

"Good day," in Russian, and then "Good-by" as we left.

Walking out of the factory, I passed small booths with sacks of potatoes piled high on them. There were special stores for the working women, operated on the principle of bringing the stores to these workers with limited time to shop, instead of obliging the workers to shop outside.

May 7 The dances at the Metropole have ended, for another serious stage of the war is in sight.

I went for a walk with Katya. She wore a yellow print dress over her trim little figure. The street scene in springtime Moscow had suddenly reversed. The crowds dressed in dingy black and brown had disappeared overnight and were replaced by crowds in white blouses and bright dresses. I could see that there were only two fashion seasons in wartime Moscow; winter and summer.

We walked down toward the Revolution Square subway station and passed the gray walls of the ancient Kitai Gorod, the Chinese town. Husky young women, dressed in laborers' clothes and rubber boots, were standing near the wall with riveting machines on their shoulders. They were building a new section of the Moscow subway despite the war and the fact that the Germans were only twenty minutes away as the bomber flies.

"Why do they call that the Chinese town?" I asked Katya.

She thought for a moment and then said: "If you had come here five hundred years ago we would have called you a Chinaman, too. In the old days every foreigner in Russia was called Chinese, and that's where the foreigners used to live and trade."

Like all Russians Katya was a great admirer of the big new utilitarian buildings at the bottom of Gorki Street. Unlike the English, the Russians seem to admire everything that is new. Tradition hasn't much interest for them, perhaps because Soviet Russia is such a new country.

We walked across Red Square, past the Troitski gate of the Kremlin, where Napoleon entered, and down to the broad, single-span bridge that crosses the little River Moskva. The narrow tree-bordered walk on the edge of the Kremlin was sprouting new grass, which looked as green as cafeteria spinach to me, because I hadn't seen grass in so long. I felt like lying down in it and rolling, it was so good to see.

I remembered that during the long, white winter I had thought that spring such as this could never come to Russia. I thought of all the hardships, frustrations, and pessimism I had gone through — the worry that there would be no Moscow by the time I arrived in Kuibyshev, the elation caused by the German retreat, and the shock of America's entering the war. Looking back, it was hard to realize how the world had changed in the past six months. I felt a compulsion to see this year of great decisions through.

May 8   The Russian spring has brought radiant optimism to Moscow. The deprivations of the winter and memories of the siege are disappearing from the thoughts of the people as the snows melt. Everyone is pleased by the news that the ugly barricades which marred the Soviet capital are to be taken down. Smiling red-kerchiefed women are helping the soldiers yank out the iron rails sunk in concrete in the streets, with gladness in their hearts and songs on their lips. Moscow is free at last from even the thought of an invasion of hobnailed jackboots across her sun-flooded streets. The old tattered muslin and gingham sandbags have been ripped open by Moscow's children and the sand dumped into vacant lots in piles for them to play in.

One of the newspapers recalls with conscious pride: "Last year when our troops retreated and not only our enemies but even many of our foreign friends sang our swan song, Comrade Stalin declared that the German advantages of suddenness and treachery would not last, but would only be an episode."

May 9   All key war factories in the
Soviet Union have started "socialist competitions" to buoy
up initiative and inject more of the game spirit into vital
work. Every branch of war industry has been asked to provide more arms and equipment for the Red Army in order
that it may carry out Stalin's victory order.

The newspapers publish on their front pages "appeals"
from one branch of industry to another to join the great
competition. The mines and foundries have been asked to
increase their production to supply the factories with raw
materials. The railroad workers have been asked to come
through with faster transportation.

The stimulation of the railroads will also be handled
on an incentive basis. Engineers will get double pay for
every trip over their monthly quota, and if they surpass
their quotas by more than ten per cent they will receive
triple pay for each extra trip. Additional bonuses will be
paid to train crews operating on overloaded lines and on
railroads near the battle front.

The war has broken out again on the eastern front. The
Germans have seized the initiative in the summer campaign
which may decide the fate of Europe and the world. German and Rumanian troops have started an offensive against
the Red Army troops who landed on the Kerch Peninsula
last December. The news is not good. Within a few days the
German-Rumanian forces under General von Mannstein
have dive-bombed and ripped the Soviet forces of General
Koslov, and the position of the Red Army troops on the
narrow peninsula is highly precarious.

The green, hummocky plains of the Kerch Peninsula are
made to order for tanks. The whole peninsula is only some
sixty miles long and forty-eight miles wide. The German
tank forces are compressing the Russian forces against the
city of Kerch and gradually denying them room to maneuver. Meantime Marshal Timoshenko has started an offensive
against Kharkov, the captured industrial capital of the
Ukraine. Everyone in Moscow is aware that the German
operations in the Crimea are intended to open a large-scale

offensive aimed at the oil of the Caucasus. Nevertheless the public is so strategy-conscious that it knows a Crimean offensive is not dangerous so long as Timoshenko can hold the German left flank in the valley of the rivers Donets and Don. Armchair strategy has become the Russian workers' "shop-talk."

During the evening we heard Prime Minister Churchill warn Germany not to use poison gas in Russia. His broadcast followed closely on the heels of the Tass report from the Crimea that the Germans were using mortar shells containing a poisonous substance that had affected the respiratory organs of several Red Army men. Said Churchill: "We shall treat the unprovoked use of poison gas against our Russian ally exactly as if it were used against ourselves, and if we are satisfied that this new outrage has been committed by Hitler, we will use our great and growing air superiority in the west to carry gas warfare far and wide against military objectives in Germany. It is thus for Hitler to choose whether he wishes to add this additional horror to aerial warfare."

Hitler took the hint. We never heard about poison gas again that year.

May 10 The second anniversary of the German invasion of France and the Lowlands was a cold, rainy day in Moscow. I slept poorly last night because it was so cold in my room and because I dreamed all night of playing poker. The strain of the big game last night was so great that I kept drawing pat straights and flushes in my dreams. We played at the Embassy with the "regulars": Captain Duncan, the Naval Attaché, a shrewd, cool-headed player who carries over to the game the dry wit with which he eases some of the problems of the American Embassy; Colonel Joseph Michela, the Military Attaché, one of the few men who was able to take a dispassionate view of the Red Army on the basis of his understanding of the Russian people; Llewellyn Thompson, the Embassy Second Secretary, who plays poker the way he handles diplomacy, unruffled and analytical, with no change in his attitude whether he is winning or losing; Henry Cassidy, chief of the Associated Press Moscow staff, the most popular foreign correspondent with the diplomats; Walter Kerr, the *Herald Tribune* correspondent, who always plays and never loses.

During the afternoon I went to a meeting called by the Komsomol of "Fighting Girls." It was held in the white and gold auditorium of the Trade Union Hall. On the platform were prominent Soviet women and young girls who had already been in battle. The appeal was for more young women of Moscow to volunteer for training in the use of modern arms.

The star of the meeting was a trim, little blonde who spoke with the inspired force of a crusader. Her sweater and skirt did not conceal her lithe, athletic figure. She was the firewoman of an armored train, but she looked like a California tennis-player. With the emotion that only a Russian can express she spoke of the time the Germans were storming a railroad station and the Russian soldiers were falling back in the face of their overwhelming drive. Suddenly around the bend the embattled men heard the whistle of the armored train. The Germans heard it, too, and with a well-placed mortar shell killed the engineer. The youthful blonde firewoman told how she took over the controls and unhesitatingly drove her iron horse into the center of the fight. The concentrated fire power of her armored train routed the Germans, and at dusk the railroad station was in Soviet hands.

May 12   Premier Joseph Stalin's May Day order to liberate the Soviet Union from the German invaders in 1942 is called: "A Law for the Soviet People." The Soviet press points out that the final defeat of the German fascist troops this year "requires from the Bolshevist press more intensified propagandism, agitation, and organization." *Pravda* says that on the pages of the Soviet newspapers even more ardent words should resound calling on the people to defend their motherland and to prepare for the victory over the enemy. "Even brighter and more enthusiastic must be the material in the Soviet press, with a depth of ideology and truth. . . ."

All along the far-flung Russian front political commissars have asked the Red Army to take an oath to carry out the Leader's order to rout the German Army in 1942.

Optimism is high in Moscow that ten months of war have caused a decay in the German Army which is not visible from the outside. Red Army experts are saying that the German Army is now largely composed of new and untrained men, some too young, others too old, and the strategic stocks of the German military machine are nearly at an end.

Germany's 1942 tanks, however, are known to be better armored and more heavily armed, especially with anti-aircraft weapons against the low-flying Russian Stormovik planes. Some of the German tanks are known to be mounting 88-mm. guns to match the heavy forty-six-ton Russian Voroshilov tanks, with their high-velocity 76-mm. cannon. The Germans are also expected to introduce many more of their newest weapons, self-propelling artillery mounted on a tank chassis.

Meantime political commissars are busy at the front lecturing the troops on offensive psychology. Steadiness in the infantry is the main consideration. During the winter Russia's factories have turned out thousands of the new two-man anti-tank rifles and a special anti-tank grenade that can be fired from the muzzle of an ordinary rifle. The Red Army believes that this strengthening of its anti-tank forces, coupled with the power of its field artillery, will allow it to hold back the massed German tank attacks within heavily defended, restricted areas.

May 13   The warm sun is stirring all the seven-month winter inertia out of Russia's farmers. For weeks I had been besieging the Press Department to arrange a trip to a collective farm, and at last it was arranged. Ralph Parker, of the *Times* of London and New York, came along with his dark, attractive secretary, Valentina. The censor preceded us in another car. After our car broke down three times on the Kalinin highway, he went on ahead, giving our driver directions to find his own way to the Red October collective farm.

Since all of the best men in Russia have been called up for service, our driver was no smarter at repairing the car than I was, so Parker and I got out and walked. We dawdled in the sunshine, watching a Red Army company of anti-tank gunners in training. The newly reorganized Soviet Army carries so much fire power now that the men were loaded down with small and large mortars on their backs, long anti-tank rifles that were as simple as a piece of iron pipe with a bolt, and automatic rifles. Very few were carrying ordinary rifles.

We watched them walk along the side of the road, keeping close to the ditches to avoid being spotted by aircraft, and then deploy over suitable tank country, digging themselves in quickly with entrenching spades. Then they cut blocks of turf and piled them around themselves until they were successfully concealed. We asked one lanky, blue-eyed gunner what he was doing. He said he was digging himself a "swallow's nest." Actually, it was different from a fox-hole because the clods of turf piled up in front of him bore a real resemblance to a barn-swallow's hide-out.

We tramped across the newly plowed fields, asking groups of peasant girls the way to the Red October farm. They had never heard of it or else they were afraid to give strangers information that might be of military value. Hungry and tired, we decided to hitch-hike home. Valentina stopped in several peasant cottages to try to buy some food, but the peasants said they had none to spare. Military cars and trucks sped along the dusty road to Moscow, ignoring our outstretched thumbs. I decided that the roadside could have been lined with the whitened bones of those who tried to hitch-hike in Russia.

Finally the lost censor arrived and drove us in his car over to the Red October farm. It was getting dark when we arrived, too late to go out over the fields, so I merely stepped into the stables and looked at the horses. They were all former cavalry war horses, sleek and slender animals, bearing ugly scars from wounds suffered during the winter offensive. The farmers had nursed them to health and were putting them to the plow. In a barn three proud old men led me into the cellar, where they had hidden a large store of seed from the Germans during the invasion. They gloatingly ran the seed through their fingers as though it were gold.

May 15 ✒ Every farmer in the Soviet Union will have to do more work. By decree the Government has drastically raised the minimum number of "work units" on which the initiative of the collective farmers is based. Although the collective farmers own the farmland jointly in perpetuity by State charter, they must complete minimum "norms" of work seasonally in order to get their share of the profits from the sale of food to the State. Depending on the crop, the farm work has been divided into units. Those engaged in sowing, for instance, must plant a fixed acreage daily to have performed a work unit. The last minimums of work units were set in 1939, but the seizure of the fertile Ukraine by the invaders has made necessary sweeping changes in the amount of work each farmer must complete in the coming year. A compulsory minimum of work has even been set for the farm youngsters. Those from twelve to sixteen will be given laborers' books in which to register their work hours and will be paid accordingly.

All those who fail to complete their minimums without good reason will be tried by a tribunal chosen from the rest of the workers. They will be punished by correctional labor. The maximum punishment will be a six-month sentence, during which twenty-five per cent of their salaries will be divided among the other members of the collective. The worst offenders may suffer the penalty of being ousted from the farm, with the loss of their homes and their small private gardens. The decree adds that those managers of collective farms who fail to turn in the shirkers will be tried the same as the culprits.

May 19 ✒ The defenders of the Kerch
Peninsula have been pushed into the sea. Von Mannstein's
tanks and dive-bombers have overwhelmed General Kozlov's insecure bridgehead at the tip of the Crimea. There
has been a minor Dunkirk carried out under the guns of
the Black Sea Fleet across the seventeen miles of the narrow straits to the Caucasus mainland. The city of Kerch
held out for a week while the Red Army men battled the
German tanks from behind the ancient burial mound in
front of the gray hill-top city. The old museum in Kerch
has been dive-bombed and many age-old relics of civilization have been destroyed.

The driving of the Red Army off the peninsula has come
as a severe blow to Moscow. This opens the way for an attack on Sevastopol, for now the rear of von Mannstein's
forces is secure.

Timoshenko's successes east of Kharkov had little influence on the Crimean situation. The people of Sevastopol
know that their turn is coming soon. The great German
troop concentrations around Kharkov, caught off balance by
Marshal Timoshenko's preventive offensive, have now recovered themselves and have started a counter-offensive on
Timoshenko's flank in the region of Izyum-Barvenkova.

German planes bombing the Soviet troops have also
dropped leaflets saying: "If you can take Kharkov, we won't
bother defending Berlin!"

May 21 ✒ Life begins at dawn in
Moscow. I am awakened every morning by the lusty voices
of soldiers. The Red Army is a singing army. They never
march through the streets without a marching song. The
composers of Russia are employed in the victory effort like
everyone else, and the songs they have written for the war
are remarkably tuneful. The main body of marching troops
sings the chorus while two or three deep-voiced men at the
head of every platoon carry the melody.

The sun is getting hotter every day now and sometimes
it's unbearably warm for my one and only suit of heavy

tweed. Several months ago I asked London to send on the clothes I left behind, but they are so long delayed that I know that they must have been sunk en route to Russia.

I cabled Ed Murrow: "Clothes unarrived should eye assume them sunk?"

The answering cable came from Kay Campbell, the efficient Scottish secretary of the London office: "Presume clothes sunk but dont worry didnt risk your good clothes sent Murrows and Collingwoods old clothes instead."

My shoes are getting so thin in the soles that my precious socks are showing through. I appealed to Burobin, the agency that takes care of the needs of foreigners, to get them soled, but they were very discouraging. They informed me that they were too busy soling the shoes of the American and British military missions.

Finally I addressed a cable to New York and handed it to the censors. It said: "Eye will soon be unable broadcast any more as shoes too outworn to walk studioward."

The censor quickly blue-penciled it, but next day Burobin phoned and told me to send my shoes along for repairing. I walked to the studio in slippers until they were ready.

The food shortage is affecting the beauty of my room. Every morning when the chambermaids come in to clean after breakfast they put the left-over slices of bread on the shelf inside my lovely gilt china-closet, a memento of some rich, pre-revolutionary merchant's home. The effect is depressing, but I'm thankful to them, for I eat the bread at lunch-time.

Like every other correspondent I always pocket the spare lump of sugar that goes with morning tea and put it inside a small glass jar to be saved for the days when no sugar is served. But I must have mice in my room, or a chambermaid with a sweet tooth, for save as I will, I can never find more than three lumps of sugar left in my hoard.

The censors promise that my clothing situation will be eased some time this summer with the opening of a diplomatic clothing store for Moscow's foreigners. I hope to be able to get a pair of blue serge trousers to go with the coat and vest the NKVD recovered for me.

The coming of spring has brought some strange sights to

Moscow. Every day from my window I see a parade of enormous, wobbling balloons tugged along the street by men and women holding them down with ropes. It looks like a string of giant perambulating sausages but actually they are the gas-bags used to fill the barrage ballons. Russia conserves metal by putting the gas in huge bags instead of steel containers. This morning the balloons were followed by a line of grotesque figures in white rubber masks with vacant goggling eyes — workers practicing marching in gas masks.

There's a vacant lot near the radio studio and little children use it as a playground. I watched one of them digging today and asked: "Where are you going?" The little smudged-faced five-year-old looked up at me seriously. "To America," he answered.

Walking back from the radio station today, I met my secretary, Lily, on the street. We stopped off in a commission shop to browse around, but I saw nothing I wanted to buy except some handsome pre-Revolutionary figurines, but I turned them down after reflecting that I had no way to get them home.

Looking at the huge papier-mâché and wax samples of fruit, hams, and sausages in the window of a food store, a common sight in Moscow, I asked Lily why it was the custom to put phony meat, fruit, or candy in the store windows. "Is that because there's none inside to buy?" I asked, teasingly.

"Of course not," she replied with some vexation. "We've always had those painted objects in the store windows as far back as I can remember. Don't forget, in the old czarist days so many people didn't know how to read that they needed huge objects in the store windows to recognize what was being sold inside. The custom still clings, I guess."

Most of the women walking were wearing the usual scarves about their heads and I thought there might be a reason for that too. Lily explained that in the old pre-Revolutionary days it was a Russian custom for all women and girls of marriageable age to cover their hair, hence the silk kerchiefs. "Before a Russian woman married, she wore her scarf under her chin. After she was a bride she put her scarf up, like her hair," said Lily. "And in some of the little villages if a girl was bad, the elders cut off her long hair so the world would know her crimes."

May 27   ✙ Everyone is depending upon Russia's peasant women to feed the nation this year. All men, except the old, have been called up for the Red Army. Because of the lack of tractors and horses which are being used to fight the war, the farm women will have to break in cows to harness. This year it must be done because the Soviet Union is hard pressed for food. There are still many "useless mouths" among the population, dependent grandfathers and grandmothers, whose lack of education, a heritage of czarist days, has made them unsuitable for work in a modern factory.

In preparation for the coming planting season, the Communist Party units throughout the villages of the hinterland have begun their task of organizational work among the farm women. They are starting competitions between the various collective farms, and because there is much extra land to be put to the plow this year, they will try to get almost military discipline from the farmers. A big competition has been started among the new girl tractor-drivers to stimulate their initiative. Their work will be judged three times a year: in the spring, at harvest time, and in late autumn, the end of the agricultural season. The leading workers will get red flags to fly from their tractors between the phases of the tournament. At the end of the year the best girl tractor-driver in the Soviet Union will get a 10,000-ruble first prize. The other competitors will divide prizes of from 5,000 rubles down.

May 28   ✙ Not much news for the broadcast tonight, so I walked to the British Mission to see what information I could pick up.

One of the most interesting characters at the British Military Mission is a little Canadian soldier who sometimes slips me a pack of English cigarettes from the Army stores. He's had a hard time in the past two years. One of the rear guard that fought such a valiant battle at Dunkirk, he was taken prisoner by the Germans and moved gradually across Europe from one prison camp to another until the Germans became irritated at his attempts to escape. They sent him to a "tough" camp in Poland. Undaunted, he finally managed to break loose, and although he could speak no Polish, he made contact with members of the Polish "underground railroad."

Hiding him in cellars and providing him with ragged civilian clothes, the Polish "underground" spirited him to Warsaw, where he spent several months walking the streets under the very eyes of the Nazi sentries. "Warsaw," he told me, "has never been blacked out. In fact, the Germans keep the street lights on all night. They are afraid of the Poles."

Finally things began to get too hot for him in Warsaw and he made his way with the aid of Polish patriots to the Russian frontier. He reached Russian territory in the winter of 1942 and the Russians, suspicious of all unidentified foreigners, put him into an internment camp. He stayed there for many months, until after Russia entered the war.

I asked him if there were any differences between the German prison camps and the Russian internment camps. He thought a moment. "The food was much better in Russia," he said, "and there was more opportunity for exercise." The Russians, he explained, were far more open to discussion over the improvement of camp conditions when the prisoners protested. He said he finally won his right to be taken to Moscow to be identified as a British soldier by going on a hunger strike. The Russian internment-camp officials took him seriously then and sent him to Moscow under guard.

He thinks there still may be other escaped British soldiers somewhere in Russia and that they will turn up sooner or later. He's a tough little tow-haired tommy and doesn't look any the worse for his experiences. The net result of his tribulations is that he now speaks both Russian and Polish badly and fluently. He is very popular with the Russian girls and attends the ballet with them at least three times a week now.

May 29   ✎ Nizhni Novgorod has certainly changed. We traveled by train with the American and
British Supply Missions to see a demonstration of Soviet
tankmen in United Nations tanks. Set in the middle of a
sandy waste, the ancient member of the Hanseatic League
of trading cities has boomed since the Soviets renamed it
Gorki. The signs of old Russia are still there in the gray, unpainted cabins of the peasants, but they surround the towering white apartment houses of the big factory city. Smoke-
blackened by the chimneys of the big plant that Ford built
here, log cabins and apartment houses alike were disgorging
workers when our train arrived in the early morning. The
street cars and buses of the old caravan city were packed
with peasant women wearing shawls and cotton dresses
whose style could not have changed very much in the three
decades since the Revolution.

There were few signs of bombing visible, although there
had been many rumors in Moscow that Gorki had been
flattened. Like all modern manufacturing cities of wartime
Europe, Gorki, too, had its airfields lined with sleek and
vicious fighter planes ready to take off at the slightest threat
to its factories.

We drove out on a sandy road leading away from the city
into a wilderness of dwarf oak and pine. A brigade of
American light and medium tanks were lined up alongside
a brigade of British Valentines and Matildas. The tank
crews had neatly fenced them in like a garden, with birch
saplings.

The men stood in front of their machines, husky and stolid
in their crash helmets, looking like professional football-
players. By their faces I could see they were from all over
the Soviet Union: Uzbeks, Kalmucks, Tajiks, Tatars, Jews,
and Russians. Talking to them revealed that none of them
had been tank-trained for less than three years, and some
of them were veterans of the days when Russia first started
its large-scale tank production, ten years ago. They agreed
that the foreign tanks were easy to master.

It was the fourth war for the commander of the American
tank brigade, Colonel Rodion Chabolin, elegantly uni-

formed, gray-haired, and gray-eyed. Now in his early fifties, he was a graduate of the Civil War cavalry, the Japanese frontier episodes, the Finnish-Russian War, and the present invasion. His only criticism of the powerful American Chrysler tanks was that they were riveted, and this, together with their gasoline engines, made them relatively vulnerable. Russia's heavy tanks, he pointed out, were welded, and equipped with Diesel engines, which reduced the fire hazard.

Someone asked if we could go for a ride across the trial grounds. The colonel nodded cheerfully and ordered one of the tank crews to wheel their American-made monster out of its little birchwood enclosure. Extra Soviet tankmen's uniforms were thrown in a pile on the ground and I donned one hastily, blue zipper overalls and sponge-rubber helmet.

I crawled inside the tank and thrust my forehead against the rubber-bolstered gun-sight. The Chrysler motors roared into life. The dark-faced little Red Army tank-driver gave his strange cargo an amused glance and threw in the clutch. We rumbled across the Russian sand, bounced through a clump of pine trees that parted like grass, and stormed up the incline. The driver shifted gears with a professional touch, and through the gun-sight I saw a blur of green and gray of trees and sand whirl past like a newsreel in technicolor. The intent little tank-driver finally brought the American machine to a halt after prodding over a six-inch pine tree as though it were a matchstick.

We crawled out and surrounded him to ask his opinion of the American machine. With a smile lighting his tanned face, he said: "It's more powerful than any tank I ever drove in the Battle of Moscow." He admitted that what he liked best about his new charge was that its seat was comfortable and it rode the bumps easily.

We spent the rest of the afternoon watching the Soviet crews destroy targets with the American 75 cannon while a comely Red Army nurse stood by with a first-aid kit in case any of us were injured.

On the train back to Moscow that night, we got off at the station at Vladimir to stretch our legs. Beside the station was a military supply dump. It was guarded by a young Red Army girl, rifle at her side, and looking every inch a soldier except for the print scarf she wore around her shining blond hair. She couldn't have been more than nineteen. She was startled when we spoke to her and drew back in alarm when I reached for the rifle at her side.

"Don't do that," she exclaimed. "It's forbidden!"

"Why," I asked, "it's not really loaded is it?"

Indignantly she said: "Of course it is," and threw open the breech to show us.

"But you don't know how to shoot it," we said teasingly.

"I certainly do," she said firmly. "I've been practicing for three months. Just touch any of these things and I'll show you!"

Her name was Natasha, and she'd been an art student in Moscow before she donned her uniform. We were disappointed when she said firmly that she wouldn't get leave in Moscow for a long time.

June 1   ✍ Marshal Timoshenko's offensive against Kharkov has been brought to a halt. The Soviet High Command says that the offensive was only a diversion to forestall a German drive on Rostov, gateway to the Caucasus, by thirty infantry and six tank divisions, and that Timoshenko did not intend to capture Kharkov. It adds that the offensive was a success because the Germans have lost ninety thousand men, killed and prisoners, while the Russians lost five thousand dead and seventy thousand missing in two and a half weeks' fighting.

June 2   ✍ Spring has brought no promise of freedom to Leningrad, but those who starved for victory will go hungry no more. Hundreds of refugees are in Moscow now, evacuated from the city of courage and tears across the secret road that stretched all winter over the eighty miles of frozen Lake Ladoga. The road was built after the first hundred days of siege by the subway workers and railroad men of Moscow.

Night after night the Red Army pushed its trucks through the frozen darkness across the Highway of Life for Leningrad. Machine-gunned by German planes because they were forced to keep one headlight lit to avoid wandering off the road to certain death, the truck-drivers lost hands and ears in the freezing drive across Ladoga, but the little lights in the tents and igloos that lined the road never faltered until the thaw came and two feet of surface water covered the ghost road. Still the trucks rolled and the Red Army men made two or three trips a night, not leaving their trucks for days at a time. As the road melted under the warm spring sun, they drove until a day came when men and trucks plunged through the ice.

Through the winter Leningraders starved on a slice and a half of bread daily, but now they have food, and some of it has a new taste. It's canned food from America.

The melting snow revealed Leningrad in all its war-torn drabness. The rubble of its battered gray marble buildings blocked the streets, twisted wire hung from the blind, gaping eyes of the shattered apartment houses. German bombers had plucked the heart out of Leningrad while the German artillery bayed like a hungry, frustrated wolf-pack on the outskirts. There were no lights, no water supply, no heat through the most terrible winter in Leningrad's history. German bombs hit all the power plants, destroyed the central heating system, and broke the water-mains.

They told me about the "days of the dead." Once monthly, on the day after the bread cards had been issued in the names of the living and the dead, Leningraders carried out the bodies and dragged them on little sledges along the snow-bound streets to the mass grave at the edge of town. Some put estimates of the dead as high as a million and a half, for Leningrad had been filled with refugees from the hinterland when the Germans slammed the door. They say thin people survived the siege better than fat ones, and women better than men.

Then came the great spring cleaning for those who were alive after nine months of siege. Old women and their grandchildren chipped the ice from the streets and carted the rubble of their city away. When the first trolley car ran down the Nevsky, it was like the first robin of spring. People cried with joy at the sight of it.

The slow, silver flood of the Neva is running clear now, but for weeks its ice floes were laden with green-gray bodies of the invaders and the khaki of the dead defenders. All that remains of the ice road now are dark hulks of log bobbing on the broad river. But still the city is under siege. A thirty-kopek ride on the trolley will take one down to the front lines. Every day the sirens sound and the Germans send some heavy shells screaming into the city. They're using 207-mm. siege guns in their fruitless effort to break the city's spirit.

They tell me that the people of Leningrad now look like a different race. They're thin and seasoned and their faces seem cut from stone, but they walk with dignity. They don't panic any more when German shells crash into the boulevards. And they know the note of their own big guns when they answer. They're very kind to each other. The little irritations of life don't count any more.

Every day the movies are crowded. And when Leningraders see the newsreels and then walk out into their own streets while the sirens are sounding and the bombers drone overhead, it seems like a continuation of the films they've been watching.

The street radio loudspeakers are never silent except after curfew time. The favorite program is a reading of letters to and from the men at the near-by front. Crowds gather to listen, for the population of Leningrad is so shrunken that everyone seems to know everyone else now.

They told me a story of a stranger who walked into a hospital near the front line. He was a big, strapping fellow but he complained that something was wrong with his heart. A Soviet doctor examined him and noticed that his Communist Party card was in the outside pocket of his blouse. The doctor knew that no member of the party would carry his card so carelessly. Communists wear their membership cards next to their skin. He ordered the man to enter the operating-room and brought out the shining steel instruments. Terrified, the husky stranger confessed. He was a member of the German Intelligence Service who had entered the besieged city for information. They never told what his fate was, but I've often wondered if the doctor completed the operation.

Leningraders are today a proud people. They know that
to them goes the honor of first stopping the avalanche of the
German invasion. Forty German divisions spent the winter
in the white trenches outside the gates of Russia's second
city.

June 3   ✍ The RAF has made the largest air raids in history on the Reich. On two out of three
nights the British have blasted the Ruhr with one-thousand-
bomber raids. The news drew large headlines in the Soviet
press, the largest accorded the RAF raids since I have been
in Russia. All Moscow is talking about the enormousness
of the air attack, for the citizens of the Soviet capital are
no greenhorns about air raids.

Those diplomats and correspondents who were here during the early Moscow raids, while the Germans were fast
approaching the Soviet capital, told me that they were frightened at the thought of what would happen to them if they
were buried under the ruins. But they were amazed and relieved to witness the Soviet organization of the people against
air bombardment. They said that no one could be better than
the tireless Russian workers at digging people out of the
ruins.

I did some research on the Soviet civilian defense organization and discovered it was based on an important
psychological factor. Virtually every person has something
to do during a raid. To this day every apartment dweller
in Moscow takes his turn at air-raid warden duty one night
a week. Even old women and men stand outside their apartment houses to challenge any stranger for his curfew or air-
raid pass. They can call the militiamen if they regard anyone as a suspicious character.

I talked to a typical Moscow family and discovered that
everyone down to the twelve-year-old children had been
trained before the war in what to do when the raiders came,
as wardens, stretcher-bearers, and gas decontaminators.
Even the elementary-school kids knew the difference between phosgene and mustard gas and how to approach a fire-
bomb. They regarded the whole preparation as a game. It

was clear that the Soviet Union expected more from its civilians than either England or America. Here in Moscow everyone took fire-watching as a matter of course and had built small wooden shelters on the roofs for the winter. But they were also expected to do their own gas decontamination and act as stretcher-bearers for the rest of the family. There is no paid civilian defense organization in Russia aside from the regular fire department.

June 4 ✍ Russian girls marry young and often, especially many of the city girls. The peasant farm girls enjoy a more stable married life. Some of the girls that I know have had two husbands before they were twenty-one. However, I understand that members of the Communist Party and others in responsible jobs rarely take advantage of the easy divorce laws any more. More than three divorces is likely to ruin their reputations as an example for the majority of the non-party people.

The divorce laws have been tightened up, too. Now it's necessary for husband and wife both to present themselves at the marriage and divorce bureau called Zaks. If they agree to be parted, the payment of a small fee will see their divorce records stamped in their personal identification "passports." Custody of the children is decided upon before the judge.

The same moral standards guide both men and women. Russian girls are highly romantic, but not promiscuous. I believe they will give a wonderful welcome to their men when they come home from the front after the war is over. As it is now, there are scarcely enough men at home to go around and the result is great "cattiness" and "knifing in the back" among girl friends, a trait which is still rare in America. It is common for young men and women to share an apartment before they make up their minds whether they will have their marriage stamped in their "passports." There is no illegitimacy in Russia, however. These realists have decided that the last persons whom society should punish are the innocent offspring. The birth of a child constitutes a common-law marriage, automatically. By law the father must pay fifty per cent of his salary for the child's rearing. It rarely happens more than once, although contraceptives are extremely scarce in Russia since the war.

Abortions are now unlawful. It's not at all difficult to prove the responsibility for fatherhood in Moscow, because the house managers in each apartment house know exactly who the tenants are, since they distribute the ration books each month. Although, naturally, there are other chances for a girl to bear a child out of wedlock, nevertheless a Soviet girl shrinks from the idea of it as much as girls do in the Western world.

Russian girls are extremely natural and, like their men, have a refreshing lack of artificial sophistication. They love above all to dance and to eat. Virtually everyone owns a portable phonograph and a tiny padded suitcase for transporting records, which are fairly inexpensive throughout the Soviet cities.

Last night Katya and Ludmilla brought some Red Army girls around to the hotel to visit us correspondents. The full-breasted soldier girls, in uniforms exactly like a Red Army man's, were rather shy about dancing in their heavy boots. They explained that they hadn't had much time to dance at the front. They wore their hair in "front bobs," rather short and uneven. They had kept it trimmed themselves.

They said that their chief amusement at the front was playing chess. Next time they promised to bring sets with them to beat us. They did. Every Soviet girl seems to be a good chess-player. I never succeeded in winning a game from any of them.

The Moscow curfew is annoying. Everyone must be off the streets by midnight, and whenever we have visitors the phone rings at ten o'clock and the hotel clerk says cheerfully: "Your guests must leave now!" The curfew is responsible for a pleasant new custom, however. When parties are held at private apartments and the guests fail to leave before the Kremlin tower clock chimes the midnight hour, everyone has to stay over. Presence on the street after twelve without a pass means being conducted by the armed patrols to the police station to sit until the curfew ends at five. Then there's a kaleidoscopic change on the stilly streets. Men and women trickle out of apartment houses all over the city and hurriedly walk home for a quick nap before going to work.

June 5   ✎ Moscow economists say that the reason the Germans have not bombed England for many months is that they are short of lubricating oil for their planes. They say that there is no ersatz lubricating oil, although during the winter the Germans experimented with Italian olive oil in the crankcases of their tanks and trucks. It flowed freely in the sub-zero temperatures, but it didn't stand up under continued use.

Russian oil experts figure that the German mechanized army and the Luftwaffe consume about a million tons of oil a month on the Russian front and one hundred thousand tons a month on less active fronts. They estimate that it takes sixteen million tons of oil yearly for Germany to fight the war and supply the factories in conquered Europe.

The Rumanian wells produce a maximum of four and a half million tons annually and other European sources, including Poland's Lwow region, another million tons. Some three or four million tons of synthetic oil are produced by Germany in her unbombed refineries, plus another million tons of ersatz benzol and alcohol. This would give Germany from nine to nine and a half million tons of oil yearly although she needs a minimum of nineteen million tons to run her war machine. The other ten million tons come from accumulated and captured oil stocks. No one knows how large these stocks are, but the Russian experts think it is doubtful if they exceed more than twenty million tons. It is known, however, that all Germans are now forbidden to use fuel for cigarette-lighters, and prisoners say that they marched from the Polish border to the eastern front to save precious gasoline for the trucks.

Germany needs the oil of the Caucasus, and needs it badly.

June 7   ⚑ Russia is now a land without a night club. Before the war there were a few restaurants and hotels open for dining and dancing, but most of them are now closed. There's little amusement for a soldier on furlough, aside from the ballet, the movies, and concerts. There's an orchestra playing at lunch-time at the huge modern Moskva Hotel, but I never saw any soldiers dancing. The doorman confided to me that the boys do dance when there's a little beer or vodka to be bought, but the dining-room hasn't had any to serve for weeks.

However, the Koktail Hall on Gorki Street has reopened and there are long lines outside every day waiting for seats. Apparently, to make a date for cocktail time an ordinary citizen would have to start waiting in line in the early afternoon.

We went around to the back entrance one afternoon and asked for the manager. He was pleased to welcome foreign correspondents. We found ourselves in a modern Fifty-second Street saloon, with a huge bar surrounded by tables and five or six bar girls and waitresses. Every table and seat at the bar was occupied, but a couple of drinkers recognized us as foreigners and politely offered us their chairs at the bar.

The menu offered the Moscow Koktail, the Kowboy Koktail, Champagne Koktail, and the Tahran. I sampled the Moscow and then switched to the Tahran. The barmaid explained that Tahran meant "battering ram" in Russian. After three I thoroughly agreed. Every Koktail has the same base, a large slug of vodka. The Tahran is a mixture of pepper vodka, Cointreau, brandy, and lemon liqueur.

The bill for three correspondents with four cocktails each inside them was three hundred rubles — about a month's pay for a Moscow factory worker and even pretty steep for the average factory manager with his two thousand rubles a month. But red-faced and pleased with the world, we argued strenuously with each other for the right to pay the bill. The Red Army officers, members of the Moscow literati and factory managers seemed to look on us benignly.

June 9   ✒ The Battle of Sevastopol has begun. After seven months of siege the forces of General Erich von Mannstein have launched their third offensive against the Crimean naval base, whose defenders have twice before compelled them to quit. After an unprecedented artillery shelling and air bombardment that lasted four days, von Mannstein has thrown his ten German-Rumanian divisions against the Black Sea fortress.

Ever since coming down the rocky Crimean Peninsula last October with six divisions and a cavalry brigade, von Mannstein had been held at bay by the defenders. In late November he reinforced his siege army to the size of two army corps, containing five divisions each, supported by tanks and artillery. By December 17 his preparations were completed. Maps of all known Sevastopol fortifications were distributed to his men, and fifty heavy guns were emplaced to each half-mile of front. In a proclamation to his troops of the Eleventh German Army, von Mannstein said: "The time of waiting is over. The necessary preparations have been made. Our attack will not fail."

For seventeen days the guns of the Black Sea Fleet, the shore batteries of the fort, and the garrison of Sevastopol battled the German-Rumanian hordes until it seemed that flesh and blood could stand no more. Wedged into the Sevastopol defenses, the Germans roamed up and down a narrow twenty-eight-mile front, probing vainly for a weak spot. Then on the night of December 30, in a heavy snowstorm, the seamen of the Black Sea Fleet stormed the beaches of the Kerch Peninsula. Frightened, von Mannstein withdrew two divisions from his attacking force to meet the threat to his rear.

The beleaguered Sevastopol garrison took advantage of the moment to launch a daring counter-attack. An armored train, built by the townspeople during the siege, steamed out of the fortress to within one hundred and fifty yards of the German positions and scored direct hits. As the climax of the counter-attack, a Russian cavalry brigade galloped out of Sevastopol while the German shock troops cowered under a hail of machine-gun fire and were cut to bits under the flailing swords of the Cossacks. Von Mannstein's Eleventh Army retreated after suffering thirty-five thousand casualties, and settled down to a blockade while their commander pleaded with Hitler for more forces. For this third offensive von Mannstein has built his army to 250,000 men armed with huge flame-throwers, the largest mortars the world has yet seen, siege artillery up to fourteen inches, and an entire air fleet of the Luftwaffe, headed by the crack Richthofen fighter squadron.

June 10 ⚑ My Birthday. The Russians welcome any opportunity to have a party, and so do we. Birthdays are occasions in Moscow. The correspondents set up a small buffet and we invited a few girls over to dance to phonograph music. Katya gave me a precious tube of Russian toothpaste. Later I went to the Embassy to play poker. Commander Allen very generously presented me with a tin of tobacco, a pint of vodka, and, bless his heart, a tube of shaving cream. I was pleased to note that it was still my birthday when we cashed in the chips.

Over the Embassy radio we heard Tokyo announce that the Imperial Navy had suffered heavy losses at Midway Island, but that they had made a landing on American territory in the Aleutian Islands.

Poring over the maps, it was easy to see that Japanese possession of any of the islands in the Aleutian chain for the purpose of building submarine or air bases means that the Russian peninsula of Kamchatka is outflanked as a possible base for a future attack on the Japanese mainland. We knew that so far as the Russians were concerned it was still "Remember Port Arthur." The feeling among Moscow diplomats was that the Russians would not object to American air bases in Siberia if they knew that they would not have to fight an immediate major war with Japan to defend them.

These geographical complications had their seed in the aggressions of 1931, the start of World War II. Japan then took advantage of every other nation's military weakness and seized Manchukuo. Now with the Japs threatening both sides of the Vladivostok Peninsula, Russian military strategy would undoubtedly be hard pressed to prevent the Japs from pinching off the Soviet Maritime Province in the same manner that the Nazis enveloped Poland.

Information here is that the Japanese have been quietly removing seasoned troops from China and adding them to the Mongolian troops now fighting under the Japanese flag in Manchukuo.

General Gregori Stern, hero of the first Russo-Japanese border clash at Lake Kassan in 1938 and prominent for his work in the Finnish War, is known to be in command of Russia's Far Eastern army.

June 11   ◤ The war in Russia took a back seat tonight. We were warned by the Press Department to expect portentous news around six o'clock and it came blaring out of the street-corner loudspeakers during the homeward rush hour. Great Britain and the United States had agreed with Russia on the "urgent tasks of creating a second front in Europe in 1942," said the announcer. I realized that the future course of world affairs had been changed because Russia and Great Britain had signed a twenty-year mutual treaty of alliance and agreed not to sign a separate armistice or peace with Germany or her allies.

From my window overlooking colorful Sverdlov Square we watched the humble, rather subdued Russian workers listen quietly to the great news. The care-worn women with shawls wrapped around their lined faces and the thin, frowning middle-aged men with kindly gray eyes stood in silent groups weighing the words of the announcer. Later we heard the BBC announce that the news had been received in Moscow with cheers. It wasn't quite true. Although they are warm-hearted and impulsive, I seldom saw the Russian people show their feelings in public.

Next day the Moscow newspapers carried front-page pictures of President Roosevelt and Molotov in the White House. The mark of a big-shot in Soviet Russia is the number of telephones on his desk, so when I showed the picture to the little old man who sweeps my room, he exclaimed with surprise:

"But how can Roosevelt be President of the United States? He has only one telephone on his desk!"

June 15   ✙ Traitors get short shrift in Russia. When the partisans retake a village, those who served the Germans as town marshals and mayors get a drumhead court martial. It's significant that the Germans never take Russian traitors with them when they retreat.

There was a story today about one factory director who failed to remove his machines when the Germans marched into a town in the Moscow region. The evacuation of the workers had been arranged in advance. They boarded the train, but the factory director stayed behind to remove the Diesel engines by truck and blow up the plant. A truck stood by with engine running, waiting for him to complete the scorching of the earth. Instead, the manager dismissed the driver and told him he would join him later. He remained in the village with the three workers assigned to help him in the demolition work.

When the Germans marched in, he offered his services if they would let him keep his job and the factory after they won the war. The Germans gladly appointed him adjutant of the factory and ordered the villagers to go to work at the plant.

Unfortunately for him, the Red Army's counter-offensive freed the village three months later and the Germans left him to his fate. Faced by the returning Red Army, the factory director claimed he had been saving the factory for Russia. He was shot for his pains.

June 18   ✙ We saw Stalin today. For the first time since the war began, the correspondents have been invited to enter the Kremlin. All week long we had wondered about the new guests at the hotel. They had arrived from all over Russia, from the hot deserts of the southeast, the still frozen reaches of Siberia, and from the factory cities of the Urals. Many brought their wives — slant-eyed Mongols in long, blue silk kimonos and black slippers, raven-haired Uzbeks in wonderfully embroidered white linen, and white-skinned, blue-eyed Russians in smart Riga and Paris clothes.

Then the Press Department gave us carefully numbered passes to attend the first war meeting of the Supreme Soviet. Carrying our typewriters, we entered the red Kremlin walls through the Borovitskaya Gate. Six separate controls manned by uniformed guards of the NKVD carefully examined our passes, discouraged us from walking through the famous Kremlin gardens, and led us through the Oriental archways of the old yellow building called the Great Palace. A small sign on the time-worn walls said: "This way to the bomb shelter." Guards made a complete examination of our briefcases and typewriters and we watched officers check their pistols at the cloakroom.

Then we were ushered to seats in the foreign press box. In back of the Great Hall, its white walls splendid with yellow silk blackout curtains, sat the prominent visitors, virtually everyone of importance in the Soviet Union.

Below us on straight-backed chestnut chairs sat the thousand delegates to the Supreme Soviet. Small white signs proclaimed the nationality of each section, but one didn't need to read the printed signs in their strange alphabets; one could tell by the costumes.

There were Tatars with little embroidered caps on the back of their heads, white-shawled, dark-skinned women from Turkomen, broad-shouldered, black-and-white gowned delegates from Buryat-Mongolia, yellow-skinned Kirghiz in blue and red kimonos, and black-bearded representatives in fine white linen blouses from Tannu Tuva. Many delegates attended in the khaki of the Red Army, while others wore their regular plain business suits. It was a gathering of the peoples living on one sixth of the world's land surface.

At exactly six o'clock in the evening Stalin made a dramatic entrance from a door behind one of the huge white pillars. A tumult of applause greeted him. He was followed by Molotov and the members of his Cabinet, the Politburo. A bell sounded to end the thunderous clapping.

Wearing his usual plain gray uniform, tucked into high black boots, Stalin seated himself next to white-bearded old Kalinin, the "Peasant President." In the favored seat on his right sat black-haired Georgi Malinkov, chairman of the Moscow Party Committee.

Stalin waved cheerfully to the audience, and although he looked a bit tired after a long winter's confinement, he smiled often and ran his hand through his stiff, grizzled hair and tugged on his graying mustache. Several times he turned to talk to one of his favorites, stocky and bear-like Andrei Zhdanov, Leningrad Communist Party leader. An "Old Bolshevik," Zhdanov is regarded as a possible successor to Stalin and one of the best students of Marxist ideals. The luster of his reputation lost no brilliance this year through his inexorable organization of the resistance of the people of Leningrad.

Then Vyacheslav Molotov rose to speak over the public-address system of the great white-domed hall. Every seat was equipped with head-phones. The bespectacled Foreign Commissar, newly returned from Washington and London, outlined the steps leading to the signing of the twenty-year alliance with Britain and stressed the role the treaty would play after the war. Apparently unwearied by his trip across the world in a Soviet bomber, Molotov spoke vigorously and denied that Russia held any territorial ambitions in Europe or Asia, "Including Iran," he said significantly.

"The problem of the second front drew serious attention in both Washington and London," he went on. "Both countries announced that there was complete unanimity over the question of a second front in Europe in 1942. Let us hope," he said emphatically, and his voice rose, "that the enemy will soon feel on his back the results of the fighting friendship of the world's three greatest powers! I ask in the name of the government that you ratify this treaty as one which completely coincides with the interests of the people."

The thousand delegates rose as one to acclaim by a thunderous voice vote the treaty and the new foreign policy of the Soviet Union. All through the meeting there had been only four persons in the Great Hall who failed to rise at Stalin's entrance, who never joined in the applause, and who pointedly left before the Anglo-Soviet treaty was acclaimed. They were Ambassador Noatake Sato of Japan and his three aides.

June 20   ✍ Some news from Murmansk. Captain Olson, youngest member of General Faymonville's supply mission, has just returned from the Arctic with some supplies and some stories. He graciously donated to me some razor blades and two bars of soap collected from the American merchant ships in the heavily bombed port. "The Russians are having a hard time beating off the German dive-bombers," said Olie. "They're using their slow pre-war 'Chika' pursuit planes and Hurricanes supplied by England, but by the time these are off the ground, the Germans have released their bombs and are on the way home to Petsamo, sixty miles away across the Finnish frontier."

He talked grimly about the sad sights in the hospitals of Murmansk and Archangel. A number of torpedoed American merchant seamen had lost their arms and legs from frostbite.

I reflected that the military situation had certainly changed since I came to Russia by convoy to Archangel. Last October Hitler was unworried over the amount of supplies that Russia's allies could send in. But now he was compelled to divert squadrons of his crack bomber pilots fom the Russian battlefront in a desperate effort to halt the ever increasing flow of tanks, planes, and food to his enemy.

June 22   ✍ The second anniversary of the German invasion. Moscow is serene and confident. The long-heralded German spring offensive is on the move in only one place — against well-defended Sevastopol. In the Ukraine the new defensive power of the Red Army is holding Hitler's mighty panzer divisions in check. Moreover,

Russia is no longer without allies, and America and Britain have "threatened" a second front in Europe within the year.

"We are entering the period of fierce battles," says *Red Star*, the official Army newspaper, "but the enemy has not succeeded in preparing for his spring and summer operations as he planned. Nevertheless, the enemy has gathered considerable forces, especially in tanks and airplanes, but these are no longer forces which could bring Germany a strategic success. It is not excluded, however, that in the course of the coming battles the Germans may secure temporary superiority and achieve partial success, but this in no way changes the general proportion of all forces, which is steadily in our favor. We must remember that whatever is ahead of us, the days of crisis of the first phase of the war have been left behind."

June 23 ☙ The Anglo-American correspondents have decided to test our new relations with Soviet Russia. Forming an association of the type which has heretofore been discouraged, we chose the occasion of the Anglo-Soviet treaty to hold a luncheon in the name of the "Anglo-American Correspondents Association." Our principal guest was Alexander Scherbakov, chief of the Soviet Information Bureau and author of the High Command communiqués. We sent invitations to a select list of the most prominent propagandists, journalists, and editors in the Soviet Union.

Following the usual Russian banquet custom of innumerable toasts, we assigned each member of the Association a brief speech. Because of my constant arguments with the censors, I was allotted to toast the Press Department. We were delighted to receive full acceptance from all our invited guests, especially since this amounted to tacit approval of the unprecedented organization. An Anglo-Russian correspondent did the translating.

All the toasts went off in perfect order. That is, all except mine. In a brief speech I called attention to the fact that "although the Press Department chief, Mr. Palgunov, and the two censors are extremely hard-working and stick to their twelve-hour shifts like factory workers, our requests for special trips, meetings with influential Russians, and visits to the front are delayed or often neglected. Unless these promises are made good, the Anglo-American correspondents do not feel that they are able to do their duty to their people." Then we drained our glasses and sat down. The Anglo-American correspondent doing the translating failed to mention the second half of my pointed remarks. The censors sitting alongside me immediately called my attention to his lapse. But by this time it was too late. The husky chief of the Soviet Information Bureau was getting up to leave for his office in the Kremlin. Annoyed, I called my Russian-speaking colleague to task. He shrugged his shoulders and said: "Oh, I'm sorry, I didn't hear all you said!" Later we learned that one of our prominent guests had remarked to a correspondent: "You fellows will no longer be troubled by such a strict censorship. We want the people of America and Britain to realize our plight more fully and our need for a second front."

June 24   Sevastopol still stands. For more than two weeks the naval base has been resisting the vicious attacks of von Mannstein's German-Rumanian Eleventh Army against an overwhelming air superiority. The defenders have an excellent field of fire against the invading army with a broad network of observation points. The great system of deep-hewn communication trenches which the mobilized civilian population — men, women, and children — dug during the winter allows the Red Army troops to transfer its men, unseen, to any threatened point on the approaches. They worked 1,500,000 man hours on it. But the impact of the mass German air raids is crumbling the Crimean granite to rubble.

During the winter all war factories of the city were moved underground into deep quarries and adapted their production to short-range siege weapons. The women and children of the besieged city live like cave dwellers in grottoes and bomb shelters. They prepare their food on camp stoves. Every available foot of land on the surface was cleared of trees for war gardens. The Germans have been dropping threatening leaflets promising extermination of those who continue to resist. Meantime Soviet civilian organizations have arranged for movies to be shown in the quarries to keep up the morale of the battered city. Communist lecturers and Komsomol agitators inspired the non-party people in the caves. Thousands of blood-donors have answered the call of their men dying on the parapets. The Communist organization of a Soviet city has never before been tested as it has at Sevastopol.

There are reports in Moscow that the evacuation of the women and children has begun on convoys escorted by the Black Sea Fleet. The cruiser *Red Crimea* has been decorated for its work.

June 25   I went back to "Sunnyside Hill" today, to Solnetchnogorsk, where the Red Army struck its first world-shaking blows against the Germans last winter. The scars of the invasion are already disappearing under a merciful cloak of thick-growing weeds. There were wild vines climbing the desolate chimney-stacks which mark the sites of burned-down Russian villages. Here and there the only trace of what once were houses is one or two tall sunflowers or hollyhocks bravely marking a former garden.

Every quarter-mile along the roadside a wrecked German tank lies rusting and sinking into the soft Russian soil. These were the odd ones abandoned too far from the road to be salvaged by the Red Army and dragged with hundreds of others to junk-heaps alongside the railroad tracks. Great piles of rusty troop-carriers, autos, and trucks with the engines removed, and tanks pulled to pieces for their spare parts, lay corroding in the little villages, waiting to be removed to the smelters of the Urals.

Old women plodded along the road, their backs bent down under heaps of faggots. We stopped once to talk to a group of peasant women. Two children tugged at the skirts of one of the care-worn, prematurely aged farm workers. Her five-year-olds were strong and healthy, but in the woman's arms was a puny, white-faced baby. It had been born during the German occupation.

"I took to the woods with my children when the Germans arrived," said the peasant mother in a weary monotone. Her voice dropped at the end of each sentence. "But I had to come back because we had no food. The Germans killed all the chickens and gave me the scraps to eat and feed the children." Then she asked doubtfully: "Do you think they'll be back? If they do, we might as well kill ourselves."

She hesitated and another old woman spoke up: "Do you think the war will be over this year?" It was the first time that I had heard anyone doubt that Stalin's May Day victory order could not be fulfilled.

We traveled on past Sunnyside Hill, and the road which six months before had been a silent, snowy waste, littered with tangled wires, sawed-down telegraph poles, and smashed-up fighting machines, was now hemmed in by a picket line of bright new telephone poles and spanned by shiny yellow wooden bridges. Like all handiwork in this country of wood, the bridges were demonstrations of the woodsmen's art, though on a massive scale.

We got out near Volokolomsk, and the leaders of the village Soviet proudly showed us how they had reconstructed the village. New log cabins had been thrown up to house the homeless.

I walked into a tiny hospital. A dozen small gray-faced children were lying in bed. Two little fellows were reading the *Pionerski Pravda* together. Each had only one eye. A German hand-grenade had been tossed into the cellar of the schoolhouse where they had hidden during the invasion.

Across the room lay an eight-year-old girl with soft brown hair, framing an almost translucent skin. She smiled as I walked over. In her hand was a small wooden object. I asked her what it was.

"A tank," she said shyly; "a soldier gave it to me."

"What's your name?"

"Natasha."

I wondered what was wrong with her. Then the nurse walked over and pulled back the covers. Natasha had no feet.

"The Germans left her lying on the field that way," the

nurse explained. "They forced the whole population of this town to walk across the field to see if it was mined. It was. Natasha lost her feet and her parents."

The nurse called another little girl over to the bedside. She wore her golden-brown hair in straight braids, Indian style. She was a friend of Natasha's. The nurse smiled at her and said: "Here's a brave girl, too. She took to the woods when the Germans came in, with her father. She carried her baby brother in her arms."

"Tell us what happened then, Tamara."

But Tamara was too bashful. The nurse went on grimly. "Her baby brother froze to death in her arms. As you can see, Tamara's hands had to be amputated because of frost-bite."

I couldn't take any more. I found my eyes and throat were not behaving. I walked out into the sun-flooded Russian spring and sat in the car awaiting my companions. I knew the war would be over some day for most people, but it would go on forever for Natasha and Tamara.

June 30 ⚓ The Germans have been trying to jolt Moscow's morale ever since the successful German offensive on the Kerch Peninsula. Several times this week the street-corner loudspeakers have interrupted the playing of martial tunes with shouts of *"Grazhdanin, Grazhdanka, vozdushnaya trevoga* (Men and women citizens, air-raid alarm)!"

Nobody hurries much to get off the streets, because after the long, raid-free winter the citizens of Moscow don't take the Luftwaffe too seriously. Sometimes the guns speak on the outskirts, but rarely do more than one or two reconnaissance planes appear over Moscow. Big German formations sometimes try to break through, according to the communiqués, but they are broken up by the Soviet fighter squadrons on the outskirts. The Red pilots maintain a highly efficient but tiring system that keeps the Germans headed off. One pilot sits in the cockpit of his fighter, while a relief pilot lies down underneath the fusilage. They trade places every hour. The heavy anti-aircraft guns in the city rarely sound any more, but at the sound of the sirens I can see scores of little fighters climbing in tight circles over the city to look for the intruders. Some people say that the reason the guns so rarely go into action now, is that the cascades of shrapnel from the anti-aircraft shells last fall and winter holed so many of Moscow's roofs that the Government has decided not to use the guns unless it's absolutely necessary.

July 1   ⚑ In a week the military situation has suddenly deteriorated. Some of the worst news comes from Egypt. Tobruk has surrendered and the German radio claims the capture of "25,000 men and vast quantities of war materials." Gloom over the British situation is widespread in Moscow. A Russian said to me today: "If they can't hold Egypt, how do the British expect to start a second front?"

Crowds in the street are intently reading the street-corner bulletin boards where the daily papers are posted. On the back page, where the foreign news is printed without comment, is the bad news that their British allies have been driven back to within seventy miles of Alexandria, the big Mediterranean naval base. However, America is getting a better press since the signing of the Lend-Lease master plan. Almost daily there have been eight-column spreads about American friendship and her enormous war potential.

Last night as I walked to the radio station after curfews, I was stopped by the Moscow patrol, as usual. Unfortunately, I had left my night pass at home. Last winter I would have had a tough time talking the militiamen and girls out of not being detained for the rest of the night, but this time the hard-boiled armed sentry looked at my American passport and said: "Ah, Americanyits," and then he smiled and gave me the international password: "Okay".

July 2   ⚑ Leo Dovotor may be dead, but his spirit still rides with the Cossack cavalry corps. The thirty-year-old half-Jewish Cossack, who rose from the rank of major to major-general in six months of war, died leading his horsemen into action and has now become a Soviet national hero. Slender, broad-shouldered, and narrow-hipped, the Cossack hero was the idol of Moscow's girls even before the war.

"How he used to look at girls!" said Katya to me, pensively. "He would stare at us so boldly at the dances and never say a word." She dropped her own disturbing black eyes and reflected. "Dovotor," she said, "was everything a man should be — 'handsome, strong, and crafty.' "

As a special treat, the entire corps of correspondents has been invited to see the famous Cossack cavalry corps whose deeds are sung in the streets of Moscow in the "Song of the Dovotorsi." We drove out the battle-scared Kalinin road to the rolling wooded hills outside Rzhev, where the Cossack corps was waiting in reserve as part of the Red Army's defense in depth.

Refilled with new horsemen from the River Don country and Siberia, the Dovotorsi Corps was conducting intensive battle practice with live ammunition when we arrived. The amount of fire power wielded by the Russian cavalry was impressive. The Cossacks still carried their famous curved swords, but they were supported by tanks, armored cars, and dive-bombers. Every regiment was saturated with tommy guns, anti-tank rifles, anti-tank guns, light artillery, and the old-fashioned "tachanka," those horse-drawn high-wheeled wagons carrying a heavy machine gun.

We watched them go into an attack. Half of the regiment dismounted, and hid their horses in a wood. The rest of the regiment circled around the enemy flank, and when an incandescent rocket arched into the sky, as climax to a thunderous artillery barrage, the Cossack horsemen charged. We watched them moving across the plain in a black, turbulent mass, shouting their blood-tingling "Oorah" and flailing at the enemy dummies with furious glittering swords. Oddly enough, the signal for the attack had come through a field telephone stamped "Connecticut Telephone and Electric Corporation." It was their only American equipment.

The sweating horsemen lined up in front of us to hear their colonel's criticism of the action. They wore black, shaggy felt cloaks that descended to the stirrups, red cowls or "bashliks" hanging down their backs, and sewn at a slant on their chests were the shining bandoleers of the Cossack plainsmen. Under their black persian-lamb hats, their tanned faces were the incarnation of all that is wild, picturesque, and romantic in Russia.

Their new general, stocky Vladimir Krukov, successor to Dovotor, invited us to ride over to the officers' mess. We mounted the slender, graceful little horses and followed them — as one English correspondent remarked, "looking like a flock of Sancho Panzas trailing a troop of Don Quixotes."

After lunch we attended a Cossack rodeo. The men rode superbly, with only a single mishap. It came when a Cossack's hat flew off as he rode at full gallop over the jumps. The general turned to me and remarked: "It's very bad form for a Cossack to lose his hat." While we watched the riding exhibition, a biplane trainer droned slowly overhead. The general looked up and murmured ironically: "There goes the terror of the Messerschmitts."

Later we dined again and toasted the Dovotorsi Cavalry Corps with vodka. Then we adjourned to a village theater to watch the Cossacks entertain. They sang, they tumbled, and played the accordion. Their dancing was an exhibition of athletic skill and co-ordination.

During the intermission I walked out for some air and noticed a Cossack private stroking the general's horses. He planted a kiss on the nose of the white one. I strolled over to talk to him and he invited me to ride. I declined because my principal experience at riding had been confined to motorcycles, but he urged me and I mounted the mild-looking white pony. Apparently it had been trained to charge at a touch, for no sooner had I climbed aboard than it pinned back its ears and started in high gear toward a gaping crowd of peasants. I forced its head around at the last moment and pelted full tilt up the hill. Gaining confidence as I rode, I headed for the hill-top with the Cossack orderly galloping behind me. Over the muddy ground we fled until I topped the rise and suddenly the white Anglo-Don pony's hoofs slipped in the mud and he went down heavily. I was underneath, but fortunately the mud was soft. The Cossack reined in sharply to avoid us, and he and his horse went head over heels in the mud, too. We picked ourselves up and quieted the horses. I knew I'd feel the bruises next day.

The Cossack explained that he couldn't bring his charges back without cleaning the mud off them. So he produced rags from the saddle bags and we walked to a nearby stream to wash the horses down. It took time, and dusk was settling when I heard the correspondents' cars honking in the distance. "*Nichevo,*" said the Cossack, "they'll wait." I couldn't demand that he allow the horses to go back dirty, for he would have been punished, nor could I face the ignominy of walking back without my horse. As we worked over the muddy horses with our rags, we heard the thunder of hoofbeats coming up the hill. Turning, I saw a group of Cossack scouts eyeing me keenly. My mud-covered windbreaker and my menial work convinced them that I was just another peasant. The band split up and made for the distant woods.

Finally we got the horses cleaned up to the orderly's acute sense of perfection and I remounted and rode slowly down the hill. I was amazed to see the entire population of the village gathered to watch my approach. Nervously I kept my horse under tight rein and managed to dismount casually in front of the censor and the divisional staff. Then I heard the news. Assuming that I was lost, the general had dispatched a whole troop of Cossacks to comb the woods to bring me back alive. The censor was furious and almost speechless. "Didn't you realize that we have to get back to Moscow before midnight because our chauffeurs have no night passes?"

But I didn't care. After all, hadn't I ridden alone with Dovotor's Cossacks, of whose feats all Moscow knew and sang?

July 3   ✎ At midnight tonight Moscow announced that Sevastopol had fallen. In two hundred fifty days of heroic resistance the defenders had cost the Germans and Rumanians 300,000 casualties. Said Moscow: "In the past twenty-five days the Germans threw 300,000 soldiers, 400 tanks, and 900 planes into the attack and lost

150,000 men, including 60,000 killed." The defenders acknowledge the loss of 40,775 casualties, not counting the deaths among the civilian population. The Germans got "nothing but ruins," the communiqué added.

Until the last moment the Germans never knew how thin the line of defenders really was, after the pulverizing effects of their siege guns and incessant mass bombardments, the heaviest yet known in this war. They finally charged through lines held only by the dead to meet the last obstinate defenders in bloody hand-to-hand combats on the streets, while rifles still spoke from the gaping windows of the defiant city. The Germans claimed angrily that they were forced to asphyxiate with smoke bombs the Red Army men who defended their city to the last from its underground passageways.

The defense of Sevastopol has held up the ultimate German drive on the oil of Baku for an entire month. Now Hitler can be expected to switch his troops against the forces of Timoshenko defending Rostov, the "Gateway to the Caucasus."

July 4 ⚑ The Russians are the same in victory as in defeat. The Red Army acknowledges that it has fallen back on the Kursk front, where a great tank battle has been raging for seven days. The Berlin radio says that the Axis troops are driving forward along a 120-mile front between Kursk and Kharkov, and advanced forces are plunging toward the River Don, 130 miles eastward.

This is such a large country that the war seems to be taking place a long way from Moscow. I can see no change in the expression or the attitude of the people. They maintain their look of stolid resignation and unshakable determination. The domestic propaganda in the Moscow papers blazes with fiery words encouraging those far from the front to do their utmost for the men in battle.

This is the most nationalistic country I have ever lived in. I remembered United Nations Day in May, when every Moscow public building flew the State flag of the Soviet Union, the red banner with the gold hammer and sickle. There wasn't an American, British, or Chinese flag to be seen in the city except over their respective embassies. Nothing is allowed to distract the public from the fact that they are standing off the main forces of the German Army alone in Europe.

When I first came to Soviet Russia I was alert for any sign that the people were in disagreement with the Communist system, but I have now almost forgotten about a possible fifth column. The impact of the war, with its tidal wave of nationalism, has cemented the public spirit so firmly that any ideas of fissures in the social structure would be far-fetched.

The people are fully conscious of the inexorable nature of the Soviet Government and the Kremlin, however. Sometimes when I have discussed the iron regimentation of the Soviet system, I have heard Russians murmur: "Perhaps it would not be like this if Lenin had lived." But I've rarely heard complaints about the ideals of the party. The few Russians with whom I have an opportunity to talk readily agree that there is no true Communism in Russia, but only State socialism or State capitalism. Then they get a far-away look in their eyes and give me the pat phrase that under Stalin the slogan is. "From each according to his capacities, to each according to his *work*." They add that when they achieve true Communism, this will be changed to: "From each according to his capacities, to each according to his *needs*." No one will venture to say when this ideal of equality for all will be reached.

The NKVD, as the OGPU is now called, is rarely mentioned. Russians don't even like to say the word "N-Ka-Vay-Day" aloud to foreigners. Someone may be listening. When I bring up this unpleasant subject, they say: "Of course, we don't like it, but we're a young country, not so settled as America and England. Some day when everybody here believes in our ideals, we won't need a secret police any more."

I was surprised and even a little disappointed to find that I was not followed around by the secret police when I arrived. They just didn't think correspondents were important enough. Like all the rest of the correspondents, I wander at will throughout Moscow, although I cannot secure a pass to visit another city unless I am conducted by an accredited Soviet representative. I suppose that my secretary and my Russian acquaintances are questioned from time to time by the secret police concerning my likes and dislikes and the subjects that particularly interest me. But since I am not a spy, this doesn't bother me. I only hope that they tell everything without appearing as though they are trying to cover up personal matters, for I should dislike arousing false suspicions. And the Soviet Russians are a suspicious people.

Actually every Soviet citizen considers himself or herself duty-bound to submit to questioning by the NKVD, just as an American citizen would answer the questions of the FBI about a foreign acquaintance. The Ambassadors of major powers are allotted six members of the NKVD to act as body guards. Lesser diplomats and foreign military men get a smaller escort, depending on their importance. Diplomatic opinion has it that the guards are provided fifty per cent for protection and fifty per cent for information, on the ground that anything or anyone visited by a diplomat is interesting. The guards follow the diplomats everywhere in full sight, riding behind them in cars when they travel by automobile and waiting outside embassies, hotels, or apartment-house doors when they go visiting. The Russian secret police is not so subtle as the French Deuxième Bureau, Scotland Yard, or the FBI. One of the British RAF officers complained to me that he got no opportunity to visit his friends of the ballet because the girls disliked visitors who always had a few NKVD men sitting outside their door.

The guards usually stand outside on the corners near the embassies waiting for the diplomats to appear. They all wear ordinary civilian clothes and the usual Russian headgear, a dark-blue cap. One night an American correspondent suggested that we all march down to the Mostorg department store, buy ourselves blue caps, and then form a group on the street corner opposite the NKVD men, stare at them, and see what their reactions would be when they thought a rival outfit was "muscling in."

July 5   ☙ Even the censors lay aside their blue pencils once a week and the vacant lots and broad squares of Moscow resound with the tramp of booted feet. Every day the shouts of battle-hardened sergeants ring out across the quiet streets. No man is exempt from the Universal Military Training Decree of the Soviet Government. Millions of Russia's office and factory men have been donning uniforms after work ever since the war began, and these are the men who will partake in the battles to come. Sometimes they go out by trucks to the suburbs and practice warfare under field conditions with trench mortars and machine guns, storming pillboxes and digging "swallows' nests" for cover.

Most of them have already had two years' compulsory training in the Army at one time during their lives and they have gone back to Army camps for at least three more years, divided into training sessions of two months until they were thirty-five and one-month camps until they were fifty.

Illiteracy has been practically banished among the males of the Soviet Union. The Red Army has educated many of its men.

Possibly they are also members of the voluntary defense organization, the Osaviakhim, which ran thousands of shooting galleries, hundreds of "aviation circles," and scores of cavalry schools from Europe to the Far East. Its membership had reached the staggering total of twelve million on the eve of the invasion. These were some of the inner muscles of the Soviet Union that accounted for her tremendous resistance.

The other day I watched Messerer, the finest ballet technician in Russia, and tall, muscular Galubin, renowned for his amazing Nijinsky-like leaps, both crawling on their bellies. A harsh-voiced sergeant was quick to remind them that they weren't on the stage now. Wielding their bayonets with determination and some grace, the male stars of the ballet could be seen stabbing straw dummies once every week in the vacant lot back of the Bolshoi Theater. You didn't need a ticket to watch.

A new call-up list has been posted on all public buildings.

Russia is combing through the lists of reserved occupations for privates up to the age of fifty and officers up to sixty. Just how many men Russia has called up from its probable maximum of 35,000,000 able-bodied males of military age is a secret of the Kremlin.

July 6   A rare treat today. I was given a few old copies of the *Saturday Evening Post* and *Life* at the American Embassy. English reading matter is extremely scarce in Moscow, and even the most ancient magazines are highly prized by us.

Katya came to the hotel after dinner and we pored over the magazines side by side, looking at the pictures. She was an unusual subject, for she had never seen an advertisement before. The Soviet magazines are devoted entirely to reading matter and the only forms of advertising in the newspapers are theater notices and the classified ads referring to apartment exchanges or factories looking for persons with specialized skills.

Pointing with her red nails at an advertisement for Listerine, she drew back in horror. It was a picture of a handsome, care-free young man unconscious of the fact that there was dandruff on his shoulders. The tiny specks on his dark suit were illustrated under a magnifying glass and revealed a mass of what seemed to be white, ugsome worms. In a frightened voice she demanded: "Does every man in America have those on his shoulder?" Nonplussed, I made a half-hearted effort to explain and then gave up.

I turned the page. We looked at a family of cartoon camels talking up their product by means of blurbs issuing from their mouths. Katya was delighted. "Ah!" she exclaimed with pleasure. "The circus! What are the animals saying about it?" Weakly, I attempted to translate the words of the camels into Russian, but went down in defeat.

I turned the page again. Here was something she could appreciate. A dozen styles of women's shoes were displayed. Bending her dark head over the page, Katya gloated over the shoes. She had never seen so many styles before. She finally selected a pair of extremely high-heeled pumps as her favorite.

We both pondered the rich color prints of strawberry shortcakes and thick, sizzling steaks with mouth-watering interest. I was hypnotized by the automobile ads, showing the absolute perfection of human existence, a happy group of extremely good-looking young men and women, all in bathing suits, admiring a shining new car. Although I couldn't really remember having ever seen such a sight, it made me homesick for America.

The waiter brought in our supper of bread and cheese, salami, and two glasses of tea. I took two lumps of sugar out of my secret hoard on top of the wardrobe.

July 7 　　　　　　　　　　　🖋 The news is getting worse. The Germans are hurling the full weight of their huge mechanized army against the south of Russia. The hope is disappearing that the Red Army, stiffened by experienced young officers and thousands of new weapons, can hold the German tanks within confined areas to deny them broad fields of maneuver.

The Germans, who defended themselves behind "hedgehogs" of fortified villages all winter, are now using a "hedgehog" system for their offensive. The march of the panzer columns is guarded on the flanks by field guns mounted on a tank chassis. These self-propelled cannon crawl along at the same pace as the tanks and defend the panzers from sudden flank attacks like a porcupine sticking out its quills.

The Germans have also come up with a new weapon. Light artillery has been mounted on the sides of motorcycles. The German riders wait in ambush in the forest until Soviet tanks appear. Then they roar out in company, attacking the big Soviet armored machines in their vulnerable sides and rears like wolves attacking a bear. After delivering a few violent blows the motorcyclists speed away out of danger. Another Nazi device is the "portable mine field." The Germans have ingeniously rigged mines on wires and pulleys which they set out in clearings where Russian tanks are likely to make an attack. When the Red Army tanks approach, the German infantry hastily pulls the wires and tries to drag the mines into the path of the Soviet machines. Still another Nazi tactic is the digging of "anti-tank cells." These are extremely narrow pits in the ground, just large enough for two men to hide in. When Soviet tanks draw near, the Germans cower below the surface and allow the iron monsters to pass over their heads or alongside them. Then the German "tank-exterminators" throw off the camouflaged cover of their pit and jump out to hurl grenades and fire-bottles at the rear of the Russian war machines.

The Russians are countering the German "tank-exterminators" by building their big forty-six ton Voroshilov tank with a limited number of open apertures and covering these with overhanging metal guards so that the liquid from the fire-bottles won't penetrate the interior.

Soviet tankmen have the highest praise for their Red Army women, who play a big role in the radio vans that accompany the Red tank columns. In the heat of a mass tank battle, when the wave-lengths are crowded with shouts by the tankmen of both sides, it is the acuteness of women's hearing that enables them to distinguish between the voices. The Germans often shout misleading orders in Russian over the open circuits, but the Russians say that their radio women can tell the difference instantly between a phony order and one radioed by their own men.

But despite the Soviet's preparations over the winter, the German tank army, paced by the dive-bombers of the Luftwaffe, is rolling relentlessly south, heading for Marshal Timoshenko's headquarters at Voronezh and for Rostov.

July 12   ✍ Heard a funny story today, or so it seems in this city, where jokes are rare. It turns on the fact that Charles Thayer, one of the Embassy secretaries, has gone to Kabul, Afghanistan, to open an American Consulate.

According to the story making the rounds, one of the Afghan attachés told him he would find living conditions good in Kabul. "The food is much better than you get in

Russia during war; your living-quarters will be comfortable; there are plenty of things to buy in the stores. There's
only one thing lacking — they have no extra women for foreigners. I advise you to take two or three with you from
Moscow. Or if you can't get them here, pick up a few in
Persia."

There's another story, not funny at all, about another of
the little independent border-state embassies represented in
Moscow. According to the legend, a lovely Russian girl was
once the mistress of one of the fierce-looking military attachés. One day she failed to appear at home. Her family
waited a few days and then made an inquiry to the police.
They had no trace of the girl. Her father then paid a visit to
the border-state Embassy and talked to her protector. The
swarthy attaché led him out to the garden and pointed down
to a paving stone. "Your daughter is under there," he said
grimly, "and there are plenty more paving stones for any
other spy I catch going through my papers."

July 13   ◪ Meetings have been held
throughout the Soviet Union appealing to all Slavs in Europe to join partisan warfare against the Germans. The censors are anxious that I don't confuse this "friendly Pan-
Slavism" with the Pan-Slavic imperialism of czarist days.
This move is designed to cultivate a bond among Europe's
Slavs against the Germanic peoples who wish to destroy and
enslave them.

The Balkans are a great problem for Soviet Russia. The
Russian press had been lauding the partisan movement in
Yugoslavia, but now they look on General Mihailovich with
a jaundiced eye. I understand that Yugoslav diplomats in
Kuibyshev regard Mihailovich as loyal to young King Peter
in London and say that the guerrilla general is trying to conserve his forces for the moment of the Anglo-American second front. On the other hand, the Russians feel that anyone who is not battling Hitler now is inimical to Russia,
because by failing to strike immediately he is helping to
weaken the Soviet Union.

Despite the diplomatic "incidents" in Bulgaria, Soviet

Russia looks upon the highly religious Bulgars with a maternal Slavic eye. Little Bulgaria, however, appears to be afraid of "Mother Russia's" embrace.

The Kremlin has already agreed to the existence of an independent Poland and Czechoslovakia after the war, and although there seems to be no intention of surrendering the portions of Poland occupied after the collapse of Colonel Josef Beck's Government in 1939, Moscow might settle the differences in direct negotiation with Poland. Russia may compensate Poland for her losses, perhaps by giving her East Prussia and the Corridor and transferring the German population back to the Reich. I know the Poles are worried about the Lwow region with its oil fields, but there's no indication in the Soviet official press as to what is Russia's attitude on this important question. It's possible that the members of the Communist Party discuss the future of Europe among themselves, but no one ever talks about it to foreigners.

Several times I have asked non-party Russians what they hope for after the war and have been surprised by their answer. They all would like to get back to the position they were in just before the war started. "Everything was so fine then," they say. "There was plenty of food and the stores were starting to fill up with things to buy." Then they look sad. "But it will take a long time to get back to where we were. We shall have so much work to build up our country again after the war."

I coaxed Katya for her opinion on Russia's plans after the war. "Why ask me?" she countered tartly. "There won't be any Russians or Germans alive after the war. What do England and America plan?" I can't answer that one myself.

July 15   At last I have a radio set. For weeks I badgered the radio station to get one for me, but to no avail. All radio sets in the Soviet Union were turned in by the people after the start of the war to keep them from listening to German propaganda and spreading enemy rumors. The only people who now possess radios are trusted officials of the Communist Party, like the leaders of town soviets. I was told by those who had seen the long lines of people standing in the rain and snow with their radio sets under their arms that the patience and willingness of the civilians to undergo the deprivation was remarkable.

The system of internal loudspeakers on street corners and in homes was immediately substituted for the independent radios, and loudspeakers were sold to the public at cost. They were instructed to keep them turned on all the time in order to hear the air-raid warnings.

I appealed to the Commissariat of Communications, which manages the warehouses where the radio sets are stored, to lend me one. Surprised at my lack of respect for private property, an official said: "But how can we lend you a radio set that belongs to someone else?" Finally I turned to Burobin and after some time I have been able to rent an excellent German "Telefunken" set. It helps pass the long hours of boredom. Nevertheless, listening to the radio is a dull pastime. All the programs are short-waved propaganda selections with entirely too much talk. It seems to me that every nation is obsessed with knocking down the enemy claims and talking its own side up.

If music is being played, I can always tell when I've tuned to a German transmitter. The Germans are completely wedded to military bands and there's no mistaking the tub-thumping "umpa-umpa." About the best broadcast to most American ears is Germany's "From the enemy to the enemy" broadcast. Directed at Australia, it consists merely in playing new American jazz records. The announcer ends the broadcasts by giving the names of a few Australian prisoners of war. He refers to them as "guests in this country." The entire program is a kind of baited hook for the German news that follows immediately.

The Germans are also responsible for the most offensive broadcast I have ever heard. Each week the announcer says proudly: "We now present the worst radio program in the world, but we're proud of it!" A skit of ancient and very dirty jokes follows. It is also beamed on the German eastern service to Australia.

There are times, although I twist the dial through every short-wave band, when I can't pick up any program except the German. The Nazis control 110 transmitters from Oslo to Algiers, Paris to Smolensk. The BBC comes through fairly well with its excellent news broadcasts, which have improved tremendously in the last year, but America is so faint that it's a great strain to listen in.

The boredom is getting me down. I take lots of walks through the sunny streets between reading the papers and broadcasting, but tennis at the British Embassy court is denied me, for I have no sneakers. They were stolen from the bag I put in the sealed car and I often ruefully reflect that someone is wearing them in far-off Siberia.

One of the world's great battles is taking place about six hundred miles away, but we can't get permission to go to the front. We'd be satisfied with a trip to one of the near-by quiet sectors, but there's no chance of that, either. The Soviet never escorts correspondents to the front unless it has won a victory. Possibly it thinks that our caravan of cars would not be safe from bombardment and their reputation might be hurt if Anglo-American journalists were killed on Russian soil. Maybe they are afraid of leaks about their military preparations even on inactive fronts. We never get an explanation.

July 16 ✠ Went to the dentist today. A filling in a tooth has worn out, exposing the nerve, but I endured days of pain before I got up enough courage to visit a Russian dentist.

I knew there were plenty of doctors and dentists administering free service to the public, but the patients have to wait in line. At the top of the street there's always a long line of people with white bandages around their aching heads outside the dentist's office. While they wait they can witness the ordeal of those ahead of them, for the dentist has put his chair right in the window. Generally speaking, it's remarkable what fine strong white teeth the Russians possess. It must be the coarse food or the plentiful sunshine. Quite different from England, where so many have bad teeth.

I learned that there were a few dentists who accepted

patients after office hours for a fee. I got the phone numbers of a few of them, but then I finally decided to call up Burobin to ask them to suggest someone to treat a foreigner's tooth. I was told to make an appointment at the dental clinic where the members of the Academy of Science are treated.

With great trepidation I entered the big gray building and sat outside a long line of dental offices with a score of Russian patients. At the appointed time the door opened and a nurse called my name. To my surprise, I found that the dentist was an elderly woman. With relief I noted that the dental equipment was quite modern. I had expected to see a drill driven by a footpress, but a modern electric drill stood at the side of the chair. When I told the dentist that I had never been treated by a woman before, she was amused and informed me that dentistry had been a woman's profession in the Soviet Union for years.

She went over my teeth with a gentle veteran's touch and remarked that I had neglected the tooth too long. The nerve would have to be killed and the root canal filled. The trouble was that she had no gold and neither did I. Patients are expected to provide their own gold, because the State used every ounce of gold produced in Russia for foreign trade before the war and for three months afterward until lend-lease went into effect. I consented to have a plastic put in my tooth and after a few exploratory drillings the kindly gray-haired woman gave me an appointment for next day.

It took six or seven treatments to get my tooth filled. I discovered that the number of waiting patients was so large that Soviet dentists made a practice of giving each one a short treatment to prevent the others from having to wait too long. This arrangement was pleasant because nothing has ever been so grueling to me as a long session in a dentist's chair.

Sometimes I walked over to the dentist's from the radio station and loitered in the sun until appointment time, watching the women working in the cellar of an old church. A huge chimney pipe had been cut in the wall of the ancient structure and I was attracted by the smoke and clicking of machines. The middle-aged women, former housewives, wore looks of great concentration on their worn faces as they energetically fashioned rings for trench-mortar shells in the made-over cellar. They didn't even notice me or the little children staring down at them through the open windows.

July 17 ⚑ The censorship has certainly relaxed. After being the most difficult I ever worked under, it has suddenly become one of the most liberal. Never so strict as the British or French about military matters, the Soviet censorship has heretofore been a "political" censorship. Broadcasts about the people and their deprivations under war conditions have been heavily cut before, but now the censors have no objection to stories depicting the hardships of the Russian workers or the defeats of the Red Army retreating across the Ukraine toward the Don.

The situation has quickly worsened in the South. Either the Red Army is making another strategic withdrawal or the Germans are unstoppable. At any rate, the Nazis have cut the main double-track railroad line leading from Moscow to Rostov at several places and hold one half of the key city of Voronezh, splitting Timoshenko's Red Armies of the south off from Zhukov's armies of the central front. The only way Moscow can reinforce the armies in the south is by sending troops along the single-track railroads that cross the steppes. All the strategic junctions of these lines are under heavy German air bombardment. Casualties among Russian troops must be heavy, because there are no woods on the steppes near railroad assembly points for them to hide in.

Virtually the entire Don coal basin has been captured by the Germans. At the pace the Germans are traveling, Rostov cannot stand up long, for its outer defenses are being stripped away by German pressure.

July 19 ⚑ Went to the circus this afternoon. We took the trolley to the little round concrete circus building with plump little Tamara, the blonde blockbuster, and Zenia, whose light-gray eyes are always a surprise under her dark eyebrows and black hair. They had been coaxing us to go for weeks because Tamara had been a bareback rider in the circus last year, resigning to study law at the Moscow Institute. I suppose this is the only country where such a change in professions would take place.

I looked around for Katya when we got inside and then saw her signaling to me from a telephone booth. Opening the door, I was surprised to find that she had taken down her night-black hair and was carefully rearranging it. She explained shyly that she'd never met the other two girls before and she wanted to be sure her hair looked just right. "Peasant!" I remarked as I waited impatiently. She was furious.

The girls warned us against the pickpockets known to congregate here, but we had no trouble except for a couple of pleasantly vodka-primed Red Army privates, who, like big children, clapped me heavily and repeatedly on the shoulder in their uncontrollable laughter at the clowns.

It's difficult not to like the Russian people. They are so impulsive, easily amused, and good-natured. All foreigners admit that the Russians show an involuntary preference for Americans because they find in them the same responsiveness, informality, and willingness to accept them as equals.

The main act of the one-ring circus hinged directly on the war. It was a scene in a captured village. During the scene when the village was invaded by Russian partisans, the performers went in for extreme realism. I dodged as they rode their motorcycles up a very steeply inclined ramp directly over my head and flinched when their machine-guns rang out in the small auditorium. Then a life-sized tank rolled out across the tanbark, spitting fire as the victorious Red Army rescued the partisan whom the Germans had buried up to his neck in the snow.

The girls told us that the show was a hold-over from last winter's siege of Moscow, as was Karandash, the extremely funny clown, who was as long and thin as his name, which means "pencil."

The Russian sense of humor is not remarkably different from ours, except that they have an inordinate love of puns.

July 20   Three of us decided to visit a Russian hospital and present ourselves as blood-donors. We chose the main blood-donation center in Moscow, the Bogdanov Central Institute.

The director, Dr. Bogdazarov, granted us an audience as soon as he was informed that we had arrived. Slender and dark-haired, he wore the rank of a lieutenant-colonel in the Red Army.

"I'm glad you came in today," he said, "because I've just returned from the front to oversee the other side of the work — transfusion to the wounded." He explained that he made frequent trips to the lines to check up on the front-line problems. "We bring blood to the southern front from as far away as Siberia," he volunteered. "And we have several new methods for preserving it. One of them we only discovered during the siege of Moscow." Particularly applicable to the Russian winter climate, the new method consisted in freezing blood plasma and defreezing it when needed. To thaw out the frozen crystals, the container of plasma had to be immersed in five different water temperatures within fifteen minutes.

"Do you know about the American method of dehydrating plasma?" I inquired.

Bogdazarov nodded. "When Harriman and Beaverbrook visited this hospital," he said, "I asked them if America would send me two dehydrating machines. You see, if we had those machines we could prepare hundreds of liters of plasma a day, for we have no shortage of blood-donors."

"Did you ever get the machines?"

"They haven't arrived yet, but we are hoping they will," he said. "We still use the ordinary flask method of dehydration, so we can make only a dozen or so liters of plasma a day. We send most of the blood to the front in the old liquid way."

We told the serious little doctor that we'd mention the lack of plasma dehydrating machines in our stories. He brightened and told us the Russians had discovered a new method of getting more plasma out of the blood after the normal separation had been made from the red portion.

"It's the Kagansky method," he went on. "We can get a second run of plasma out of one donation of blood." He hesitated a moment and then gave us the newly discovered formula. It consisted in mixing the left-over portion of the blood with a solution of salt, magnesium sulphate, potassium chloride, and water.

I asked if it was true that Soviet doctors got a great deal of blood for transfusion from newly dead bodies. He shrugged his shoulders and said that the method had been tried, "but it's only effective when the person has been killed instantly by electrocution or another form of sudden death."

Bogdazarov was enthusiastic when we told him we would like to become blood-donors. He conducted us to a room where we put on white orderlies' smocks and caps. Then nurses escorted us to a laboratory to have our blood tested. As distinguished visitors we were permitted to forgo the usual physical examination.

A cheerful-looking high-cheek-boned blonde quickly typed my blood and led me to a hospital cot. I felt rather apprehensive — I'd never been a blood-donor before — but it turned out to be painless. Masked nurses jabbed the needle into my vein and joked until I was as much at ease as a blood-donor can be.

The chief nurse shyly asked us if we cared to send the customary message along with our blood to be read by the wounded man who received it. I could think of nothing clever or witty to say, so I merely wrote: "To the Red Army man who receives this blood: This is a donation from an American in the fight against Hitler. I hope it will bring you back to good health. Sincerely, Larry Lesueur."

Then the smiling nurse handed me a small printed card that went to all voluntary donors. It said: "Proletarians of all lands, unite! The bearer has the honorary title of blood-donor. He contributed 225 cubic centimeters of blood without charge to a hero injured in the battle for the freedom of our land. The Central Institute for Blood Transfusions."

Our surprises weren't over. We were escorted downstairs to a crowded restaurant where every blood-donor was being given an extra-special meal to replenish his or her blood.

Ninety-five per cent of the donors were women. The meal was one of the best I had eaten in weeks — cabbage soup, pork chops and browned potatoes, sliced lemons covered with sugar to provide us with vitamins, stewed fruit, bread, a big square of butter, and tea.

As we left we got another of the gifts to blood-donors. It was an extra war worker's monthly ration card, entitling us to extra butter and meat.

Going back on the subway to the Metropole, I thought about the nurses at the hospital. Most of them had been ordinary peasant girls who had studied to become laboratory assistants, yet they had been as efficient as any nurses I had ever known. I considered the mistaken judgments I had made in Archangel nine months before. I knew that with proper education the hillbillies of the White Sea would be anyone's equal.

July 24   ✙ The Soviet press daily gives strong hints to the Russian public that a second front may shortly be opened in Europe. The latest indication is based on the announced arrival in Northern Ireland of one of the largest convoys of American troop ships ever to cross the Atlantic. The official press of Moscow apparently regards the June statement issued in Washington and London regarding "agreement on the urgent tasks of creating a second front in Europe in 1942" as a promise, or at least it's giving the Russian public the impression that the promise still holds good despite the British defeat in Egypt.

However, the German Army is discounting the chances of being attacked in the west or refuses to be shaken by the United Nations' "war of nerves." The pattern of the German drive is now becoming clear. One huge armored force is aiming for Rostov and the oil of the Caucasus while an even larger weight of metal and men is advancing on the River Don and Stalingrad, the lusty new Soviet industrial center on the Volga. Stalingrad, the pre-Revolutionary Tsaritsin, is one of the greatest tank-manufacturing cities in the Soviet Union and commands a strategic position between south Russia and the rest of the Soviet Union by its position on the backbone of Russia, the River Volga.

Today I noticed a new poster on the streets. It shows a Red Army man bayoneting a Nazi soldier in Europe while just across the English Channel a pipe-smoking English officer stands watching and waiting. In the distant background of the Atlantic are a number of ships, so distant, however, that the American flag they bear is just a blur of red, white, and blue, too small even to see the stars and stripes.

July 25   A book fair has opened in the little park near the radio station and on my way home each afternoon I join the throng poring over the second-hand books and the new Soviet pamphlets. The Russians are great readers and there is no end to the flood of pamphlets. Books are the only commodities that are really plentiful in Moscow, and the second-hand shops on the Kuznetsky Most are always crowded. Almost every other street corner has a small bookstand, run by tall, blonde, sunburned Komsomolkas, back from their work on the labor front, where the new fortifications of Moscow are being dug to replace the torn-down Moscow barricades. The pamphlets they sell are singularly unemotional and range from booklets detailing "what every partisan should know" to military treatises on "the use of tanks in modern warfare" and instructions on "how to plant a war garden." The prices are rarely more than one or two rubles. This is the only country I've seen where there are long lines in front of the bookstands each day buying the newspapers and pamphlets.

I am told that the most popular book among Russian soldiers at the front is a new adaptation of *The Good Soldier Schweik*, the Czech whose heart wasn't in the last German war. A Russian author has written a comic version of the misadventures of an Austrian soldier in this war, battling the Red Army on the eastern front. But the most popular book of all since the war, both at home and in the trenches, is the Great Book of Russia, Count Leo Tolstoy's *War and Peace*.

Almost every Russian loves and quotes poetry, and their old favorites, Pushkin and Lermontov, have not been for-

gotten since the invasion. Perhaps the most popular of all
the new poems which stud the Soviet newspapers daily is one
by K. Simonov. It was cut out by wives and sweethearts and
mailed to their men at the front, and Red Army men in the
trenches tore it out of their newspapers and sent it home. It
is called "Waiting."

Wait for me, and home I'll come
Though 'twas hard to part,
Wait when dreary raindrops drum
On your very heart.

Wait when blizzards whirl the snow
And when summer's in,
When with waiting weary grows,
All my kith and kin.

Let my son and mother grieve
That I am no more,
Let my dearest friends believe
That all hope is o'er.

Let them to my memory drink,
Wrapped in silence pained,
Wait — and when their glasses clink
Yours you'll leave undrained.

Wait for me, and home I'll come
Ever spiting death.
"Wondrous luck," will every chum
Think with bated breath.

Not for me it is to see
Those who did not wait,
'Twas your waiting so for me
Saved me from my fate.

Why unscathed I've passed through hell
I shall never know — nor you
Just because, like no one else
How to wait you knew.

I was amused to read the *Komsomolska Pravda* today.
This young people's newspaper, far more lively than the
dignified *Pravda* or *Isvestia,* has been running a campaign

to encourage young women to "wait for" their men at the front. One young lady has written a most serious letter demanding to know, "if Soviet girls can learn to drive a tractor, fly a plane, and jump by parachute, why can't they learn to be faithful?"

July 26   ✄ Premiere Ballerina Olga Lepischinskaya gave us an interview today. Twenty-eight years old, blue-eyed, and snub-nosed, she is the best-dressed woman in Moscow. She wore a smart black hat, silver-fox scarf, and Persian-lamb coat. Gleaming silk stockings covered her shapely legs, and her opera pumps were quite new. I wondered where she got her clothes, but guessed that they were left-overs from a pre-war wardrobe. Now at her peak, Lepischinskaya is the foremost ballerina in Moscow. No dancer approaches her in vitality and élan as she spins across the stage like a bit of white thistledown. She told me she was also very fond of adagio dancing, but her favorite ballet role was in *Don Quixote*, the longest ballet given in Russia. It has four or five intermissions and lasts four and a half hours.

The Russian ballet differs decidedly from American ballet, as I remembered, in that the Russians place great emphasis on verve and dash. The Soviet ballet dancers seem to be chosen more for their dancing ability than their looks. But the greatest difference is the audience. Dancing is a part of Russian life. Almost every worker is a balletomane. In America the audience is dignified, self-conscious, and mink-coated. In Russia the audience is almost part of the performance. The people seem to find complete expression in the gyrations of the dancers. They applaud almost continually and cheer unselfconsciously, while the high-school girls run down the aisles at each curtain, shouting themselves hoarse for their heroes and heroines. They even cheer a striking new stage set. They never seem to tire of the limited bill of fare at the Bolshoi Theater — *Swan Lake, Coppelia, The Hunchbacked Horse, Don Quixote,* and *Vain Precaution.* I was disappointed to see ballets demonstrating only the past periods of European culture. There was no ballet based on modern life in Russia. No new ideas. However, there was gossip among the ballet girls that an entirely new ballet reflecting the war was being composed, called *The Land of Miracles*.

The Stanislavsky Theater dances more pantomime and satire. It is more experimental than the classic school of the Bolshoi Theater, but never goes over the heads of its popular audience. They were doing an amusing *Merry Wives of Windsor* and *School for Scandal* and light opera coupled with *Chopiniana* and *Straussiana*. Nevertheless, the light-hearted Stanislavsky company has no such claim on the affections of Moscow as the classic Bolshoi Ballet with its acrobatics and superb character dancing.

The average ballet dancer enters the Bolshoi School of Choreography at the age of eight and studies three hours a day, six days a week, for seven years. Every dancer also takes regular school courses in her spare time, generally until she's fourteen. The wages of an average dancer are not higher than a good factory worker's, about 450 rubles a month, but premiere ballerinas like Lepischinskaya, Galina, Ulanova, Marina Semenova, and Sulamith Messerer average about 2,500 rubles monthly, which would be top salary for a factory director, and they are paid additionally for extra performances over their monthly "contract."

Lepischinskaya, Moscow's First Lady of the Ballet, told us that there had been only one new ballet conceived since the war. It had been given at the front to the troops. She and three other girls had danced an abbreviated version caricaturing the Nazi leaders. "I played Hitler myself," she said. "It wasn't difficult, you know. He's given to feminine hysterics and I mimicked his desire to emulate Napoleon. Goebbels was a cinch, too. We danced him as the little monkey man. And all that was needed for Göring was a little padding. Himmler, of course, was the incarnation of all evil. It was pretty difficult dancing on the back of an army truck," she said, "but we had Hitler and his three comrades appear at a frontier post of the Soviet Union. They made frantic gestures toward the east to indicate the invasion. We had a tree in the background whose leaves kept falling off to indicate the passing summer. Finally the Nazi leaders appear at the front and Hitler sees what a miserable state his soldiers are in. He flies into a rage and wants to kill Göring."

Lepischinskaya laughed delightedly and went on: "All the Nazi leaders are in rags by this time, but Göring manages to find a silver scarf to throw round his neck. Their quarreling ends in a battle royal, in which Himmler and Göring fall down across each other in the shape of a swastika. Then the frontier post collapsed and fell down and killed me — I mean Hitler."

"What happened to Goebbels?"

The blue-eyed ballerina smiled sweetly and said: "Oh, he just gives a squeal and falls dead, too." Lepischinskaya is well known as an organizer of the Young Communist League and many times I heard her giving propaganda talks in English on Moscow Radio's North American broadcast. Her English is quite good, with a slight American accent. There's a Moscow rumor that she learned it as a friend of Ambassador Bullitt when she was eighteen.

July 28 ✍ The Russian big-shot is a man easily recognized in the crowd. The factory manager, members of the literati, and the artists, the journalists, the bureaucrats, all wear better clothes, for they have access to special stores where higher-quality goods are stocked. Most of the members of the Communist Party have won themselves good jobs by virtue of their organizational abilities and their ambition.

I remembered that in America and England a Communist invariably wore old clothes and a shirt which hadn't seen a laundry for a few days to denote that he was on the side of the workers in the "class struggle," but here the Communist is usually the best-dressed member of the community. Without exception Communists are the pick of the people in the Soviet Union, the brightest and most intelligent men, whose talents would earn them good livings in America or England.

If a party member holds a responsible job, he gets various perquisites: a pass enabling him to eat in a better-class canteen, an automobile and chauffeur for business use, and sometimes a rent-free apartment. Few Communists abuse their privileges. The penalty of being ousted from the party is not to be considered lightly.

Not all executives in the Soviet Union are party members; some decline to take on the extra responsibilities of doing outside organizational work among the people after working hours. Since the war the pressure on the party members has been very heavy. Some of them never leave their factories and offices for days at a time, sleeping on cots and eating at the factory canteens.

Many of them wear plain khaki uniforms and high boots to work, like soldiers. I asked one of them the reason for this and got the answer that "ever since the days of the Civil War against the Whites and interventionists, the Bolsheviks who fought in uniform and ran the country at the same time have regarded a uniform as a Revolutionary tradition." However, while looking through an old Baedeker guidebook published in 1914, I ran across an item saying: "The Russians are very fond of uniforms. They even wear them to work. Uniform is the Russian's passion; it stamps him as a member of the governing class. To be a plain civilian is to be nothing."

Not many Soviet bureaucrats have ever been outside the frontiers of Russia, for it is not possible to leave the country voluntarily unless one is sent on a *komandirovka*, or Government mission, with all expenses paid. Since the Russian ruble is a managed currency, it is not exchangeable for foreign money outside the Soviet Union. Moreover, the Soviet customs officials take pains not to allow travelers leaving the country to take any rubles with them in order to sell them to foreigners coming in.

When a Soviet woman marries a foreigner and leaves the country, it is understood that she will not be allowed to come back. Except for sailors and soldiers, usually only picked members of the party and Komsomol, experts in their particular field, are sent to foreign countries to bring back industrial and cultural information to aid the growth of the Soviet Union.

Few foreign movies are shown in the Soviet Union, and although, since the war, British newsreels are exhibited, the foreign movies are invariably the product of Hollywood. Generally they are musicals or costume pictures. In the past year Moscow movies have publicly shown the perennial favorite, *The Great Waltz*, and also *The Melody Waltz, The Champagne Waltz, One Hundred Men and a Girl*, and *The Three Musketeers*, featuring the "Three Stooges." Lines formed all around the block to see the last. Communist Party members often see private showings of other American movies not publicly exhibited. Charlie Chaplin's *The Dictator* was one of these. The Communists enjoyed it, but for some reason it was not passed for public view.

Every person in the Soviet Union carries a personal identification card which is called his "passport." It contains his picture and life history. All marriages and divorces are entered therein, as well as all criminal offenses. The passport must be carried at all times, for it may be demanded by the police or militiamen as well as the secret police. The pre-Revolutionary Russian saying that the body consisted of three parts: "body, passport, and soul," still holds good. The passport must be presented when registering at a hotel so that the NKVD will have a check on all guests, in case of thefts or disorders. Since the war a double check is kept on Moscow hotel residents by requiring Russian guests to present a special pass allowing them to rent a room. Such passes are usually given to executives on business missions and to officers and men on leave.

No railroad or airplane travel is now permitted in wartime Russia without a special pass, given only when the nature of the mission is important enough to warrant the occupation of valuable transportation space. Passes are required for many things. It recalls another old Russian saying: "What is life without documents?"

The problem of a lazy and complacent bureaucracy is constantly under attack by a flexible merit system. Changes on the commissariats are publicized frequently. Generally the notices say that a commissar has been "freed" from his job and often that he has been demoted to the rank of second or third commissar in the same industry. Since the war every Soviet bureaucrat is on the alert, for drones are likely to be sent to the front.

The Soviet Union is now a completely socialized state. Virtually every citizen is a "buyer," and the State is the only "seller." Except for the State-controlled barter stores for farmers there is no private or foreign-controlled industry in Russia. Even the shoeshine stands on the street corners are part of a State "trust."

I asked a Communist Party member what he thought about Soviet regimentation. "We are not a people given to method," he replied. "Our past shows we had no natural gift for organization. We need a strong leader and Bolshevik organization, but some day we will relax. We are very young yet."

"Who will succeed Stalin when he dies?"

The answer came with a look of shocked surprise: "How can you say such a thing? Our great leader Stalin dying at such a time!" He admired Stalin the way men admire strong, hard, and inexorable men.

Then I asked: "What will happen when America and Russia go to war against each other?"

The Communist laughed and said: "America and Russia fighting each other? Don't be silly. We both own a world to ourselves. We'll never want to take anything from each other."

July 31   Red flows the Don. The Germans are on the threshold of the Caucasus after forcing the withdrawal of the Red Army from the entire Ukraine and from Rostov. German armored divisions claim to have engaged in bloody fighting at the Big Bend of the Don, only fifty miles from the strategic city of Stalingrad.

The Soviet press, abandoning the optimism of its propaganda which raised so high the morale of the people during the long, hard winter, has taken a different line. It threatens and warns. "In this war many *brave* men may die," says one editorial, "but *no cowards* will escape. . . . Every inch of land the enemy takes from us now is our bread and our future. The very existence of the Soviet Union is threatened. Red Army men must die rather than retreat. Not one step backward!"

The Army newspaper *Red Star,* circulated only among
the military and read to the men by the political workers,
delivered a scathing rebuke to the officers of the southern
command. It claimed that lack of decision and determination on the part of the officers permitted the Red Army to
flee from the defenses of Novocherkassk and Rostov, defenses constructed within the past six months. The editorial
was the harshest criticism of the Army Command that I
had ever seen in a country at war. From the tone of the editorial, there could be little doubt that high-ranking officers
would be relieved of command. Timoshenko's name has not
been mentioned in the Soviet press since the Nazi June offensive started. There has been a question in everyone's
mind as to whether he was to be replaced.

Pravda began publication of a play by Alexander Kor-
neichuk, called *Front.* It looked to all of us like a potent
domestic propaganda effort to show the Soviet people why
a general reorganization of the Red Army would take place.
The chief character was depicted as an Old Bolshevik who
had fought well in the Civil War, but who failed to learn
the new methods of warfare in the present conflict. He was
replaced by a young and ambitious general.

It was rumored around Moscow that a great reorganization of the command was actually under way and that neither Army seniority nor position in the Communist Party
would enter into the selection and promotion of youthful
generals.

Daily the newspapers stressed the message that although
Russia appeared to be an enormous country on the map,
nevertheless the Germans were now penetrating regions vital to the Soviet economy. Warned *Pravda:* "There is no
longer room to retreat."

Ilya Ehrenburg, the most prominent Soviet war correspondent, who frequently handles directives from the Kremlin, wrote: "The Germans have stripped their forces in western Europe to reinforce the eastern front." This left only
two infantry divisions remaining in Belgium, he declared,
and only twenty-six in France. "Where are our allies?"
he asked.

August 1   ✍ I visited one of the Moscow hospitals today. It was filled with Red Army men in bed and convalescing in the small, wooded park outside. Their heads were shaved and they wore hospital smocks and cotton slippers. Potted plants stood all around the corridors. In the small wards a cross-section of the Red Army lay wounded. There were Ukrainians, Jews, Tatars, Cossacks, and representatives of the hundred races that make up the Soviet Union. The shaven-headed men were quartered four and six to a ward. At each bedside was a plate with an orange and a piece of brown bread.

I offered a cigarette to a simple, weather-beaten peasant. He thanked me profusely, but explained that only the most seriously wounded were allowed to smoke. The woman doctor whispered in my ear that this fellow would never fight again. I turned to him and asked: "What are you going to do when you get well?" Without hesitation he answered: "I am going back to fight, of course." I smiled sympathetically and said: "Don't worry, Russia has plenty of men to take your place." He gave me a puzzled look and said. "But you don't understand. In a battle no one can take your place. Every man must fight for himself."

In the next ward was a vital-looking, square-jawed officer. A Communist, he had the rank of colonel of the Political Department. Like all political commissars, he would have made a fine salesman. He spoke with the ease of a practiced orator, pounding his hand to lend emphasis to his spirited words.

"What about a second front?" he demanded.

I told him about America's and Britain's shortage of shipping.

"Perhaps that is so," he said. "But, at least, I should like you to carry back a message to the American workers. They must enter a competition with us in the Red Army. We'll kill the fascists and they'll supply us with the machines." He was tremendously earnest about his request. "You'll do this, won't you?" he pleaded.

I asked him what work he did among his own Red Army men. He said that as a colonel he had under him a number of what he called "agitators," or political workers, of lower rank. He and his agitators were in charge of keeping up morale and advising the men. As a colonel commissar his principal task was to explain the military tasks set before the troops. He said he had found that such big problems were best explained by illustrations from life. He added that there was no room for vague terms in his work, and all his lectures had to be very concrete.

"In a way," he went on, "I am a front-line lecturer. We get copies of the papers from Moscow and also a limited number of copies of a special newspaper published for each major front. Then there are also divisional newspapers. Because of the limited number of copies, it is my work and the work of my assistants to read the papers to the men and give them the news of the whole world. We also read special inspirational articles on the war while the men are eating or during a lull in the action. It is my duty to know every man in my unit," he added,"and to illustrate all my talks with living examples. Another side of my work is the organization of Communist Party members within the unit and the taking of applications from Red Army men who would like to become candidates for the party. As you know, Communists are expected to be models of discipline and to help the command in any way they can."

His speech contained all those elements in the personality called "Russian" which I thought were a key to the mystery of the country — the fierce Russian pride, the egotism, the optimism, love of exaggeration, the hardness and the sentimentality, the effusiveness of speech. At the other end of the scale was an acceptance of life, seen through the eyes of a people who are close to the soil, the endurance and patience of peasants who accept the realities of nature as part of life to be endured without escapism or rationalization. Superimposed on this was the extraordinary organization of socialism and Marxism, which combined to make a Soviet Russian.

The colonel said he had been wounded on the Finnish front. He said he had learned from prisoners that the Finnish division in his sector had been filled in with youngsters, old men, and some convicts. It was his job to organize the propaganda directed at them over loudspeakers. He decided first to work on the convicts, and by leaflets and broadcasts he advised them that their only hope of being rescued from completion of their jail sentences was by surrender. Then he addressed special broadcasts to the very young soldiers and others to the older men.

"That differentiation showed immediate results," he said like an American advertising executive. "In three weeks I got two dozen Finns to surrender. The Finns," he said optimistically, "can't go on fighting much longer. They've already mobilized eighteen per cent of their manpower."

"What's the most difficult job for a political worker?" I asked.

He reflected. "The biggest problem of all is preparing green soldiers for combat. These unseasoned fellows who have never been under fire take an unreal view of the war. Some of them see the problems too simply. They think of it only as a question of advancing and retreating. They don't know the stresses and strains of fear and how their imaginations can run wild. To others, war appears too complex. They exaggerate its problems, and when they think of the technicalities of tactics or even firing a cannon, the whole task seems impossible to fulfill. They are afraid they won't make the grade. It is important to get these men before they go under fire and give them lectures on military psychology, to tell them what they are going to come up against, how they are going to feel, and try to rid them of the terrible fear of the unknown. One of the best methods I found is to line them up and then parade some newly captured prisoners before them. 'These are the invincible enemies you have been hearing so much about,' I tell them. 'Is this what you're afraid of?' When they look at the bedraggled prisoners, it gives them a feeling of superiority and self-confidence. They've already won half their first battle."

August 2　　　　　　　　⚑ The short northern summer is in full bloom. From south Russia come reports that the battle is going on under a burning sun, but here in Moscow the temperature has not gone above 75 degrees. Katya took me out to Khimki today. It's the Coney Island of Moscow, only there are no amusements aside from swings, rowboats, and a big swimming pool on the edge of the Moscow-Volga Canal. The trip costs only three rubles by trolley-bus from Moscow, but just down the road is the high-water mark of the German invasion, where the German motorcyclists came nearest before the tide of history turned in front of Moscow.

We walked through the big, white Dynamo Stadium, crowded with young workers on their day off. Every young man wore wool bathing trunks and the girls wore full-length black bathing suits. I was rather disappointed when Katya explained that everyone wore bathing suits around Moscow. It was only down on the Black Sea coast that people used to depend merely on coats of tan. When we sat down on the edge of the grass near the pool, however, three factory girls casually took off their dresses alongside us and stretched out in the sun in their plain blue rayon underwear. Nobody paid any attention to them.

Although one of the great battles of history was making the earth tremble on the Don steppes, six hundred miles to the south of us, the scene here was remarkably unwarlike. We could faintly hear the shouting of the bathers in the pool and once a Soviet fighter roared low overhead, but otherwise we might have been back in America listening to the sleepy summer chirp of the crickets. Katya was afraid to go in the green smooth-flowing canal. "Everybody knows," she said, "that it's full of dead German soldiers from last winter." I dove deep, but didn't see any.

On the way back to Moscow, our trolley-bus was halted on the city outskirts and an armed Red Army man went slowly through the crowded bus examining everyone's identification "passport." The authorities were taking no chances on German spies entering the city the easy way.

August 4 ✍ From partisan information here I gather that Hitler's personal representative in the Ukraine, Erich Koch, is making an intense effort to get a crop out of the conquered land this summer. Orders have been given to the Ukrainian peasants that they must till the land in "comradely fashion." After this summer Koch has promised that he intends to give parcels of land to those who have worked best for the German Army, and thus reestablish private landownership. Young Ukrainians, born under the Soviet, will have to work for the new landowners at least three years until they prove themselves. However, it looks as though the land tenure of peasants who believe him will be short in any event, for if the Ukraine is not recaptured by the Red Army, Koch has promised land scrip to German soldiers after the war. A printed handbill signed by Koch and found on the body of a German officer read:

"I, as Commandant of the Ukraine and by the Führer's will, must open her up and make her useful for the New Order in Europe. The question is to bring in a new population, which will be the greatest work in European history. I am doing it for you and your comrades in arms. I don't want your names or your money. I ask only for your faith in National Socialism."

The Germans plan to bring in Netherlanders to the Ukraine. The partisans say that some families from Holland have already arrived.

August 6   One of the correspondents has come back from Teheran with clothes for the winter. He has brought back a load of cigarettes, razor blades, and shoes from the Iranian capital. Shoes are the scarcest goods in Moscow. Almost everyone's are ragged, scuffed, and worn out, except for Red Army men's. The only choice a civilian has is to get his or her shoes repaired with old leather from a pair of even older shoes.

Katya, Tamara, and Zenia have been anxiously awaiting the shoes from Teheran after carefully furnishing paper tracings of their feet for sizes a month ago. Mary Brock, the only American girl in Persia, had been entrusted to choose shoes suitable for a young lady of Moscow. She selected stout, low-heeled walking shoes of a decidedly collegiate cut.

We decided to give a presentation party to the girls. After dinner we proudly displayed their handsome, new, utilitarian footgear. To our great surprise, their faces fell. None of them spoke for a few moments. Then husky-voiced Zenia broke the frigid silence.

"Why did you get us shoes to play football?" she accused.

Katya chimed in. "Where are those high-heeled models I asked for?" she demanded coldly.

Tamara, the blonde bombshell who could give Lana Turner two sweaters and still come out ahead, struggled into the offending shoes, and limped noisily around the room. Black-haired Katya rolled a paper wad and threw it on the floor with dramatic bitterness. Tamara kicked it out the window like a football.

Then they huddled together and wailed loudly. "You Americans are trying to make the most beautiful girls in Moscow look like Kolkhozniks (collective farmers)," they mourned. In mock tears, gray-eyed Zenia sadly put the shoes back in the suitcase and then turned suddenly to hurl it at our heads. But next time I saw Katya she was wearing the "footballist" shoes. She reluctantly confessed that her father thought they were "very sensible."

August 8 Despite the great battle for the Don, life goes on as usual in the Soviet rear. The Government is cracking down on unsanitary conditions on the home front. The chief of the Sanitary Department of the Tashkent Railroad has been accused of sending several trains from Samarkand loaded with sick passengers and in an unsanitary condition. The War Tribunal has sentenced him to five years' imprisonment. The director of the Tashkent Trade School and the commandant of the refugee dormitories in the big evacuee city on the Afghanistan border have been put away for four years apiece.

Near Moscow a Sanitary Department chief did not give the people an opportunity to use the public steam baths. He's getting two years in jail.

Out in Siberia, in the boom city of Novossibirsk, where so many of the factories from the west have settled since the war, the commandant of the refugee dormitories failed to provide boiled water and "elementary comforts" for the factory workers. He will pay for this with a year at forced labor, giving a percentage of his salary over to the State for the next twelve months.

A colleague of his, in one of the unmapped cities of the Urals, which is called "the city without a name," has supplied sanitary conditions which are described as "miserable." He will serve six years' imprisonment, and his assistant three years.

August 9 ✒ Major General Follett Bradley of the U. S. Army Air Forces has landed in Moscow after a record flight from America. His B–24 Liberator bomber made the trip from Washington in ten days. Handing out the first American newspapers we had seen for months, the tall, gray-haired general denied that he was in the Soviet capital to attend a "second front" conference. He explained that his mission was only "to expedite aid to Russia in every possible way," despite rumors that Prime Minister Churchill is also on his way here to talk to Stalin.

With pride I told Katya about the remarkable speed with which the general had flown from Washington. She was not impressed.

"Everybody knows," she said, "that Soviet pilots are the best in the world."

"Better than Americans?" I demanded with patriotic spirit.

"Of course," she countered. "Who were the first men to fly across the North Pole to America? The Russians, the most courageous pilots in the world."

"Yes, but who were the first to fly around the world?"

"Who cares?" said Katya scornfully.

August 10 ✒ The German offensive is rushing like wildfire across the rich wheatlands of the northern Caucasus, more than a hundred and twenty-five miles southeast of Rostov. Cossack cavalry is making mounted raids against the rear of the German tank columns, but they can't stop the panzers on this flat "parade ground," the dream battlefield of the German tank commanders. The Nazi forces are driving on toward the high Caucasus, the snow-capped mountain range that walls off the narrow isthmus which joins Europe and Asia.

Their obvious strategic plan is to cross the Caucasus along the Caspian Sea, the traditional route of Genghis Khan, seize the oil of Baku, then meet Field Marshal Rommel's forces camped at El Alamein in Egypt. If they can cut the British Empire in half in this fashion, it looks as though they'll join with their Japanese partners in India.

The triumphantly advancing Germans are dropping leaflets over the retreating Soviet troops that say: "And the Second Front?" One of the secrets of the rapid German advance is their new "airfield" maneuver. The Nazis are flying engineers in transport planes up to the front lines to level field air bases on the smooth Don and Kuban steppes. Gasoline and ammunition dumps are hurriedly established and the Nazi Messerschmitts are quickly transferred to the new fields directly behind the front lines. They are so close that the German troops can summon their protecting fighter planes by signal rockets when they spot Russian bombers approaching.

German parachutists are being landed in the rear of the retreating Russian troops to set fire to the rapidly ripening grain fields, hoping that the huge clouds of black smoke will panic the Red Army men into believing that they are surrounded.

The Germans are also demonstrating their slyness by pulling columns of cardboard tanks along the roads with tractors. This is done at sunset to give the Red Air Force planes the impression that they will mount an attack in that sector at dawn. During the night the Germans switch their troops and tanks to another point and launch a surprise attack.

August 11   So there's not going to be a second front in Europe this year! We got the big news today when Ambassador Standley came up from Kuibyshev. I walked over to Spasse House in the hot August sunshine after my broadcast. White-haired Admiral Standley was waiting for us in the big white-columned room of the American Embassy, the handsomest building in Moscow.

The California-born admiral remarked that he had very little news to give us.

"What about the second front?" someone asked.

The cagey Mr. Standley replied: "You know, boys, the people here seem to be under the impression that the statement of agreement on the urgent task of creating a second front in Europe this year was a promise. Now, I don't think it really was. Frankly," he added, "if I were you I wouldn't go around saying to these people that you think a second front is going to be opened in Europe this year."

We were silent for a full minute. Then I asked: "May we quote you on this, Mr. Ambassador? "

His wise blue eyes twinkled. "Sure," he replied. "If you think it's important."

Admiral Standley is not a "correspondent's diplomat." He doesn't take us aside and "spill the dirt," nor does he play any favorites. He treats all correspondents equally and he never gives us a "wrong steer." He can be counted on for advice on delicate problems. The dignity of his former post as highest-ranking United States admiral gives him the respect among Soviet officials that he enjoys among his own staff and the correspondents.

Sage old Standley has probably had more audiences with Stalin than any foreign diplomat of equal rank in Russia. But diplomacy counts for little now. Military action is everything here. He is a widely traveled realist like most naval officers, and his most obvious characteristic is his complete loyalty to his Commander-in-Chief. Few wiser choices could have been made than the sending of this four-star admiral to Russia at this time, when the military is all-important.

With a fine sense of humor that lightens his dignity Admiral Standley is at heart very fond of the Russian people.

He has come to know them during his long, monotonous stay at Kuibyshev, a city much more typical of Russia than Moscow. I know that he is much concerned with getting the Russian people to know that the American people are their friends.

Weeks later, when he flew to Washington on a short visit, I saw him off at the airport. Standing under the wing of the plane, out of the cold driving rain, Standley said to me: "One thing I've got to impress on the people back home is that we can't neglect these people after the war. We can't let them down. They deserve a lot."

August 12   ✍ The landing of American marines in the Guadalcanal, Tulagi, and Florida areas of the Solomon Islands drew prominent headlines in the Moscow press today. It is the first American offensive of World War II.

My Russian friends refuse even to comment on the possibility of a Japanese attack in the Soviet Far East while the Red Army is in such a desperate position on the European front. But I know they are worried about it. The Chungking radio has repeatedly stated that Japanese combat divisions are being withdrawn from China to the Manchurian front, but my Russian acquaintances are adamant. They simply refuse to believe it. We Anglo-American correspondents, however, can go nowhere in Moscow without being asked: "What about the second front?" and I don't want to comment on that any more.

Actually, there is no Soviet spokesman to whom an Anglo-American correspondent can direct a question for even semi-official comment. Solomon Lozovsky, Vice-Commissar for Foreign Affairs, has his headquarters in Kuibyshev with the diplomatic colony and there hasn't been a press conference in months. Except for the newspapers, there is no place for us to turn for official Soviet comment.

A joke is going the rounds in Moscow about the second front. It seems that a group of Russians finally turned to an old priest to find out if he could tell them anything about the possibility of a second front in Europe in 1942. The priest reflected and then said: "A second front can be established in two ways, the natural way and the supernatural way. The natural way would be for God to send down 150,-000 archangels to open it. The supernatural way would be for the Americans and British to do it."

August 13   ✒ While we walked across sun-flooded Sverdlov Square, the heavy rumble of four-engined bombers filled the sky. Looking up, we saw three American B–24 Liberators cruising low over the roof-tops, escorted by seven small Soviet pursuit ships.

So the rumors were true. It could be none other than Prime Minister Churchill arriving on the first trip that a British Premier has ever paid to Moscow. Excitedly we ran over to Gorki Street, the direct route from the Moscow airport. Within twenty minutes a line of big, black limousines rolled swiftly through the traffic lights, and in the first car, a shining black Packard, we saw Churchill himself, in the back seat, getting his first sight of the Russian capital through the bullet-proof windows and leaning over in a well-known posture, lighting up a big black cigar. None of the Russian pedestrians paid any attention to the line of cars, but we watched them turn the corner and speed into the great gate in the red walls of the Kremlin.

We rushed over to the British Embassy to ask when Churchill could see us. The Embassy officials were taken aback, invited us to have a drink, and then called up to check the news. The Embassy attaché came back from the phone a chastened man. This time he said: "Just whom were you asking to see?"

We repeated: "The Prime Minister, Mr. Churchill."

"Really," he said, "I know nothing about it. Who told you he was in Moscow?"

"Nobody told us. We just saw him."

"I'm afraid you're wrong, gentlemen," was the abrupt answer.

We walked back to the hotel annoyed and frustrated. It was bad enough to be ignored by the Soviet authorities, but that was normal. Now even our own circles seemed to have turned against us. Here we were in the midst of the biggest story in the world. Virtually nothing was taking place of decisive military importance to the world except in Russia and we couldn't go to the front. Now the world's most important diplomatic conference was taking place and we were getting the old "revolving door" treatment. I was jittery and nervous from the inner tension of trying to dig out enough news for two broadcasts a day. I didn't want to go back to the hotel for supper. The arguments among the fifteen or more correspondents who ate three meals a day together were getting out of hand. We were tired of looking at one another.

Then at nine that night the phones rang in our rooms. "Would the American correspondents care to drop over to the diplomatic guest house? Someone would like to see them."

The Moscow subway never seemed to go so slowly and we fairly trotted along the street to the spacious old merchant's home that had been turned into a guest house by the Soviets for distinguished foreign visitors.

We shook hands with Averell Harriman. None of us had seen him for almost a year and he looked much older. He had a tired and careworn expression, yet there was also a new poise and stature about this handsome man who had played a large role in the diplomacy of the first three years of European war.

He greeted us and said: "Boys, you understand my position. I'm merely accompanying the Prime Minister. This is really Churchill's visit. I'm just on the sidelines."

Our questions led naturally to the second front.

"I can't say anything about it," said Harriman frankly. "But what makes you think that the landing of our marines on Guadalcanal isn't a second front? It could be, you know."

August 17   After four days on Russian soil, in which he did no sightseeing except between the British Embassy summer house, nine miles from Moscow, and the Kremlin, the leader of the British Tory Party has shaken hands in farewell with the leader of the Communist Party. Prime Minister Churchill has flown back to Egypt.

Intense digging among our sources of information revealed that for the first three days Mr. Churchill was in a black humor. On the fourth day, after a night-long session with Premier Stalin, Churchill came back to the Embassy, threw himself on a couch, and said to Ambassador Sir Archibald Clark Kerr: "Everything is fine now."

Churchill had lost no time getting in touch with Stalin within a half-hour after his plane landed in Moscow. The first meeting between the son of Lord Randolph Churchill and the son of the Georgian shoemaker was brief and colorful, according to report. Joseph Stalin had left few words unspoken and no doubt as to what was on his mind. Churchill's angry mood, as demonstrated among the members of the British diplomatic colony, indicated what had occurred.

Next day the two realists met again to discuss the Battle of Europe. In the evening Stalin gave one of his famous banquets. As usual, the meal began with a dozen hot and cold "zakuski" or hors d'œuvres. Three choices of soup followed, then a selection of meat, game and fowl, ending with cakes and four or five flavors of ice cream. Vodka and wine were drunk throughout the meal in scores of toasts. Stalin seated Churchill on his right and Harriman on his left, but frequently the Soviet Premier rose from his chair and walked around the table to throw his arm about the shoulders of one of his favorites who had made a brilliant speech.

Stalin wore his usual costume, a plain beige uniform with breeches tucked into polished Russian boots. Churchill countered with his famous blue zipper overalls, leaving his ten-gallon hat in the Kremlin cloakroom.

Toasts were offered on every side, but the second front was not mentioned. Stalin was cheerful and in a joking mood. Toast followed toast and then Stalin rose to praise the intelligence officers of the United Nations. "There's no answer to this toast," he said. "The men who do so much to win a war receive no recognition." He used this as a springboard to recall that the British intelligence officers of the last war had vainly informed London that the Turkish defenders of Gallipoli peninsula were running out of armor-piercing shells, implying pointedly that he had read Churchill's critical military study of the last war.

British Ambassador Clark Kerr rose to address an eloquent toast to Stalin. As all the guests lifted their glasses to their lips, Churchill bluntly informed the Ambassador that he had bungled protocol. The Prime Minister insisted that Clark Kerr repeat his toast and direct it to Vyacheslav Molotov, Commissar for Foreign Affairs. The British Ambassador's neck was described to me as :"so red you could have lit a cigarette on it." He repeated his toast.

Captain Duncan, the undauntable United States Naval Attaché, made the hit of the evening when he rose, glass in hand, and announced he could answer Stalin's "unanswerable" toast. "I'll confess that I'm an intelligence officer myself," said Duncan dryly, "but if we make mistakes it's because the only information we can get is what your liaison men give us and that's not very much!"

Laughing, Stalin left his chair and walked all the way over to the side table where Duncan sat, put his arm around his shoulder, drank a personal toast to him, and said: "If you want information, just come to me next time." When the banquet ended, after midnight, Stalin and Duncan walked out of the room arm in arm.

All reports agreed that it had been a fine banquet, but back at the Metropole Hotel the correspondents were the only ones aware that the ham and cheese had been removed from our hotel's limited menu to feed the visiting celebrities.

Our appeals to the British Ambassador to get Churchill to grant us a press conference were answered the next day. We were to see him at three in the afternoon. I was at the American Embassy as conference time approached. As we said good-by to Admiral Standley and told him we were seeing Churchill, he said: "I don't think you are. I just saw Churchill and he said he was allergic to the press."

Admiral Standley was right. The British Ambassador conducted the Churchill press conference. He explained that the Prime Minister felt that he couldn't talk to us because if he did, he would also have to hold a press conference when he got back to Cairo.

We asked Sir Archibald what the Churchill-Stalin talks were about. "All I can say," he answered, "is that the meeting was epochal. And that is a word I use very infrequently." He paced back and forth across the carpet: "If I could only tell you. It's on the tip of my tongue." He didn't.

That evening the Prime Minister returned to the Kremlin again to take tea with Stalin. The Russian leader's daughter, eighteen-year-old, red-haired Svetlana, was hostess. The men who planned to crush Hitler talked far into the night and then Churchill returned to the Embassy in a better mood than he had been in on the entire trip. Without getting much sleep, he boarded his plane for Egypt next morning.

Next day the Russian public learned that Churchill had visited Moscow. The Soviet press blossomed with front-page photographs of Churchill, Stalin, and Harriman. The newsreels of Churchill's arrival at Moscow airport, one of the best examples of newsreel photography I have ever seen, were released in Moscow's "Kino" theaters. For a week thereafter small boys gave me the "V" sign as they had seen Churchill do in the newsreels. But to the Russian public Churchill's two raised fingers meant only the "second front." There is no "V" in the Russian alphabet. The Russians would have understood the British "thumb's up" sign; it's also a tradition in Russia.

Visitors who came to Moscow weeks later from Egypt told us that to Britishers in the Middle East Churchill had reportedly referred to Stalin as "that monster." When the report reached England, Churchill sent a cable to Ambassador Clark Kerr calling the rumor "a ridiculous lie."

August 19   British troops have stormed across the Channel to Dieppe. When we heard the exciting news over the BBC, many British correspondents were convinced that the second front had been launched. Nine hours later, when the British withdrew, the atmosphere was gloomy in Moscow's British colony.

The news had little effect on the Russian public. They didn't hear about it while it was taking place. Next day, on the back pages of the Soviet papers, devoted to foreign news, the press carried a brief two-column story. It ranked no greater in importance than previous commando raids on the Continent. The Russians got the news as an entire story, so they had not been raised to a peak of expectancy and then disappointed when the Allied troops withdrew.

Churchill had undoubtedly told Stalin that the raid would be a reconaissance-in-force, but since every successful military strategist has an alternate plan, I assume that the British would have tried to seize the Dieppe peninsula if they had found German resistance weak.

I listened to the German radio gloating over its defense. They put a purported "Luftwaffe pilot" on their eastern service. "You've got to hand it to the RAF," he said. "They certainly can fly. I got on the tail of a Spitfire and almost had him in my guns when he pulled away in a neat stall turn and then got on my own tail. He surely would have got me if it hadn't been for a greenhorn Yankee pilot getting in his way. I shot the American down myself. He was easy."

The announcer broke in. "Yes," he said, "I talked to that American pilot myself. His name was William Beard, of Texas. He said he'd like to congratulate the man who shot him down, but he never wants to fly with the English again. He said he wouldn't have been shot down if the RAF hadn't deserted him."

And so on, far into the night, the German radio spread its poison, trying neatly to split the Allies.

Like all the Russians, Katya was not very much impressed with the Dieppe raid. I boasted, however, that the RAF had knocked out one third of the German fighter planes in the west.

"How long were the British troops fighting the Germans?"

"Nine hours," I said proudly.

She gave me a sidelong glance from her dark eyes. "They're almost as good as our partisans," she said.

August 21   It's dangerous for politicians to write a book. I found a copy of Churchill's book on the last war, entitled *The Eastern Front, the Unknown War*. I had an idea that Stalin might have read it before mentioning British intelligence officers in Turkey at the Churchill banquet.

Churchill had fully described therein the failure of the British offensive against the Gallipoli peninsula. Then he spoke of "Russia's agonies" in the last war and how her peasants had fought with "supreme devotion." Writing of the Russian Revolution, he added: "It was not until a fearsome set of internationalists and logicians built a subhuman structure on the ruins of Christian civilization that any form of order and design emerged again. . . . Vainly did the great men of action strive to marshal the social revolutionary forces in defense of Russia. . . . All fell headlong into the depths where Lenin, Trotsky, Zinoviev and other unnatural spirits awaited their prey. . . ."

I smiled as I thought how little Churchill had realized that the day would come when he would propose a twenty-year alliance with the "fearsome set" and pay an urgent visit to one of the "unnatural spirits." I remembered my great admiration for Churchill's realism when on June 22, 1941, without consulting Parliament, he had broadcast to the world that Britain would give "whatever help we can to Russia and the Russian people. . . . Any man or state who fights against Nazidom will have our aid." And he added that he would "unsay no words" he had already spoken about Communism. "All this fades before the spectacle which is now unfolding," he said. "The Russian danger is our danger and the danger of the United States."

August 23   The members of the British mission are feeling rather on the defensive about the lack of a second front, but they haven't lost their sense of humor. A British officer told me the latest joke in Moscow.

"God was becoming annoyed at the noise of the war down on earth," he said. "He couldn't sleep at night because of the racket. So he called in Saint Peter and asked him who was responsible. Saint Peter thought it was Stalin. God ordered Stalin to appear in heaven. He ordered the Russian leader to halt the war immediately. Taken aback, the Russian leader declared: 'It's not my doing. We're only defending ourselves. Hitler attacked us.' Hitler was called in. He listened to God's accusation and said meekly: 'But it's not my fault. It's Churchill's.' Churchill then answered God's summons, heard the charges, and said with surprise: 'But it can't be my fault, sir. You won't find a British soldier fighting anywhere!' "

I rewrote the joke in a modified version and handed it in to the censor. He passed it. My Russian friends were surprised, not because the censor passed it, but because the name of the materialistic Stalin was permitted to be linked with God's.

August 25 ✒ Stalingrad is besieged. The crack German Sixth Army, conquering veterans of Poland, the Low Countries, and France, have drawn up outside the Volga city under direct command of General von Paulus. Marching in two columns, they have cut off the city from the rest of Russia on the north and southeast. The people and the defenders of Stalingrad can be fed and reinforced only by the broad, serene Volga.

Opposite Stalingrad burns the sun-baked wasteland of the Transcaspian Desert. "There is no land on the other side of the Volga," the newspapers state grimly.

Gigantic preparations are being made to defend the young metropolis, for Stalingrad, like Leningrad and Moscow, will never be declared an "open city." "Panic-mongers, cowards, and the craven" are being cleared from the civilian population under Stalin's orders. Housewives, old men, and children have become dock workers, straining their backs to lug crates of food and ammunition up the high, steep, sandy Volga bank to the plateau that supports the city. The big, American-made freight conveyer belts have now been bombed into twisted, blackened wreckage.

The brown bosom of the Volga, on which the great river boats once swung lazily in the current, is a scene of dynamic activity. Small river boats, cutters, and even rowboats scuttle back and forth like beetles to a supply base being frantically built on the eastern shore. The workers of the big Volga arms and tanks plants, Red October, Barricades, and the Stalin Tractor Plant stop work only when they rest beside their machines. But at dusk, just before the blackout starts and the whine of night raiders begins overhead, the Stalingrad band plays in the Central Square to boost civilian morale. Profiting by the experiences of Odessa and Sevastopol, the Red Army Command and the Soviet Party organization are placing their stores and headquarters in extremely deep dugouts, impenetrable even to armor-piercing bombs.

The Sixty-second Russian Army, under the command of forty-two-year-old Lieutenant-General Vasili Chuikov, has been deployed in the narrow triangle in front of the city to serve as a "meat-grinder" between the German armies and the city, falling back a mile or so a day, but inflicting terrible losses on the Nazis who are advancing under orders to take the city at all costs. Another military miracle will have to occur if the Volga is to remain out of Hitler's hands. Stalingrad will have to prove another Moscow.

An artillery expert, the gold-toothed, dark-haired commander of the Sixty-second Red Army, has introduced a new artillery maneuver against Field Marshal von Paulus's advancing hordes. He has strung out his light and heavy artillery in lines across the flat Stalingrad steppes. Each group of guns is elevated so that the shells fall within a narrow area. The concentrated explosions of the flying steel shards is even more devastating than a mass air bombardment. The high-explosive shells are fused to burst before hitting the ground, while air bombs bury themselves in the earth before exploding.

Taking up their positions behind the huge tank trap dug by the Stalingrad civilians, the Sixty-second Soviet Army is employing many "Katushas" against the tank-paced German Sixth Army. The Germans, in turn, subjecting the Red troops to intense dive-bombing, and crawling ever ahead, use the very bomb craters as fox-holes.

A dispatch from the front tells of a raid by Kalmuck cavalrymen against a German garrison near Elista, capital of the Kalmuck Republic, which lies between Stalingrad and Astrakhan. Several of the Kalmuck riders failed to return, and when scouts discovered they had been tortured and killed, they planned a massed night attack on the German garrison. Slaughtering the German sentries, the fierce horsemen of the steppes stole into the German barracks and slit the Nazis' throats, hanging them up by the heels to bleed like sheep. Then they buried their tortured companions and cut the throats of their horses across the graves in the ancient Kalmuck custom.

August 26   🚩 Another convoy of war supplies to Russia has arrived at the northern ports. This one suffered considerable losses from a heavy and sustained German submarine and torpedo attack.

The English commodore of the convoy attended the Saturday afternoon movies at the American Embassy and told us something of his experiences. "The German planes kept shadowing us for days and made six separate torpedo attacks," he said. "When we got out of range, they directed their submarines to our new position. It was hell. Whenever a bomb or torpedo scored a hit on one of our TNT-loaded ships, there was no time to take to the lifeboats. Just a tremendous explosion and a wall of yellow flame. No survivors."

He revealed a new German trick. "When the torpedo bombers came over simultaneously with the high-altitude bombers, we discovered that some of the torpedo planes were just dropping logs in the water. We were trying to dodge what we thought were torpedoes when we should have been zigzagging to avoid the bombs dropped from the high-level raiders. The air attack was so constant that some of our ships had to stop firing. They ran out of ammunition."

The commodore revealed that when the German torpedo bombers dropped real torpedoes, they no longer aimed them straight at the merchant ships. The cunning Nazis had adjusted the rudders so that the torpedoes would travel in concentric circles. Then they dropped them ahead of the convoy, confident that the constantly circling torpedoes would hit some ship in the packed group.

The "local hero" of Murmansk and Archangel was in

town, too: gray-eyed, cleft-chinned, and curly-haired Lieutenant Commander Sam Frankel of Staten Island and California, the Assistant United States Naval Attaché. He told us that times were hard at Murmansk. "It's a little too close to the German bombers based on Finland," he said. "We cleaned all the buildings off the docks to avoid the danger of fire-bombs, and after every raid the Russians worked hard clearing up the damage."

In answer to our questions Frankel modestly revealed that he was the only man living directly on the much-bombed docks, that he was active after every raid putting out the fires, and that he did a bit of first aid, too. He had been cut about the face by glass and suffered burnt hands.

The Russian Government had built an International Seamen's Club for the Anglo-American sailors, he told us, but it had been leveled by the Germans along with the only hotel in Murmansk. The morale among the American seamen, under fire for the first time in their lives, was excellent, he said. The Soviet Government showed its gratitude by rewarding them with an extra month's pay when they landed, and the sum amounted to about $3,000 a ship. This was besides the bonus paid to the American sailors for landing in a foreign port.

August 27   ⚑ The Moscow papers report that Wendell Willkie is going to visit Russia. I said in my broadcast: "Nobody here is quite sure just when Wendell Willkie will arrive, but some of the reporters who went around with him in London are here to welcome him now. They could tell him that he won't need a tin hat this time, because air-raid alarms have been few and far between in Moscow this summer. Mr. Willkie probably will want to visit the famous Moscow subway, but he won't find anyone living there or in the air-raid shelters as they did in London.

"The special representative of the President will have to be home at midnight, when the curfew chimes. Even if he is armed with a diplomatic passport, he will be stopped every block or so by the Moscow patrols, who will read every word on his passport before they let him proceed.

"It will be a good idea if Mr. Willkie brings a supply of American cigarettes; otherwise he'll have to roll his own, the way every man and woman in Moscow does now that cigarettes are scarce.

"And then there's the language. Mr. Willkie may have difficulty with the Russian language because it's difficult to pick up in a short stay. But there's one word that will come in very handy. It's *'nichevo'* and it means 'no matter' or 'all right,' depending how you say it. Perhaps the best advice to Mr. Willkie when he gets to Moscow is just to sit tight and say *'nichevo.'* "

August 28   ✍ Took a walk to the Park of Culture and Rest with Captain Glasser, a member of the U. S. Army Air Forces attached to the Supply Mission. We strolled in the summer sun along the river boulevard past the unfinished steel skeleton of the Palace of Soviets. Before the war the Soviet Government planned to make this the tallest building in the world, higher even than the Empire State Building, but now Moscow's dream building is being torn down to be melted into steel for the winning of the war.

We leaned over the river parapet to watch oarsmen sculling their slender craft like water beetles along the placid Moskva River. Great rafts swung lazily in the water in the wash of the paddle-wheel tugboats, and a pack of sunburned little boys were swimming in the small pool near the largest apartment house in Moscow. Scores of automobiles were parked in front, for this is where the minor commissars and their families live. They belong to the rowing club on the river.

The Park of Culture and Rest was not very crowded. It was a week-day and most people were working. The kindergartens were open and scores of toddlers were riding the park's toy automobiles under the watchful eye of their mothers. Red Army men on leave crowded the motorcycle bowl, where "death-defying Vovo" whirled his machine around at right angles to the ground. The parachute jump was doing a good business, as usual, and remembering an experience at the World's Fair in New York, I suggested to Captain Glasser that we try a jump.

"Not for me," he said, looking over the parachute with a professional eye; "I'll sit this one out."

I bought a ticket for half a ruble and walked inside to get a harness strapped on. The assistant manager was surprised to see a full-grown man in the midst of all the children. He frowned and said: "You're too heavy."

I was willing to take him at his word, but the manager came out, looked me over, and in his robust Russian way clapped me on the back and said: "*Nichevo,* you won't hurt yourself much. Just keep your feet together." Then, before I could answer, he strapped a harness on me.

With a feeling of foreboding I climbed the tower and joined the line of children on top, like Gulliver among the Lilliputians. I had never realized before how high the tower really was. I could scarcely pick out Captain Glasser in the crowd below.

Then to my horror I noticed that a side of the extended parachute had torn away from the frame and I realized why the assistant manager thought I was far too heavy. Moreover, unlike the World's Fair jump, this was a "free" parachute; that is, it had no guide wires, only a slender rope on top to haul it up and down.

The line of little boys and girls jumping with gay screams was rapidly melting in front of me, and I could escape no longer. It was my turn. The plump Russian girl shook her head as she hooked the parachute to my harness. "You're very heavy. Be sure to keep your feet together."

I said: "Thank you," and was surprised to find that my voice was already hoarse with fright.

She slammed the gate behind me and I looked down a hundred feet to the ground. All the muscles that I had trained in a career of newspaper typing and radio broadcasting pulled me back from the edge. I just couldn't do it.

I stepped back and the girl looked at me with surprise.

"What are you?" she asked bluntly.

"I'm an American," I answered, smiling wanly.

"America! America!" she said with a far-away look. "How much I want to go there some day! And some day

I will." Then she looked at me again and said: "But you're not an American. You must be an Englishman!"

"No," I said with determination. "I'm an American."

The honor of both America and England were at stake now. I had to jump. I dropped off the edge of the platform with my eyes closed and I opened them only when the parachute harness jerked. With relief I saw that I hadn't snapped the rope after all. The parachute was following me. Looking down, I could see the ground approaching me at high speed. The manager and his assistant were standing with frantic expressions and outstretched arms to catch me. The ground was hard, but I rose with a feeling that the good name of the United Nations had been preserved.

Captain Glasser helped dust me off. "Gosh," he said, "You were up there so long that I thought the Soviet Union had reversed the law of gravity."

August 30   There are rumors in Moscow that Stalin has flown to Stalingrad. The censor carefully deleted all intimations of this from my broadcast.

It would not be the first time Stalin had gone to the front. An oil painting hanging for months in the famous Triatiakov Gallery shows him conferring with his staff by the light of a kerosene lamp in a cottage at Khimki, five miles from Moscow, the nearest point reached by the German motorcycle scouts before the collapse of the Nazi attack on Moscow last winter.

There is no man in the Soviet Union more experienced than Stalin to direct the defense of his name city. Twenty-two years ago Stalin personally directed the Battle of Stalingrad, then called Tsaritsin. That was during the Civil War of 1918 against the Whites and interventionists. According to Soviet histories, Stalin was sent by Lenin to organize grain-collections on the Don steppes to feed the cities in the rear. When he arrived, he found the Red Army Command confused and panicky. Stalin immediately placed the artillery staff and part of the General Staff under arrest on a barge in the middle of the Volga. His next step was to rid the city of cowards and frightened civilians. Even before his reported arrival in Stalingrad this time, Stalin had telephoned the chairman of the Stalingrad Soviet from the Kremlin and advised him that his first move in readying the city for defense was to clear it of panicky civilians.

As in 1918, the Red Army defending Stalingrad has heard Stalin's order that all Volga ships and barges will be sent north up the river. There is no retreat left.

Stalingrad's civilian population have undergone the worst daylight raid on any Russian city since the war began. The German bombers dropped threatening leaflets warning that if they resist, the mighty Luftwaffe "will turn your homes into rubble and you into corpses."

The German Army is complaining of the terrible heat, profound and incessant. The parched, dry-lipped men are fighting desperately and dying for small wells. Capture of a well often means that the losers must retreat twenty miles to the next watering-place for their tanks, horses, and men. At night heavy skirmishes are fought even at the captured water-holes, and the clanking war machines are incongruously loaded down with iron buckets and barrels filled with the water that has become so vital.

The Red Army has also organized special combat units to penetrate no man's land at night to rescue damaged tanks and send them back to the beleaguered factories in Stalingrad. Tractors guarded by tank-destroyers explore the battlefield during the darkness while the Red Army engineers jump off to examine abandoned tanks to determine which are worth salvaging. These they drag back with tractors, like ants tugging at a dead beetle.

Striving desperately to hamper the transfer of German troops to the Stalingrad front on the long line of captured railroads, the Russians have launched a series of diversionary attacks all along the tremendous front from Leningrad to Voronezh. The heaviest of these limited offensives is on the central front toward Rzhev under the direction of the newly appointed Vice-Commissar of Defense, General Georgi Zhukov, the dynamic shaven-headed hero of the victory over the Japanese at Khalkhin-Gol in 1939 and the

German failure near Moscow. Zhukov now outranks all marshals of the Red Army, and is second only to Stalin, the supreme Commander-in-Chief.

September 1 🖾 The Red Army's diversionary offensive toward Rzhev has scored a minor victory, so the correspondents have been invited to visit the scene of action. So many correspondents have come to Russia for the summer that we must travel in a convoy of six cars, signifying that we will not get very near the front. The uncamouflaged cars would be immediately spotted by enemy aircraft, which might mistake us for high-ranking officers.

As we journeyed out the Kalinin highway toward Rzhev, I noticed a significant change from the winter. All the German graveyards of the Battle of Moscow have been cleared away and their occupants buried in common graves. One of the Red Army officers conducting us explained that the Nazis "had been poisoning the earth." The crosses put up by the Germans had been very neat, but the graves were too shallow.

In the fields, now dappled with flowers, were the patient hard-working peasant women, putting the last touches on the harvest. We saw no men working on the edge of the central front except the very old, and those, of course, in Red Army uniforms.

On the dusty road were Russian peasants walking back to their homes in the recaptured villages. The women wore their heavy quilted winter jackets and felt boots, to save themselves the trouble of carrying them, I suppose. The rest of their belongings they had packed on their backs. In the little villages they found most of their log cabins wrecked. But we watched them sitting around the shell-torn houses, poking in the blackened ruins, cooking over campfires, and demonstrating the impressive Russian capacity to take punishment without wilting.

We talked to a group of thirty or more youngsters standing at the roadside. Recently freed from German bondage, they stood with bundles at their feet. The Soviet Government was sending them to trade schools in the rear. They said the first thing the Red Army men did when they stormed the village was to use bayonets to cut off the wooden tags the Germans had forced each Russian villager to wear around his neck. The purpose of the wooden tags had been to prevent the captured people from going from one village to another, so that any stranger could be identified as a partisan.

Our heavy cars bumped over mud-covered, corduroy roads to a control point where armed guards demanded our military passes. The guards clicked their heels and saluted smartly, asking the major who was escorting us correspondents: "Tovarisch Major, your pass, please." After scrutinizing everyone in the car, the sentry said: "Please separate your cars by 1,600 yards because this road is under enemy observation."

Rain was falling now and the deep-voiced major observed that this was bad luck since mud would bog down the Russian war machines and give the Germans time to regroup forces and close the gap ripped in the first days of the Red Army's offensive.

Our cars bumped and skidded over steep hills and for the first time the bellow of distant field artillery became louder than the noise of the logs bouncing under our car wheels. We halted ten minutes once while Red Army engineers put the finishing touches to a small bridge recently smashed by a low-diving Stuka.

Somebody pointed out a dead body sprawled in a muddy field near a working party of Red Army men. "Probably killed by a bomb," one of the correspondents remarked. But the Red Army sappers worked stolidly, not even noticing death in their midst, while they chanted their Red Army marching songs in time to the beat of their axes.

Then suddenly our lurching, skidding, wheel-spinning cars topped the rise of a hill and the gross, incessant beat of heavy guns grew even louder. Another correspondent called our attention to the white plumes of smoke from the guns in the distance.

We piled out of the cars and slogged through some woods to a green-turfed mound which the major said was an artillery observation post. Some of us clambered up to listen to the major's explanation of the battle in progress. Below us spread ten miles of rolling countryside, once rich and checkerboarded with collective farms. But now it was a no man's land of weeds and barbed wire, laced with water-filled trenches and pockmarked by the shell-holes of Russian artillery.

"German spies learned that our offensive would start within five days," said the major, "but they didn't know the direction, so the German High Command hastily concentrated four hundred bombers in the Smolensk-Vyazma airfields to slow up our offensive and give them time to concentrate their troops. We immediately launched fighting patrols against the enemy lines to scare them into bringing up their nearest reserves. Two hours later, when we were sure the Germans were waiting in the front lines, we let loose with one of the heaviest artillery barrages of the war, advancing nine miles over German dead in the first day alone."

Our cars got stuck in the mud before we could move on to a reconquered village, so the major summoned a tractor from the working Red Army party, and, along with some other officers, he pitched in with the privates to get us moving.

Among the wrecked and blackened ruins of a reconquered village stood peasant women who had for many months lived under German Army law on the eastern frontier of the Nazi New Order. We were standing at the edge of "Fortress Europe"!

One old woman pointed out the gallows where Germans had hanged five men suspected of being partisans. I asked her what she did when the Germans entered her village. In a shrill voice she damned the Germans and said: "I hid in the near-by woods until I was starved into returning home. I found Germans in my house. They took all the food, even my chickens. I lived on left-over scraps."

I walked with her to the ruins of her wrecked log cabin. She kicked at the dirty green-gray uniforms on the floor and shrieked when I stooped to pick one up. I was startled. "It's poison," she said. "Look at the lice. If the Germans ever come back here, I might as well kill myself."

I turned to a crowd of little boys and asked: "What did you fellows do?"

They were bashful. Then one little tow-head spoke up. "I was a partisan scout," he said proudly. He couldn't have been more than ten. "My father was a partisan scout with the others in the woods. I would sneak out at night and take him food. I even told him where the German guns were and where the sentries walked."

Another ragged youngster pointed to a grave eleven-year-old next to him. "Ivan was a scout, too," he said admiringly. "He blew up a German ammunition dump. It even blew off his arm!"

The other boys laughed delightedly, the way children do. But Ivan didn't laugh. He looked uncomfortable with all this attention focused on him. We noticed his empty little sleeve and turned our eyes. As we walked away, I heard Ivan cry out after us: "They killed my little pig, too."

September 2   ✍ The latest edition of the new weekly British propaganda paper has embarrassed the British correspondents in Moscow. Printed on glossy paper, the *British Ally* enjoys a wide circulation in the Soviet capital. This week's edition, however, carries a spread of lovely English countryside scenes, with happy villagers strolling through the peaceful streets. Meanwhile the Germans are bombing Stalingrad into rubble. The answer lies in the fact that the British editor in Kuibyshev has little control of the articles appearing in his Russian-language paper, for the articles and pictures are forwarded from London.

The Red Air Force has launched a series of night raids on the eastern cities of the Reich: Berlin, Königsberg, Danzig, and Stettin. The number of planes partaking in the raids is not mentioned, but they are given equal prominence in the Soviet press along with the RAF raids on Germany.

The tone of the Moscow newspapers has become desperate, even foreboding. The second front is no longer mentioned. The stress now falls on the responsibility of the Red Army to save Stalingrad. The fate of the Volga city, the people are told, "is a question of life and death for the Soviet Union, slavery or freedom for its citizens. German control of the Volga at this strategic point will mean cutting off south Russia from the rest of the Soviet Union, new life for the German Army feeding on the oil of Baku, and a broken back for Russia."

But the Kremlin studies the reactions of the people carefully. Every day we see and hear more military bands and parades through the streets of Moscow. Every afternoon at the beginning of the rush hour, a regiment of mounted Cossacks, led by clashing cymbals and drums of a Cossack band, rides through the streets. They are impressive in their colorful, red-striped breeches, long black cloaks that reach to the horses' tails and red, blue, and gray cowls thrown over the back of their fierce, aloof faces. "Have confidence," the parades seem to say; "Russia still has men to defend her."

September 3   ⧙ Every day through the dusty summer streets march little lines of boys and girls, two by two, sometimes singing, sometimes not. They always wear black, brass-buttoned uniforms, high military boots, peaked hats for the boys, and blue berets for girls. They are the children of the trade schools, the boarding schools of the Soviet Union, and one of Russia's stakes in the future. By a 1940 decree, the trade schools were established to train apprentices in factory work. The children were first selected from volunteers of fourteen and fifteen who preferred to abandon their regular studies for technical work. After the war began they were mobilized if they showed no special ability for higher education as engineers or in other professions.

I was granted permission to visit one of the schools, on a Moscow side street. The school director was Mikhail Tophler, a thin, wiry man, wearing the ubiquitous khaki uniform of a Communist Party member. He told me modestly that he was chosen for the task because he held an advanced engineering degree. He had the studious appearance of a professional man. The boarding school had been a former warehouse. Now it was fitted out with workshops and classrooms.

"My children work ten hours a day if they're over sixteen," explained the director, "or eight hours if they're under that age. Before the war," he went on, running his hand through his thick black hair, "all of them worked only eight hours, but the war has forced us to make the work day longer. Our only product now is war munitions, and the boys and girls learn while they make ammunition for the Red Army."

"Half of my boys and girls live in Moscow and they go home every night, but the other fifty per cent come from other parts of Russia and they live in the school dormitories. The State," he said with pride, "provides them with everything — uniforms, boots, underwear, and all other essentials. They pay the State back fifty per cent of their wages for their tuition and living expenses."

"How much money do they make?" I asked.

"After two or three months the new kids make only about a hundred rubles a month," he explained somewhat apologetically, "but by the time they graduate, many of them are making up to seven hundred rubles a month on piece work. They average from a hundred to three hundred rubles a month, according to their initiative and ability."

The intelligent-looking, dark-eyed director added that the trade-school training was considered completed by the time a youngster could turn out a factory worker's norm. He stopped talking to roll a cigarette, carefully tearing a strip from an old *Pravda* for cigarette paper. "However," he continued, "there have been cases where factories in the Urals and Siberia needed apprentices immediately, so we sent out some of our best sixteen-year-olds to finish their training at a regular factory."

"How many youngsters are there in the Moscow trade schools?" I asked.

"In Moscow alone there are about 80,000," he replied. "Throughout the Soviet Union there are almost a million. We get volunteers all the time."

The director escorted me through some of the classrooms. I thought most of the boys looked much younger than their stated age, but the director assured me that every boy was at least fourteen and the girls at least fifteen. Soviet youngsters are smaller than American kids of the same age.

"What about the Army?" I asked him. "Are the boys drafted when they reach eighteen?"

"No. The Government has exempted all trade-school youngsters for the next four years."

It was plain that despite the casualties among mobilized factory workers in the Red Army, the Soviet Union will have an appreciable bank of well-trained factory workers to run its industries after the war.

Boys and girls worked in separate shops. Adult foremen superintended the classes, and talking was not encouraged among the apprentices. There were little boys and big boys, boys with wavy brown hair and many with their heads shaven. They seemed to be enjoying their work and only a few looked up with interest at me from their machines turning out trench-mortar shells.

Some of the youngsters had the ever present little red flags standing on their work tables. "Those are my Stakhonovites," the director explained earnestly. "They've outdistanced everyone else on production. This fellow here discovered how to run two lathes at once by putting one atop the other."

I talked to the hard-working little fellow. He was about fifteen, small and slight.

"Do you like the work?"

He nodded silently.

"What is your day like, here at school?" I asked. "I mean, what time do you get up?"

He said that the bell rang at seven o'clock in the morning and everybody did setting-up exercises out in the hallways and then went in to breakfast. "After that," he said, "we work until two o'clock. Then we eat lunch and go to the classrooms. At four o'clock we go back to work until six, when we have our supper." He said the food was based on a war worker's ration plus extra bread and butter. "We can rest, or read, or rehearse with the orchestra in the evening."

"What do *you* do?" I asked.

He said shyly: "I play the saxophone. And on Sundays we have our day off and I go to the movies or take a walk in the park."

"What do you like to do best?"

The youngster knitted his brow for a moment and said: "I guess I like the military training best, because I like to shoot in the rifle range."

On my way out of the building I glanced at the school's wall newspaper. It was written by hand by the student editor and was changed twice a month. There were childish caricatures of Hitler and the articles ardently declared that the school would help the Red Army beat the Germans. The line was exactly like that of the regular Soviet newspapers.

At the doorway I passed two rosy-cheeked fifteen-year-old girls standing in their black uniforms with brass buttons, rifles pressed to their sides. The only thing wrong with their military appearance was that they both wore earrings of the five-and-ten-cent-store type.

September 6   I hear that prices are soaring in the Moscow public markets. These are the stalls where the collective farmers who have excess food products, raised in their back-yard gardens, can offer them for sale at any price the market will bear. These small amounts of food are outside the control of the Government, and the price is governed only by demand.

The central market is located back of the Arbatt subway station and I dropped in on the way back from my afternoon broadcast. Flower-sellers had taken over most of the big stalls, and the market was bright and redolent with piles of cut gladioli and wild flowers. Even little peasant boys and girls were selling small bouquets.

Eggs were going for 10 rubles each, raspberries for 15 rubles a glassful. I bought two bunches of radishes for 15 rubles, or about $1.50.

The market was crowded, but there were more buyers than sellers. I watched a pair of rubbers go for a month's pay, five hundred rubles. One woman bought an old pair of shoes without even trying them on.

It's obvious that even with its managed currency, the Soviet Union faces the threat of inflation. Almost no consumer goods are being made now because of the war, but there's no holding back the tremendous demand. The Soviet Union is using four methods to control inflation: first, by direct taxation; second, by manipulating the prices of "luxuries"; third, by selling war-bond lottery tickets; and latest, by Red Army Defense Fund drives.

The Soviet income-tax structure extends to even the lowest-paid workers, those making one hundred and fifty rubles a month. The tax rate increases proportionately from four to eight per cent as incomes mount, until those Soviet citizens in the high-income brackets, like commissars, artists, writers, factory managers, and those on the stage, are paying impressive taxes. On top of this a new war tax has been added that has the effect of at least doubling the income tax. In addition, all defense workers, artists, writers, and entertainers who are exempted from military service, like Shostakovich, the composer, and Galubin, the ballet dancer, must pay for the privilege by adding fifty per cent to their income tax.

By manipulating the prices of extra food, clothing, and vodka and in restaurants which sell unrationed meals, the State tried to adjust the situation to meet the demand and supply. Sometimes the prices are doubled overnight. Sometimes they're cut in half. The Government also controls the prices for second-hand goods in the commission shops, and during my stay in Russia I saw them mount over one hundred per cent. But the latent purchasing power of the peasants and workers and the Red Army officers who receive generous salaries but have no way to spend them has risen tremendously since the war. The Government war-bond lottery, to which every loyal citizen subscribes on the installment plan, with an outside chance of winning 100,000 rubles at each drawing, was over-subscribed in the first two days, and it dragged a lot of cash out of old stockings. So did subscriptions to the Defense Fund, for which Stalin thanked the group donors with personally dictated telegrams.

In the cities of the far north and on the edge of the Siberian wilderness the Government has lowered the prices on consumer goods as some compensation for the hardships of existence of the people sent there by the State.

There are indications that the trend of Russian State capitalism is moving a little bit toward the individualism of the West. On the Soviet collective farms, where members of the collective work for group profit and sell their produce to the State, pure Communism has not worked. The realistic Government met this factor in human nature by conceding to each farmer the right to a private plot of ground, with a cow, chickens, beehives, and an orchard. In the village "artels," handicraft shops, canneries, and pottery mills are operated by groups of peasants who are permitted to barter their wares for other products. This is very much like the cottage industry in England which later gave way to pure individualism. There is no question that under Stalinist socialism, complete equality of the workers does not exist, nor is it meant to exist. Under the factory piece-work system the workers are prodded to produce more goods and make more money as a patriotic duty. Those who prosper can buy better apartments or summer houses in the country.

Students above the age of fourteen enter the factories upon graduation. Those who wish to pursue a higher education or enter the professions must either win scholarships or have their tuition paid by their parents, as in America. The Stalin Government started out with free education through college, but soon discovered that many of the scholars were sluggards and the only way to make them study was to give their parents the responsibility, by paying nominal tuition for higher education.

September 8   ✒ There's a touch of autumn in the Moscow air. Katya and I walked up to the Ermitage, the amusement park in the center of Moscow, where all the young folks of the city go to promenade after work and school. "You ought to come here on Sundays," Katya said. "Then you would see the best class of people in really fine clothes."

Nobody looked worried about the Battle of Stalingrad. Pairs of girls walked slowly through the gardens, their fine figures showing through their thin summer dresses. I spotted two members of the U. S. War Aid Mission, in their American Army uniforms, striking up a conversation with a couple of the girls.

There were crowds standing in line for tickets to the outdoor theater and we could hear the voices of the singers above the blare of the band on the opposite side of the park. Katya insisted on our going to the movie, although she had already seen the picture five or six times. It was an old favorite in Moscow called *The Circus* and had been running for about ten years.

I found out why she was so eager for me to see it. It was about two American circus performers who came to Russia. The picture opened with a scene in one of our Southern states. A howling mob was pursuing a handsome blonde young woman across a railroad platform. Only when she reached the safety of the observation platform of an outgoing train did she consider herself safe. Clutched in her arms was a little half-Negro baby.

Next she appeared in a Russian circus as a trapeze artist. The hero, a strapping Nordic Russian, was the star performer. Equipped with batlike wings, he soared miraculously through the circus tent and won the applause of all and the admiration of the beautiful American outcast with her half-Negro child. Her American partner, stung with jealousy, decided to denounce her in public. He strode into a crowded restaurant, bearing the child in his arms, and announced that she was the mother. To his amazement, the Soviet orchestra, instead of being shocked, formed a smiling circle around the child to serenade it. The astonished American withdrew in discomfort. The picture closed with the scene of a great May Day parade, with the blond Russian acrobat, now a Red Army parachutist, and the American heroine marching side by side as thousands cheered.

"Wasn't that a wonderful picture?" asked Katya. "Is it really true that in America there are signs up in the parks saying: 'No dogs or Negroes allowed'?"

"No, it isn't," I replied. I could see she didn't believe me.

September 10 ✍ The Germans have almost succeeded in making the Black Sea a German lake. Breaking into the outskirts of Novorossiisk, the last big Soviet naval base on the Black Sea, the Nazis have denied its use to the Russians. The Soviet Black Sea Fleet with its crack cruisers like the *Krasny Krim,* or *Red Crimea,* will now have to base themselves on Sukhumi. This means that their operating range will be so reduced that they'll have difficulty attacking German convoys of tanks and ammunition feeding the troops on the Stalingrad front. Those long overland supply lines which have held up the Nazi advance all summer have been greatly strengthened by the withdrawal of the Red Army outside Novorossiisk. Now the Germans can run barges directly down the Danube and from Odessa and sneak them along the edge of the Crimea under air cover through the Strait of Kerch into Rostov, the big port on the Sea of Azov.

The danger to Stalingrad has grown almost overnight. The Germans have succeeded in crossing the Don in great force and have come up against the main defense lines of the Volga city. No more of a fortress than Chicago is, Stalingrad has a bad defensive position. Stretching over a plain on the near side of the Volga, it has no defense line of hills or water barrier in front of it. But the mobilized population of the city, digging day and night, has turned up the Don steppes into trenches and tank traps. Yet this has failed to stop the vicious rushes of Hitler's panzer armies. They claim to have entered the western suburbs of the city.

To allow the Nazis to control the Volga not only will mean the cutting off of eighty-five per cent of Russia's oil supplies, but will permit an advance southeast of Moscow to the vital railroad lines leading from the arsenal of Russia, the Ural factory cities. If the Germans can accomplish this, the Red Armies on the eastern front will be left stranded without food or munitions.

The mystery of how the German tanks forced their way across the River Don, the best defense line in southern Russia, is revealed. The Nazi ground command, getting complete co-operation from the Luftwaffe, established the crucially important river crossings by flying German and Italian fighters directly over the ferries. Systems of high and low anti-aircraft guns were set up all around the bridgeheads, while German bombers machine-gunned and bombed every road within a radius of thirty to forty miles to hold back Red Army reserves from attacking the Nazi engineers, frantically laying pontoon bridges. Skillfully the Nazi engineers sank their bridges under two feet of water. This served to conceal them from Soviet planes or made them look already damaged, but the water did not bar the passage of tanks and trucks.

The citizens of Stalingrad are now preparing to receive the same brutal bombing meted out to Rostov before occupation of the city. The entire center of Rostov was wiped out before the Germans entered.

September 13   ✒ The flood of refugees is on toward the Caucasus Mountains. A tired-looking Georgian radio engineer who has just flown up from Vladikavkaz wearily described the scene to me.

The roads into the mountains are clogged with heavily laden wagons, pulled by ancient horses, oxen, and even cows. On the side roads, moving in their own clouds of dust, go flocks of refugee cattle and meek-faced sheep driven by sun-blackened Cossack boys and girls. Southeast of Pyatigorsk, toward the melting-pot of the world, swarm the anxious women of many races — velvet-eyed Azerbaijans, blonde and brunette Cossack girls from the Don and Kuban plains, and white-skinned, blue-eyed Russians, watching their men move up to the front, plodding foot-soldiers and the iron-faced mountain Cossacks of the Caucasus. Toward the mountains go high-wheeled wagons loaded with wounded.

The Germans have announced that a party of mountain troops have scaled the snow-capped peak of Mount Elbrus and planted the swastika on the highest mountain in Europe, which rises like a sentinel more than 18,000 feet above the Kuban plain. From here they can see the savage spike of Kasbek, on whose sheer slopes legend tells us that Prometheus was bound. Hitler's outriders are the first invaders since Alexander the Great and Genghis Khan to look gloatingly down on the very birthplace of the Aryan white race.

September 15   Mikhail Romm, chief director of the Soviet moving-picture industry, is in town. I visited him in his room at the Moskva Hotel. He was deeply tanned from a summer of making pictures near the Chinese frontier.

"At last," he said with pleasure, "the Germans have got us movie men what we wanted — a Hollywood." All the Russian movie industry, formerly centered at Kiev, in the Ukraine, has been removed to Alma-Ata, just across from China's Sinkiang Province. "It's like California," he said; "we can shoot films there the year round."

"What kind of pictures are you planning this season?" I asked.

"War pictures, of course," said the slender, dark-eyed movie executive.

"That's just the trouble," I suggested. "I hear a lot of complaints around Moscow that the people are getting tired of war pictures all the time. Aren't you going to make any 'escapist' pictures?"

"Yes," he replied. "Our productions in 1943 will contain plenty of 'escapist' movies. You see, our problem in the beginning of the war was to make the happy-go-lucky Russian people war-conscious. We had to change their attitude of nonchalance into hatred of the enemy and concentration on the tasks ahead of them. In 1941 we showed many old historical films and next year we'll give them more to make them appreciate their great heritage. Naturally, we are not going to neglect films on military topics, but we feel there's a need for comedies and straight love pictures. Our people have worked very hard this year."

Fixing me with his intense, dark eyes, Romm said: "In 1942 we want our people to feel optimistic. All our pictures will try to inculcate this hope for the future. My people have gone through a lot," he said; "we want them to laugh more. They will have plenty of comedies. They will see a comic fantasy called: *The Wonderful Violin.* Then there will be one about air transport after the war, called *The Air-Taxi Man.* That will be very funny. Another will deal with the comic exploits of a Red Army man at the front. They will laugh in these very difficult times. And we cannot forget Zoya, our martyr Komsomol whom the Germans hanged," he said gravely. "We are doing a picture on her life."

"What about after the war?" I asked.

Romm was thoughtfully silent. "The end of the war," he said, "will not necessarily mean that Fascism will be dead. Europe has been poisoned by it. We will make anti-Fascist films to be shown everywhere. America must help us. Hollywood makes wonderful pictures."

"Do you think more American movies will be shown in Soviet Russia?" I wanted to know.

The Soviet film man nodded. "Yes," he said; "after the war, maybe even next spring, we will show more American films. We are thinking of John Ford's *Young Abe Lincoln* for public release. It's a very fine film. Have you seen it?"

I confessed I hadn't. "Have you seen the new American animated cartoons?" I asked him. "Like Walt Disney's *Fantasia?*"

"Wonderful! Wonderful!" Romm answered. "A great medium of expression. You know," he confided, "we are opening big studios for animated cartoons in Central Asia. I'm flying down there tomorrow."

We shook hands, and as I walked out of the hotel, I considered the Soviet propaganda methods. The smartest people really did the thinking for the masses. Every medium was hitched to the ideology of Russia, like the operating of a jack-knife switch on an electrical circuit. The newspapers, now conducting a great drive to teach the Russian people to hate the Germans, and the radio, the movies, the schools, all were hitched to the propaganda machine. On top it all was the inexorably efficient system of the secret police "to defend the ideals for which the Revolution was fought."

Back at the hotel I asked the girl in the Intourist office: "Do you believe the news on the Soviet radio?"

"Of course," she answered. "We know that very often they don't tell us all, but what they do say is true. We know it."

September 17   ✍ The Germans have broken into Stalingrad. Under the impact of thousand-bomber raids the handsome, tree-lined city now stands like a skeleton on the cratered banks above the Volga. The two columns of the German Sixth Army, led by the extremely tall, pale, thin, and calculating General von Paulus, joined hands outside the city, consolidated, and struck at both ends.

The Sixty-second Soviet Army is fighting back fanatically in the southern suburbs, and the Soviet High Command has sent General Rokossovsky's Sixteenth Army down from Moscow to concentrate north of the city and keep up pressure on the German left flank. Bloody hand-to-hand combat has broken out in the big factory settlement in the northwest of Stalingrad, where the workers' apartment houses cluster around the Red October and Barricades munitions plants.

Many of the Stalingrad women and children have been evacuated across the Volga to the east shore, on ferries making countless trips throughout the night. Yet there are those who elected to stay on with their husbands. They have hollowed out caves on the high Volga banks, throwing logs and tarpaulins over the open holes to protect their children.

In desperation the Germans have almost entirely abandoned their night raids and, risking heavy losses for their depleted Luftwaffe, are hurling their bombers in daylight against the battered city. A thousand bomber flights a day over the city are becoming common now that Hitler has concentrated an entire air fleet of the Luftwaffe against the lone Volga city. It is now commanded by General of Air Forces Wolfram Baron von Richthofen, son of the World War ace. The Eighth Air Fleet has been in action at Leningrad, under Moscow, at Kerch and Sevastopol, and now at Stalingrad.

The German fighter pilots have been newly equipped with the most advanced pursuit plane on the eastern front, and they have won air supremacy over the Volga. Their new Messerschmitt 190G can outspeed any of the defender's planes above fifteen thousand feet, including the Curtiss P–40s and Airacobras. The new German fighters stay high in the sky unmolested by the frustrated Red Air Force pilots, who cannot reach their altitude. Then the Germans dive out of the sun, take one burst at the Soviet planes, and climb back to the safety of twenty thousand feet.

The ground is so flat on both sides of the Volga at Stalingrad that bombing of the landing fields has become useless. Both sides disperse their planes over areas ten miles wide, which are still termed airfields because direct contact can be made with each plane by radio-telephone. The Red Air Force has set up a system of radio communications all over the east bank of the Volga. The Soviet planes are never out of touch with the scattered radio control points. By this means Russian officers on the ground can warn pilots in the air of the approach of German planes from any direction and counter the German method of bringing in fighter reinforcements when the first wave of attackers has exhausted the gas and ammunition of the defending fighters. By the extended system of radio-telephone points, an entire air battle can be directed by men on the ground.

The squeezing of Lieutenant-General Chiukov's Sixty-second Army into the streets of Stalingrad has forced the Red Army to move its field artillery across to the east bank of the Volga, where it is safe from enemy tanks. The Red guns now fire from across the river, subjecting the massed German troops to a murderous barrage. Major-General Nikolai Pozharsky commands the trans-Volga artillery. The firing is directed by radio-telephone from observation points in Stalingrad.

The Sixty-second Soviet Army and the Stalingrad garrison have received much-needed reinforcements from the far bank of the Volga. Major Alexander Rodimtzev's 13th Guard Division has crossed over in boats. The new division went into action immediately, for the Nazis on their first rush into the city had captured its dominant height, the Mamayev Kurgan, or Hill 102. From the 350-foot-high double-ridged crest of Hill 102, German artillery observers could look far to the north at three great factories, Red October, the Barricades, and the Stalin tractor plant; east over the battered homes of the factory workers; and southward to jagged walls in the city's center, six miles distant. Possession of Hill 102 gave the German batteries the opportunity to shell the vital river ferries from the Soviet supply base across the Volga. Its recapture was crucial to Stalingrad's defense.

Rodimtzev's 13th Guards Rifle Division, forced to split up under the heavy shellfire, advanced cautiously against the Kurgan on two sides, two regiments going to the north and the third to the south of the hill, crawling under cover of darkness. To reach it, the crack Soviet division had to advance over about a mile and a half of gently rising land covered with partially demolished houses, stores, and small buildings. Then in front of the hill lay three lines of railroad tracks with a large meat-packing plant in between the first and second lines. This was the only cover the attacking army had. The last seven hundred yards were straight uphill.

Rodimtzev's men charged up the first ridge, ejected the Germans, re-formed, and charged the second crest, finally reaching the summit, where the Germans had dug in, using the concrete water towers as fortresses. Deprived of this observation post, the German artillery now has to fire blind.

The thirty-six-year old, athletically-built general with the short-cropped blond hair has become the hero of Moscow.

September 18   ✍ Re-reading the dog-eared bundle of year-old letters I carried with me on the convoy from England, I decided to send a cable to Ruth Woodward, the Massachusetts girl who gave me a lift out of Paris just before the Germans marched in. Garbed in a British officer's uniform as a war correspondent, I might have had to do a lot of explaining to prove I was an American, and her timely aid was heaven-sent in the middle of the panic. Her last address was the Ritz Hotel, Madrid, so I presented a brief cable to the Moscow cable office addressed to Spain, sending regards to Ruth and her mother, "Skippy."

The girl at the desk looked at the address and handed the cable back to me. "We don't accept cables for Spain," she said firmly.

I asked Llewellyn Thompson, Second Secretary at the Embassy, if he would put a diplomatic stamp on the cable and send it to the Madrid Consulate. After assuring him that it was perfectly harmless, he agreed. Next day he telephoned me to explain.

"Sorry," he said, "even the Embassy can't get in touch with our Spanish Consulate. The Soviet Union has absolutely no relations with Franco, including the sending of messages by wireless."

The stenographers of Moscow are being turned into amateur lumberjacks. All factories and offices are getting a final combing over to complete the army of 80,000 who have been sent to camps in the near-by forests to chop wood for winter. Mayor Pronin of Moscow says that eighty-five per cent of his lumberjack army is composed of women. The German occupation has put central Russia in a bad way so far as coal supplies are concerned, so the mobilized women's army has been entrusted with the task of cutting down enough logs to keep all Moscow and its factories warm this winter.

For months now the suburban bus lines have been jammed with groups of girls carrying their bedding and work clothes out to the labor front. They board the Volga Canal boats at Khimki, and most of them won't be home until November.

However, the woodchopping is being done on an "incentive" basis and anyone who cuts her quota of wood before the allotted time may go home immediately. The factories and offices continue to pay the women their regular salaries while they are away.

The task is being organized according to each worker's abilities. The weakest girls do the trimming of the trees, while the stronger women and the men do the chopping and sawing.

Correspondents who have been out to watch the work tell me that the food provided for the workers is very good, even better than we foreigners have been getting at the hotel. Our fare this summer has been rather flat-tasting, but it's much better than the eternal meat and rice of the winter months. We are now served cabbage soup, potatoes, meat, tea, and cake for lunch, the main meal of the day in Russia.

During the spring we were favored with strawberries, and although everyone suffered from a mild dysentery after eating them, we who had not eaten any fresh fruit for seven months could not resist their red ripeness. The food served to us foreigners is far different from that available downstairs in the canteen for Soviet citizens. They get weak soup, cold-storage fish, or ersatz meat croquettes, made of barley with a suspicion of meat, and tea without sugar.

At the factories the workers eat once a day. They also have the opportunity to buy four pounds of potatoes a month to take home to their families for supper. Otherwise there's little available in the rationed food stores except bread and some American lard shipped in through Lend-Lease. Most of the factory workers take home any pieces of bread left on their plates at the factory canteen and many housewives save a slice a day out of their ration. They are drying it for the winter, for no one knows what the food situation will be like after the city is snowbound.

There's a great match shortage in Moscow and I am stopped a dozen times a day for a light from my cigarette. Sometimes a peasant seems to puff so long while lighting his hand-rolled cigarette, that I suspect he's smoking half of mine. Every day you can see men leaning out of windows with glass watch crystals filled with water, trying to get a light from the sun's rays.

There's absolutely no cigarette paper in Russia and no one thinks anything of rolling a cigarette out of today's *Pravda*. The newspapers have other varied uses. Every housewife wraps food in them when she goes shopping with her string-net bag. Eventually the newspapers become a valuable bathroom accessory.

September 19   I am going home. CBS sent me a cable today saying: "When would you like to be relieved?" I answered: "Octoberish if possible." I knew that the battle of Stalingrad would be decided one way or another by then.

One of the censors had introduced me to a Red Army courier who had just come up from the embattled city. Over a carafe of vodka in the hotel dining-room he told a little about the situation. So far as we knew in Moscow, the battle was just vast and impersonal. The newspapers told us little more than the daily toll of German dead.

The thin, tired-looking courier was optimistic, though. "The Germans will never hold their positions at Stalingrad," he said. "Their tanks outnumber ours six to one, but they can't knock out our guns on the other side of the Volga." He smiled grimly and patted the Luger pistol he had taken from a German officer. "I got three of them myself. And they didn't find any trees out on the steppe to make crosses for their graves."

I asked if the Germans had actually reached the Volga. The Red Army man nodded. "Sometimes they do," he answered. "And then we drive them back again." He shook his head in wonderment over some of the events he had lived through. "You know," he said, "it's like fighting for a football field. Almost the whole war is now confined to a battlefield about two hundred yards long in the northwest of the city. For two months the Germans have been trying to reach the Volga here and get our river ferries under fire."

"When do you sleep?" I questioned.

The man from Stalingrad rubbed his eyes unconsciously

at the question. "Sometimes I don't think I slept for seventy-two hours. Once I remember sleeping for twenty-two hours straight when I was relieved." Then, with a gesture of his hand, he said: "But you don't think so much about being tired. You're almost afraid to sleep. You might never wake up." He laughed, and added: "As long as you get hot food you're all right. We still eat three times a day in the lines."

Later that day I told Mr. Polikarpov, chief of the Radio Committee, of my decision to go home in late October. He surprised me by looking disappointed, even after all the trouble I had given him in order to be heard in America.

"Why don't you stay and see the war through with us?" he asked.

I explained that I hadn't been home for three and a half years and I was longing for a sight of my family and my own country.

The blond, uniformed radio chief nodded sympathetically. "We Russians know how you feel," he said.

Every night now as I walk back to the hotel through the blackout, guiding myself by the lighter line of night sky above the roof-tops, I think of home and wonder if America has changed very much.

I know that I've changed. For one thing, I've become highly nationalistic, perhaps as a counter-reaction to the waves of nationalism I've witnessed in England and Russia. I know that the Russians I talk to are not interested in me as a personality; they think of me only as a representative American. I'm so used to giving my opinions as to the way I think the majority of Americans feel that I'm beginning to believe that I have few opinions of my own. Informally, I've been representing America for a long time now.

Russia doesn't seem so mysterious to me any more. Almost unconsciously I've grown into the life here. I take for granted the little annoyances of existence that often disturb those who come to Russia on short visits — the trouble with the telephones, the difficulty of just getting things done with the bureaucracy, the word *"saftra"* which means the tomorrow that never comes, the endless *"Nichevo nyet,"* meaning the cupboard is bare. I've grown into the life here. I understand now what people are saying as I mingle in the crowds. I push my way into the street cars and subway as though I were one of them. I dress just as carelessly as they do. I understand the Russian saying: "Have a heart and have a soul; all else is passing fashion."

I have a pretty good idea now why the Western world was mistaken about the Russian will to resist. We misjudged by appearances; we compared this industrially backward country with ourselves instead of with America one hundred years ago, or with czarist Russia before the first World War. A lot of us thought that a people who had exiled or destroyed their cultured classes, a people who started from scratch with their education, would be incapable of resisting an invader who had beaten the best armies that the rest of Europe could put in the field. We thought that the purges of the Red Army in the late 1930's had reduced the Russian Staff to the impotence of party "hacks."

The Finnish War confused us, too. There are indications now that misguided Soviet intelligence misled Moscow, also. They didn't believe that the Finns would show such spirited resistance. As a result, during the first months of the Finnish War the Red Army used only reserves drawn from the Leningrad area. The Soviets did not use blitz tactics and had no intention of smashing Finland. It's clear now that the Red Army used the Finnish War as a test for its theories of winter warfare. After 1939 all Red Army maneuvers were held in the winter.

But perhaps the prime reason for our belief that the Soviet Union would collapse was due to lack of understanding of the remarkably efficient methods of the Communist zealots in organizing the civilian population for total war, together with our unbelief in the incredible sacrifices the Russians would endure to defend their land.

There's no doubt that our conviction that the Bolshevik State would collapse was based partly on wishful thinking. We don't like dictatorships. We believed that the Soviet Union was run on principles contrary to the laws of society, morality, and nature.

The Western world was blinded to the effectiveness of the massive logic of the complete materialists who run Russia, ruthless men who cut the cloth of their policy to fit the change in conditions as they see them; materialists who believe that history is not a fixed condition because it is inscribed in history books, but that history is made by man and that men can make it to suit his own purposefulness.

I know that the future course of history has changed, too, since I've been in Russia. America entered the war at a moment when Japan believed that Moscow would fall and control of the Soviet armies be destroyed. Then the military miracle of Moscow took place and Hitler's dream of world domination was shattered. Another military miracle is taking place at Stalingrad. The cold breath of winter is in the air of the Caucasus and Hitler is forced to weaken his drive on Baku to reinforce his fanatical drive on Stalingrad and the Volga. And the days are getting short at Stalingrad. Even if Hitler straddles the Volga, he can no longer advance this winter. And next year America and Britain will be ready to attack.

But were it not for Leningrad, Sevastopol, Moscow, and Stalingrad, the armies of the Axis would control all of Europe, Africa, and the Middle East and most of the valuable land in Asia. The New World would have been surrounded by the New Order.

September 20   The four-engined B–24 bomber *Gulliver* rolled over Moscow Central Airport and big, shaggy, travel-tired Wendell Willkie stepped out, an air-spent look in his usually twinkling blue eyes. A small Soviet reception filed in front of him and mechanically he murmured: "I'm delighted to meet you." Then he spotted Eddy Gilmore, the AP correspondent who had crossed the Atlantic with him to England the previous year. "Eddy," he cried, "God bless you. It's good to see you again."

For the past few days Willkie had been in Kuibyshev, where Admiral Standley wanted him to see a "typical Russian city." We were still in doubt as to how the Russians viewed the visit of President Roosevelt's opponent. After all, there was no "opposition" in Russia.

The Soviet newsreel cameramen who had photographed Churchill and Harriman were staying away in droves. And upon his arrival in Kuibyshev, Willkie had been met only

by Solomon Lozovsky, the Soviet spokesman for correspondents and Assistant Vice-Commissar for Foreign Affairs. Willkie himself had called on First Vice-Commissar
Andrie Vishinsky.

We drove over to the guest house set aside for Willkie and
his traveling mates, Gardner Cowles, Jr., and Joseph Barnes,
both on leave from the OWI. While he ate, Willkie talked
about his visits to Africa, the Middle East, Turkey, and Iran.
One of his companions told me that the Republican leader
had run into heavy censorship in Egypt and the British censors had unceremoniously blue-penciled his press statement
on grounds of security. Willkie hadn't liked it. I had to leave
before he finished his remarks in order to make my afternoon broadcast.

September 21   Went to the ballet to see
Lepischinskaya dance *Swan Lake*. Almost the entire roster
of the foreign diplomatic corps was there, expecting to see
Mr. Willkie. We had heard that he jumped up on the stage
in Kuibyshev to present a bouquet and had kissed Tiko-
mirova, one of the prettiest ballerinas in the Soviet Union.

What the Russians call "the second front" of Anglo-
American military men were in attendance. I never saw a
ballet when they weren't there. They have little else to do,
since they never visit the front. Their monotonous Moscow
life consists mainly in translating military articles from the
newspapers. They have seen *Swan Lake* so often that some
of them are said to have been unofficially awarded their
"gold" swans. You get this honorary title in the Moscow
diplomatic set after you've seen *Swan Lake* thirty-five times.
Brigadier General Philip Faymonville of the United States
Lend-Lease Mission holds the record. He has seen *Swan
Lake* so many times he's lost count. Admiral Myles, chief of
the British Mission, is a "gold swan." Captain John Cooke
of the American Mission, the former sergeant who gave Howard Hughes the opportunity to make his round-the-world
flying record, when he repaired Hughes's plane after it
cracked up on Le Bourget in Paris, is a "silver swan." He's
seen this ballet just over twenty-five times. Since the war

began, the Russians have given *Swan Lake* an optimistic twist; they've changed the ending so that the Prince triumphs over the Evil Black Swan. The Russian audience never tires of it. At every curtain the aisles are jammed with high-school kids who rushed to cheer like the jitterbugs who applaud dance orchestras in New York's Paramount Theater.

A little Russian kid about ten years old who squeezed himself in back of my chair kept screaming in a shrill treble: "Lepischinskaya! Lepischinskaya!"

The Red Army officer sitting next to me turned around with a mock frown and said: "You're too young to be calling for a ballerina. You must keep quiet."

"I'll cheer for anyone I like. Lepischinskaya! Lepischinskaya!" the little boy replied spunkily. I heard a high-school girl murmur to the girl next to her as she looked at muscular Galubin, the male dancer: "He certainly looks strong enough. He ought to be at the front."

September 23   Breakfasted with Willkie this morning. He appears excited over Russia, and when I arrived sleepily at eight a.m., after getting home from the night broadcast at half past four, Willkie was just coming in from a walk.

"I talk to people every chance I get," he said enthusiastically. "Why, just out here on the corner I talked to two men on the way to work." He paused and added as an afterthought: "One of them spoke English."

All through breakfast we talked about the Russian situation and its prospects. "What I want to know," said Willkie, "is whether we should continue sending aid to Russia. Do you think it's too late? Will it fall into German hands?"

We were all surprised to learn that doubt still existed in America over whether Russia could continue standing against the Germans. We knew that Stalingrad was not a decisive battle for Russia, but a decisive battle for Germany. If the Germans couldn't secure their eastern flank and grab the Caucasus oil, the prospects of a short war would be much better.

I replied that we might as well send what aid we could

because it was being used up so fast that the Germans could never get it.

"What do the Russians want most from their Allies?" Willkie asked.

There was only one answer. "A second front," we chorused.

"I must tell that to the American people," said Willkie.

I suggested that the best way to appeal to America was on the basis of "What's in it for us?" Mr. Willkie seemed more of an idealist than that. He shook his shaggy head thoughtfully.

"No," he said. "The American people must be aroused like avenging angels. Avenging angels! That's when they're at their best!" He brushed the vagrant lock of hair out of his eyes. Then he added: "I'm going to give you people a strong statement and see that it gets through the censors."

After breakfast Willkie and his party visited a factory. The correspondents were not encouraged to go along. His advisers were making every effort to avoid the "political junket" atmosphere which had surrounded Willkie's visit to London the previous year.

In the evening we were invited by the American Embassy to Ambassador Standley's cocktail party for the President's special representative. Food and drink stocks were so low at Spasse House that only vodka punch and bologna sandwiches could be served the attending diplomats.

A discussion between Willkie and Admiral Standley grew heated. I resisted the temptation to eavesdrop. There's no doubt that the Embassy thinks that Willkie's presence in Soviet Russia is harming the American policy of representing the United States as a direct, positive power completely behind the Commander-in-Chief. Yet Willkie had Roosevelt's blessing on this trip and a letter of introduction to the Kremlin. It was hard to figure out what that astute politician in the White House was up to.

September 26   Mr. Willkie has presented the President's letter to Premier Stalin. The Soviet leader acceded to the suggestion that the Republican leader and his party visit the front. Admiral Standley apparently has asked that Willkie take with him the American Military Attachés and Major General Bradley and Brigadier General Faymonville, who enjoyed their first visit to an active front. They went to command headquarters near Rzhev.

Upon their return Willkie, his companions, and a few more Americans were banqueted by Stalin. Admiral Standley attended with British Ambassador Clark Kerr, the only Englishman present.

My informants reported that the main toast of the evening came when Stalin raised his glass to the "Airmen of the United Nations." He added pointedly that Britain was holding up a shipment of 152 American aircobra fighters consigned to Russia.

The British Ambassador had no information on the subject, so Willkie eased the strained situation by remarking that the Soviet Premier "always kept his eye on the ball." Stalin didn't get the American slang, so Willkie drew a laugh from him when he explained the term in American sport. Stalin added: "I hope I always keep my eye on the ball." Clark Kerr then replied that if any planes were diverted from Russia, it would only be to further the cause of the United Nations. "Nothing the British Ambassador has said will be taken amiss," said Stalin.

I was told by an irritated American Embassy man that as the vodka-primed party left the Kremlin, one of Willkie's traveling companions clapped Molotov on the shoulder and, pointing to Willkie, said enthusiastically: "There's the next President of the United States!" As my informant heatedly related this I noticed a picture of President Roosevelt hung over his writing-table.

We correspondents strained the slender resources of the Metropole Hotel's larder to give Mr. Willkie a cocktail party. Joe Barnes handed some of us a typewritten statement from Willkie beginning: "I am convinced we can best help Russia by establishing a real second front in Europe with Britain at the earliest possible moment our military leaders approve. And perhaps some of them will need a little public prodding. . . ." We had no trouble getting the censors to pass it.

I gave Gardner (Mike) Cowles, Jr., the large, battered,

and ancient ikon I had picked up at the wrecked Monastery
Museum of New Jerusalem. It was from Middle Asia and
depicted events in the life of Saint Nicholas, patron saint of
old Russia. The ikon-painters of that part of Asia had never
seen a mountain, so they had painted them the way they
thought they should look, like a series of fish scales, one on
top of another.

I asked Willkie if he had room in his plane to take my
ikon collection to America for me. He gladly assented and
the ikons traveled with him to China, across Siberia and
Alaska, to New York.

We saw Willkie off from the Moscow airport. I had a
profound conviction that the future of the world would be
faced with better understanding if more politicians took
such an opportunity to see the world. Forthright and ambitious Willkie had a new outlook on world problems. He
was learning what so many of our ferry pilots already knew:
that the world had suddenly shrunk and brought its peoples
close together — so close that the American continent is no
longer isolated.

September 30   ✄ The Germans are getting
nowhere in the Caucasus. Strain as they will, they cannot
bomb the Russian troops out of the mountain fastnesses.
The battle sways back and forth in the valley of the turbulent Terek. The German losses have been so great on the
Stalingrad front that Hitler must make a decision. He cannot be strong everywhere at once. So it looks as though he
is aiming only for limited objectives in the Caucasus, trying
to get his tank forces over to the southern slopes of the mountains before the winter snows set in. Then he will attempt a
winter offensive against Baku if and when he conquers
Stalingrad.

Opening the Winter Help Campaign in Germany, Hitler
said: "I can assure you of one thing. Stalingrad will fall.
My program for next year is to hold all important objectives and let the enemy take the offensive if they want to.
We will bleed them white and wait and see who tires first."

Significantly, in the audience sat Field Marshal Erwin

Rommel, home from the Egyptian front. Military observers here say that Rommel's presence in Berlin when the fighting season is starting in the desert can mean only that the front dispatches in the Soviet Press are accurate when they say that some captured German tank-drivers and pilots have just been flown in from Egypt. No general, least of all a military man of Rommel's caliber, would leave his army at such a crucial moment. The leader of the Afrika Korps has gone to Berlin to find out why Hitler is weakening his forces in Egypt.

October 1 　　　　　　 ✎ One line in a dispatch from the Stalingrad front reveals that Stalin's twenty-four-year-old son, Vassily, now a colonel in the Red Air Force, has assumed command of a Red fighter squadron in defense of his father's native city. I remembered seeing him back in Kuibyshev during the long winter. Dark-haired and medium-sized, he was then a captain in charge of communication planes between Kuibyshev and the Moscow front.

He often went to the ballet, sitting with a red-haired, stocky eighteen-year-old girl with gray eyes and strong, grave features. Few persons knew them or paid any attention to them, but we correspondents were interested in the girl's unusual face. They both thought Lepischinskaya was wonderful and clapped enthusiastically at every curtain.

I used to see the red-haired girl going to P.S.26, a three-story, whitewashed schoolhouse on the main street. It had been set up to accommodate refugee students and their teachers from Moscow. She wore plain dark clothes of good quality. Each afternoon you could see her motor away from the school in a small gray coupé driven by a chauffeur. When May 1 came, the quiet girl went out to the airport and boarded a plane to see her father in the Kremlin. Her name was Svetlana Djugashvili. She was Premier Stalin's daughter.

Her stepbrother, Jacob, an artillery officer, was claimed a captive by the Germans in the Ukraine.

Stalin has never been seen in public with a woman since his wife Nadezhda (Hope) died, in November 1939. Twice a widower, he was left with two youngsters and their step-brother, "Yasha." Stalin has not appeared in public since the beginning of the war except for his speech at the Red Army parade on November 7, 1941, when he sprang a surprise on the German bombers by holding the traditional parade in the early morning. He has not even appeared at the theater during the war, although the best artists of the Soviet, its ballerinas and singers, give private performances in the Kremlin. Stalin has a small summer home just outside Moscow, surrounded by a white picket fence, but he has not visited there since the invasion began. He rarely leaves the Kremlin, nerve-center of the gigantic Soviet Union. When he does so, he rides in a big black Packard limousine with bullet-proof windows and the rear curtain drawn. He is followed by guards of the NKVD.

All foreign observers who have talked to Stalin tell me that calmness is his most outstanding characteristic. He takes good and bad news alike, with a controlled attitude that bespeaks great powers of concentration and iron nerves. They speak also of his grasp of the smallest details of a situation, of his dislike for generalities, and a desire for straight, blunt talk without diplomatic trimmings. He has a remarkable knowledge of technical subjects, especially aerodynamics. Fast fighter planes are his hobby, and the desk in his private office always has one or two new models standing on it. He frequently confers with Soviet airplane designers.

He does most of his great volume of paper work during the night and the early hours of the morning. He never receives visitors before six o'clock in the evening. Dawn is rising over the red Kremlin walls and the hundreds of black jackdaws that roost in the Kremlin gardens are chattering before Stalin has finished his tasks. He is beginning to look worn, gray, and tired from his war labors, but despite his sixty-three years he appears fresher after long hours of negotiations than some of his younger cabinet members. His thick, wiry black hair, brushed straight back from his forehead, is heavily touched with gray now, his swarthy complexion has become paler, but his short stocky figure is still erect and there are no signs that his physical power is diminished.

Work is his only hobby. He generally sticks to Georgian wine on the occasions of his State banquets, but he never fails to drain the scores of toasts "bottoms up" and no one has ever seen him drunk. In his early youth he was fond of fishing and hunting, but he has neglected these sports since becoming Premier. The Russian classics are his favorite relaxation. *War and Peace* is his best-liked book and he has re-read it many times.

Hundreds of letters are addressed to him every day from all over Russia and the little post box on the Kremlin wall is always filled. A score of secretaries keep up with the correspondence, turning over the most important letters for him to read.

The Russian people admire him as a strong, inexorable man, who acts for their own good. The respect with which they regard him is decidedly tinged with awe.

Stalin, born in Gori, Georgia, speaks Russian with an accent. It is known that he once took English lessons from a professor at the Moscow Institute, but he never uses the language except to surprise his foreign guests with a pleasant "Good night."

October 2   Took a bus out to the Lenin Hills, the renamed Sparrow Hills where Napoleon obtained the first view of his splendid prey. If Hitler had been able to look down from those hills today, his heart would have beat high in exultation.

Factory chimneys blackened the sky and huge apartment houses that would have provided pillage and quarters for his soldiers loomed in every sector of the city. Many of the four hundred and forty ancient churches and chapels are still standing from Napoleon's day, their domes thrusting into the sky. All but twenty-five or so, I am told, are now museums or factories. Down the river, in the clear September air, was the mighty citadel of the Kremlin, its red walls pasted against the blue sky in a stirring Asiatic pattern.

Standing here with Napoleon's ghost in the pleasant wooded park, with the Moscow-Volga Canal running green below, I asked myself: "What would have happened if Hitler, too, had marched into the Troitski Gate of the Kremlin as the Frenchman did?" Soviet Russia might have become another China, fighting forever with a horde army directed from behind the Urals, but with few railroad lines to transfer troops and almost no way to obtain war supplies from her Western Allies. Japan would have had her heart's desire, India and the Soviet Far East. Hitler would have walked through the Caucasus and clasped the hands of the Japanese at the crossroads of the world, the Middle East. The Mediterranean, Africa, and the South Atlantic bases would be German now.

But Moscow stood. And now the Battle of Stalingrad is months old. The first wet snows have fallen on the Volga. I know that Russia has not committed her reserves, massed on the inactive fronts from Leningrad down to Voronezh. Although these may be fateful days for Russia, they are even more fateful for Germany.

October 3   ✍ I was sitting in the censorship office typing my broadcast at twelve thirty a.m. last night when Henry Cassidy walked in. He was somewhat out of breath, having walked a mile and a half from his apartment in the blackout.

"What's up, Henry?" I called.

"I don't know. The Press Department wants to see me about something, but they wouldn't tell me over the phone."

In five minutes Cassidy was back in front of me, his eyes sparkling. "I just got a letter," he said. "Look who it's from!"

Glancing at the signature, I received a shock. It was stamped: "J. Stalin," in bright blue ink.

"I dropped a letter in the Kremlin mailbox yesterday," said Cassidy, his hair standing up like a ruffled chipmunk's, "and look what I got today."

We read the authorized English translation together. It said:

Dear Mr. Cassidy, —

Owing to pressure of work and consequent inability to grant you an interview, I shall confine myself to a brief written answer to your questions.

1. "What place does the possibility of a second front occupy in Soviet estimates of the current situation?"

Answer: A very important, one might say, a prime place.

2. "To what extent is Allied aid to the Soviet Union proving effective and what could be done to amplify and improve this aid?"

Answer: As compared with the aid which the Soviet Union is giving the Allies by drawing upon itself the main forces of the German Fascist armies, the aid of the Allies to the Soviet Union has so far been little effective. In order to amplify and improve this aid only one thing is required:

the full and prompt fulfillment by the Allies of their obligations.

3. "What remains the Soviet capacity for resistance?"

Answer: I think that the Soviet capacity of resisting the German brigands in strength not less, if not greater, than the capacity of Fascist Germany or of any other aggressive power to secure for itself world domination.

With respect

(signed) J. Stalin

Cassidy and I understood without putting it in words that I would not broadcast the letter or intimate its contents that night. Trying to look casual, Henry got about five feet from the office door and then bolted.

Later that night in the hotel Cassidy was busy on the telephone taking changes in the authorized English translation from the censors. The main change was that instead of "the full and prompt fulfillment by the Allies of their obligations," Stalin's answer should be translated: "that the Allies fulfill their obligations fully and on time."

October 4   ✍ There is no absenteeism in Soviet factories since the war. Workers who take a day off without permission or a doctor's certificate face a factory tribunal. If guilty they can be sent to jail, where they will not be just getting a rest. The cots are taken out of the cells during the day and they must stand from early morning until late afternoon. Few factory workers are sent to jail for absenteeism, however. Their production is too badly needed. They are usually fined a percentage of their wages and pay off the fine while they continue at the work-bench.

There's very little lateness in the war factories, either. Tardiness up to twenty minutes draws a bawling out, but anything over that without sufficient excuse will bring a worker before the factory tribunal.

When Willkie left from the Moscow Airport, I noticed a newly delivered American "Boston" bomber standing near by. It still bore the white star of the U. S. Army Air Forces. Today when I looked, it had Soviet markings. Mechanics were carefully going over the white American star with red paint. It's too bad it's not that easy to get them here.

I'm told that numbers of bombers are now being flown into Russia across the narrow Bering Strait between Alaska and Siberia, where the nearest Russian and American islands are only a mile apart. Scores of planes are also coming in across the Caucasus Mountains from Teheran after flying across a series of South American and African air bases all the way from Miami. The Soviet Union is continually expanding its tremendous Red Air Force to supply pilots for the front and to fly the machines in from Alaska and Persia. Some women are being used as aerial navigators on the ferry flights. It's clear that after the war the Russians will possess one of the largest corps of trained pilots among the United Nations.

October 6   ✒ Went up to Katya's house to say good-by to her school friend Maya, a strapping young Kimsomolka who's going to the front as a "polytrook," or junior political worker.

Katya's family shares five rooms with a factory engineer, his wife, and their two children. They use the kitchen and bathroom communally, but stick to their own living-quarters most of the time without infringing on each other's privacy. I made the mistake of ringing the doorbell twice instead of once and the wrong family came to the door.

Carelessness about ringing the doorbell is considered a breach of etiquette in Moscow, for the number of rings is plainly marked alongside each name in the overcrowded apartment houses. Even the evacuation of Moscow during the siege failed to ease the housing shortage.

Large family pictures stared down from the walls, and everyone was talking as I walked in, as conversation is and always has been the chief Russian sport. The silver samovar was steaming, with the china teapot sitting on top to warm.

Rosy-cheeked Maya was back in uniform after her spell in the hospital with a mine fragment in her side. An ardent Komsomolka, she had been a nurse during the winter until a sledload of wounded she was bringing back from the front ran over a mine. She didn't call my attention to the new red and yellow wound stripe she was wearing on her blouse, but once in a while I saw her glancing at it proudly, so I made the appropriate comments.

Katya's cousin Nadya was at the little party. A handsome girl, who wears her black hair drawn back severely from her pale, sweet face, Nadya always has a sad expression in her dark eyes. Her husband was called up the first day of the war and she never saw him again. The Army notified her that he was killed at Bryansk last October. She gets a tiny widow's pension from the state, but it's hardly enough to support her and her four-year-old boy. So she has taken a job in a factory and works eleven hours a day, six days a week. She takes her son to the factory nursery every morning and brings him home at night. The yellow-haired pudgy little fellow certainly looked well fed.

They said I made him cry for the first time in months. I had asked him what his name was and misunderstood his answer. "Jura," he had replied in his baby Russian. "Julia?" I exclaimed in surprise. "Why, that's a girl's name!" That was too much for little Jura and he burst into tears. His mother patiently explained that I was a foreigner and didn't understand Russian, but that didn't serve to quiet him. Between sobs, he stared at me with a reproachful, tear-stained face.

While she petted his tousled yellow hair, Nadya smiled and said he often leaned out the window and pointed to soldiers on the street. "Is that Daddy?" he would ask her.

"But when I tell him no," she said, "he always cuddles up to me and says: 'Well, I can get another Daddy some day, but I can only have one mother.' Isn't that smart?" she asked me proudly.

"What's Jura going to be when he grows up?" I asked, awkwardly changing the subject.

"An engineer, just like his father."

There was a pause in the conversation and we sipped our tea and ate the little cakes I had bought in the diplomatic store.

"What front are you going to, Maya?" I asked.

"You know I can't answer that," she said indignantly. "It's a military secret." She said the words "military secret" the way I had heard so many Russians say it. It has a special meaning for them — something sacred. The Russians are the best keepers of secrets I've ever known.

She tilted her black Cossack hat on her shining brown braids and I helped her put on her heavy winter overcoat.

"What do you carry in that map-case of yours, Maya?" I teased. "Your lunch?"

"Don't be silly," she said tartly. "I carry maps and things in there."

"Let's see," I challenged her.

She opened the shiny old leather case slung from her Sam Browne belt and drew out some old letters, a lipstick, her red Komsomol card, and a dozen pictures of her family. Blushing, she said: "Naturally, I don't have my maps with me now."

After the third glass of tea we said good-by to her. When she left, Katya looked at me sadly.

"She won't be back. Everybody knows that 'polytrooks' get killed right off. They have to be the first in every attack. They keep putting in new ones all the time."

October 7 ✍ The lines of men and women looking over one another's shoulders at the street-corner bulletin board of today's *Pravda* are smiling at the outspoken cartoon on the back page among the foreign news items. It's entitled the "Meeting of Military Experts on the Question of the Second Front." It shows two smart-looking young Anglo-American officers, labeled "General Decision" and "General Courage," pointing at a map on a table where five elderly fat-bottomed officers are seated. The old duffers, with long walrus mustaches, are labeled "General Maybe we'll be beaten," "General Is it worth the risk," "General No need to hurry," "General Let's think it over," and "General Maybe something will go wrong." There's a calendar on the wall reading "October 1942" and a wall clock points to half past the eleventh hour.

October 8 The night skies over Stalingrad have been made hideous by the yellow flares dropped by the raiders.

The Russians are showing their talent for improvisation by rushing scores of old mail planes to the front, some of the first ever used for civil flying. The Germans call them the "flying bedsteads" because they go so slow that by the light of flares the Red Air Force bombers can pick out the separate houses in the gray skeleton city and avoid bombing their own men.

Twenty-three days have passed since the Germans first broke into Stalingrad and they have completely demolished the city, but the fanatical defenders are still holding them at bay. Moscow estimates that 200,000 Axis troops have been slain before the city. Stalingrad is the scene of the costliest and most stubborn struggle of the entire war. In all history it is without parallel in its intensity and destructiveness. The entire war in Europe is now concentrated within the blackened, jagged walls of the bomb-wrecked city on the Volga bluffs. The full strength of Europe's two largest armies is engaged in a life-and-death struggle for a decision that will affect the course of the world.

Hitler could retreat in front of Moscow but from Stalingrad there is no retreat for his armies. The city is a symbol for both Hitler and Stalin and has settled down to a test of endurance. But already the first wet snow of winter has fallen.

Von Paulus is unable to use the mighty tank forces which smashed their way to the city gates. The narrow confines of the demolished streets give the Nazi panzers no room to maneuver and they cannot escape the grenades, fire-bottles, anti-tank rifles and rifle-bombs of the defenders. This new Soviet weapon, developed since the war and especially designed for short-range work against tanks, is a small explosive bomb fitted with a tail. It can be placed on the end of an ordinary rifle and aimed like a bullet. When it hits a tank, the effect is impressive.

The defenders have sustained an incessant and almost unendurable pounding from another complete air fleet sent in by Hitler after his boastful speech on September 30, when he assured the German people that Stalingrad would be theirs. Two thousand separate bomber flights over the city within twenty-four hours have become normal. A choking smoke pall obscures the sun, and the earth never ceases trembling from the concussion of bombs and the thud of exploding shells.

The modern factories, the apartment houses, the parks and tree-lined boulevards where 500,000 men and women and children once worked and played have been turned into twisted chaos. The wrecked schoolhouse near the bath-house ravine that separates the Red October factory and the observation hill of Mayayev Kurgan has changed hands more than twenty times. The land next to the famous Stalin tractor plant, built by American engineers, is the scene of the bitterest hand-to-hand fighting now, Russian and German blood soaking a strip of land one hundred yards wide. A front dispatch says that Russian and German soldiers are falling into the same shell-holes to escape the rain of bombs.

At night Soviet nurses cross the Volga in small boats under cover of smoke screens to bring back the wounded. They are using strips torn from their uniforms to bandage the men on the ground.

General Rodimtsev's headquarters, deep in a log-bolstered dugout, is so near the German lines that a rampaging tank smashed across it and the tank crew threatened to capture his staff. At a critical moment the tank itself was blown up with a grenade.

The heart of the city still beats in the bomb-proof military headquarters. Tommy-gunners are posted at ground level to show officers how to get to headquarters without being seen by the enemy. Casualties among these sentries are so high that they must be replaced three and four times a day. Where the Red Army men cannot dislodge the Germans from a building, they enter it with dynamite and blow up the building and themselves.

There are no more simple inhabitants of the city. All who have not been evacuated are defenders. Barricades are built of anything available — old boilers, furniture, burnt planks, anything. Women bring up ammunition to their husbands, and factory girls carry away their wounded fellow workers. The Red Army's ace in the hole lies in the fact that their artillery is massed on the far side of the mile-wide Volga and the German tanks are thwarted from their usual attacks on the Soviet guns.

October 10 ✠ This is a day of great change for the Red Army. The system of political commissars has been again abolished as it was in 1940 after the Finnish War. Ever since the second month of the Russo-German war, the political commissar has been a figure of great power and prominence in the Red Army. His authority and that of the military officer commanding were equal. But today Commander-in-Chief Stalin has decreed that commissar's authority is to be "liquidated." All the political commissars will be withdrawn and trained to be commanding officers. The highest-ranking commissars will go to the Kremlin Staff College. Thus the Red Army has secured two valuable measures at a stroke. The number of high officers has been increased at a time when casualties among officers are high, and, second, the decree has established singleness of command for the Red Army in the field. Alexander Scherbakov, new chief of the Political Department of the Red Army, however, had previously announced that the number of junior political officers would be greatly increased and thousands of these "chaplains who carry a gun" are taking their places in the Red Army from the ranks of the Komsomol. They will lecture the men on military psychology and advise them about their families in the rear, write letters for them, and do the old work of the political commissar's staff, with one important difference. They will no longer have the power to share command. Theirs will be the duties of Communist "evangelists."

October 11   The Soviet children are still the "pets of the State."

I talked today to the Commissar of Education, Vladimir Potemkin, former Vice-Commissar for Foreign Affairs, who has been entrusted with Soviet Russia's stake in the future. The plain khaki uniform of a party member looked incongruous on this gray-haired scholar. He is famous in Moscow for his culture and his ability as a linguist.

"The war has thrown tremendous burdens on our educational system," he told me. "Hardest hit were the classrooms we established during the last ten years in our backwoods farming villages. The teachers joined the partisans when the Germans marched in and our children have been sent to work in the Reich."

He sighed and continued: "Our youngsters will be confronted by great tasks after the war. They must rebuild our cities, our factories, and our destroyed Soviet culture. But I'm glad to say that our evacuation of the big schools was accomplished according to plan. We shortened our educational front. We moved the schools with their books and papers, teachers and children to the Urals and Siberia. Then we were faced with the problem of mobilized mothers. We had to treble the number of kindergartens in the factories.

"The war has been responsible for a great deal of heartbreak," he reflected. "Never before in our history have there been so many orphans. We've had to establish asylums for them in the east and we sent thousands to collective farms to be cared for and adopted by the peasants. We want to place as many as possible in homes. That is better for children." He took off his gold pince-nez, wiped them, and replaced them. Then he went on. "The food shortage has added to our difficulties, but through our socialist organizations we've succeeded in getting many collective farms to sponsor the schools in the rear. They provide the extra food to keep our children nourished and fit for the enormous tasks that face them in the future."

Mr. Potemkin called to a middle-aged woman, who returned with cakes and glasses of hot tea.

"What about the homeless children you see around the railroad yards in the Urals?" I asked.

"That's part of the horror of war," he answered, puffing on a long Russian cigarette. "We are faced with homeless, wandering children, just as we were during the Civil War. But this time we have organizations to combat this destruction of our youth. We've put up reception points at every big railroad yard, and the NKVD round up these *bisprizorni* who ride the rods and live by their wits, and we send them to our trade schools to make useful citizens out of them."

His voice became emphatic. "But we want to find homes for them. We've organized a lost-and-found bureau for children right here in Moscow. It does marvelous work tracing parents or finding their children for them. I wish I could tell you some of the miracles our volunteer clerks have performed, checking everyone who last saw a child or a parent during those unavoidable panics when a city was being evacuated."

I questioned the commissar about Soviet educational plans after the war.

"One thing we will do," he said thoughtfully, "is readjust our present system of study. Our leading educational circles have reached the conclusion that it is better for boys and girls to be separated in the higher school grades. Just as in the Army men do one kind of work and women another, so it is in civilian life. We will give our girls more courses in household economy and the rearing of children." It appeared to me that the Soviet Union would place a great deal more emphasis on family life in the future.

I asked what courses the Soviet schools would specialize in after the war.

"It's hard to see the shape of things to come," the commissar said. "We have first to win the war. This year we have especially glamorized our cultural past, with emphasis on Russia's great writers, her musicians and military leaders. It is more than just nationalism. We want to raise our children's self-respect and their devotion to the motherland."

"What languages will be studied in the future?" I inquired.

"As always," he answered, "our children will study German and French. Now German is important. It is the language of our enemies. But French, I think, will always be the international diplomatic language. However, I look forward to establishing more English courses, now that we are allies."

"How about your new military schools that I read about in the papers?" I queried. "Will these be continued after the war?"

"Certainly," he answered, somewhat surprised at my question. "We need more trained officers after the losses we have suffered. After all, they are not much different from your American military academies. We take volunteers with the highest school records, if they can pass the physical examination. The boys enter when they are thirteen and take regular cultural courses in addition to artillery, air, or naval training. The schools are run under military discipline, of course. Then after three years the boys go on to higher military academies." He added: "Since the war we have had more volunteers than ever before and we have met the demand by opening more military schools."

"Does that mean that you will have another huge army in a few more years?"

"No," said the gray-haired commissar, sipping his hot tea. "We will naturally demobilize our Army after the war. That will not be difficult, for half our men are peasant boys, and they'll go back to the farms. The other half are trained factory workers and we shall need them in the rebuilt factories. But naturally a country with such vast frontiers as Russia has cannot liquidate its Army." He smiled reassuringly and added: "For the most part, though, I am sure we will beat our swords into plowshares."

Surprised, I said: "Mr. Potemkin, you're quoting from the Bible!"

"A good Bolshevik can always quote the Bible when he needs to," replied the commissar, laughing.

October 12   This evening Moscow welcomed back its famous Mali (Little) Theater, which has returned from a year's absence in the safety of the Urals. With the exception of Simonov's play *The Russian People*, this is the first straight drama to be performed in Moscow since the siege. The appearance of these cherished actors in the capital is a sign that Moscow is now considered entirely safe.

To celebrate their home-coming the Mali Theater has dramatized Russia's widest-selling book, Tolstoy's *War and Peace*. It gave a four-hour performance, but even at this length it was impossible to encompass the broad sweep of the great novel. An interlocutor was used to introduce each scene by reading passages from the book. It was more like a pageant than a play. Napoleon's role had been enlarged out of proportion to his importance in the book to point up the failure of another would-be world conqueror.

The well-dressed first-night audience, composed mostly of the privileged intellectuals of Moscow, laughed several times in the wrong place. They were amused at the sight of Napoleon served real food in his headquarters tent, wolfing it ravenously. The audience appreciated his pangs of hunger.

I was surprised at the emphasis placed on the religious scene when General Kutusov, commander of the Russian forces, kissed the ikons and received the blessing of the priests before the Battle of Borodino.

During the promenade in the intermissions I heard sharp criticism of the performance. Every Muscovite has read *War and Peace* so many times that he considers it almost a sacrilege to try to constrict it within the confines of the stage.

October 13   The people are looking forward to the winter with uneasiness. The old Russian proverb: "Summer and Russia do not get along well together," has come true again. The harvest of the black-earth region has been ruined by the invasion, and the rich wheat and tobacco crops of the Caucasus are in German hands. This is a giant country with a giant's appetite, but much of Russia's vastness is infertile. There is a certain amount of irritability in the air. I hear more people saying: "I don't know what we're going to do this winter."

The first wet snows of the year have fallen as a warning of what is to come to the "Queen of the Snows." If this is anything like last year, the people know that the electric lights will be turned off in their homes for days at a time and they will sit in the dark through the long winter nights. Already gas service is discontinued without notice for hours to save fuel. Every apartment-house dweller has received a notice that his or her electric light consumption is not to exceed a fixed minimum. Even the largest room in any apartment is restricted to only a single electric-light bulb. We correspondents are on the same basis so far as light goes. The hotel has removed all but one overhead bulb from each of our rooms. But as everything in Russia is done for the mass rather than for the individual, the street lights of Moscow have suddenly blossomed with long rows of yellow "star lights" that go far to lighten the gloom of the city's blackout.

We had some news from the north today. The besieged people of Leningrad are preparing for another winter of holding the Nazis at bay and are decking themselves like explorers preparing for an expedition.

The last harvest of cabbage and potatoes is being gathered by a weary people who must walk all the way out to the tiny triangle of suburb held by the guns of Lieutenant-General Govorov.

All the wooden houses of old Leningrad are being torn down by order. Every male citizen must cut two cords of wood, one for his own home and one for the public buildings of the State, the movies, theaters, libraries, and bath-houses. On all important street corners long lines stand in front of huge posters studying how to make the simplest forms of wood stoves for their apartments. All the old trees of Leningrad's historic parks are being felled for firewood, for Leningrad will never fall.

October 14 ⚒ The barricades of Moscow have long been removed, but every morning the streets are blocked off with great piles of cut logs, the product of the army of amateur woodchoppers. Buses stripped of seats, trolley cars hitched three in a line like freight cars, and captured German trucks towing lines of trailers, all are bringing in the wood from the banks of the Volga where it has been dumped in towering piles from the paddle-wheel steamers.

The tenants of the apartment houses are notified when their load of wood arrives, and at all hours of the day and night I see them dragging it upstairs to their apartments, despite the midnight curfew. Elderly men, grandmothers, even little children carry the winter's fuel in their arms. The entire *corps de ballet* has turned out to help load wood on the trucks at the riverside. Today at the ballet it was announced from the stage that the premiere ballerina, Messerer, was unable to appear. She was too stiff from hauling wood. Even the members of the American Military Mission have filled their big Ford truck with wood for the Embassy.

Moscow is beginning to sprout stove pipes from each apartment. Crude wood-stoves have been provided by the State to keep the city from freezing this winter. The apartment-house furnaces will be shut down for lack of fuel, now that the coal of the Don Basin is in German hands.

October 15 ⚒ Made an appointment with Dmitri Shostakovich today to ask him if he would accept the invitation of the New York Philharmonic Orchestra to conduct a series of nine concerts in America.

Like generals and commissars, composers are "State

property" and a correspondent must make arrangements to see them through official channels. The Society for Cultural Relations acts as their publicity department. Shostakovich is also sought after for interviews by reporters for the Soviet press.

I visited him in his big room in the Moskva Hotel. A slightly built man came to the door, peered at me nearsightedly through horn-rimmed glasses, and led me to a chair. It was the man who had composed his Seventh Symphony during the first winter of the siege of Leningrad.

His features were cameo-sharp; his pink complexion made him look boyish, younger than his thirty-eight years. He gave me an impression of youthful shyness, and his light-blue eyes carried more than a hint of nervousness. Shostakovich wore an ordinary business suit, with a carelessly knotted tie.

"I should love to go to America," he said, "but unfortunately I have never learned to conduct an orchestra." He turned to his quiet blonde wife, Irina, who sat knitting at another table. "Wouldn't we like to go?" he said feelingly, and she returned him a bright smile.

"Yes, I must learn," he said, "but I have little time to do so because I am now working on my next symphony in honor of the twenty-fifth anniversary of the Revolution."

His thin face never lost its look of inner preoccupation as he talked and drummed the table nervously with his slender fingers.

"I understand you are a football fan," I volunteered.

"Ah, I would rather watch a football game than compose," he said, and added proudly: "You know, I am the football correspondent of *Red Sport*."

"Tell me something about your experiences in Leningrad," I suggested.

He seemed a little reluctant, but then spoke. "When the Germans came to our beautiful city," he said, "I tried to volunteer, but after a medical examination I was turned down. I joined the Home Guard and they accepted me until they found out who I was and they turned me down too, because they said I was too valuable to lose. So I became a fire watcher. We had many air raids. From the roof I could see our factory workers in uniform marching to the front. My classes at the conservatory shrank until there were only four pupils. Everyone was digging tank traps and working on the barricades." Shostakovich ran his hand through his tousled brown hair. There was a distant look in his light eyes.

"In the suffering of my people I saw the music of Leningrad. I started work. There was no heat, but I had my warm overcoat to wear while I picked at the piano. Twice the windows blew out and my wife and I boarded them up." He looked over at his silent wife with a smile. Then he turned to me and said with great intenseness in his voice: "But I could not hear the finale. It just wouldn't come. Then one day I heard a shouting in the streets. When I looked out, I saw a surging crowd around a group of German prisoners. Some of the wolves had been caught and they were being marched under guard through Leningrad. From that cry of triumphant anger that rose from the throats of the crowd came the music I had searched for in vain. It was the triumph of light over dark, of good over evil.

"It was agonizing work, but concentration helped me forget what the people were going through. And when I finished, I got an order to leave the city. We flew to Kuibyshev. I had to do it for my wife's sake."

He hesitated and crushed out his cigarette.

"I am glad my Leningrad Symphony has been a success in America. Some day I will visit your country."

The shy composer spoke very rapidly, with a look of concentration on his face as though he were making an effort to keep his thoughts from running away.

I shook hands with him and his quiet young wife and asked her about their son's health. "He's very well, thank you," she said in a low voice.

I thought about Shostakovich as I typed the cable of his inability to go to America. He was the most sensitive-looking man I'd ever seen in Russia, this hard country whose leaders usually carry a look of physical power and great energy. The true ancestor of most of the Russian people is the grim land that fashioned them.

October 18   ✒ In front of Moscow lies a desert, a wasteland of shell-torn cities and villages obliterated by the German scourge.

The European Russia that the Soviet power took over after the Revolution had changed little physically in the twenty-five years of the Soviet regime. Factories had been built and new cities laid out, but the essential city structure of the centuries of czarist rule underlay it all.

I wondered what the future held for the Soviet architects whose task it would be to build the new Russia. A committee headed by Eophan, the Armenian architect, had already been set up to consider the future, and I talked to him about it. He sat in his office in the square gray modernistic Architects' House just off Gorki Street. Pleased with my interest, the slender, swarthy man leafed over page after page of plans embodying the new ideas.

"I was in America in 1939 for the World's Fair," he said. "We got many ideas from your architects and their plans for model villages. We are taking them and adapting them to our people and the Russian scene." He pointed at an old photograph of a simple settlement. "You see, our villages grew up at the sides of farm paths, one house added to another in a line on both sides of the lane. Then horses gave way to trucks and some of the highways were paved, but the houses didn't move. The villages grew but the peasants continued to build one house after another until they straggled out in a long line on the historic highways." He thumbed over his book of plans and said: "Now, here is what you are doing in America. Building model towns on one side of the road in a semicircle with a by-road coming off the main highway, half-circling the center of the town and joining the highway farther along. That is what we will do, too."

He pointed out that old Russia had been built around the czarist system and the Church. The rich landowners had built large houses, and their serfs lived in one-room cabins. "We will build the new Russia around the Soviet system. In the center of our villages will be the social buildings of Soviet Russia — the town Soviet, the club and the schools and theaters. In back of those will come the individual peasant houses with their private plots of land in the rear. And nearest the road will be the collective barns and garages."

The peasant houses would not change very much in appearance, he said. "Our peasant houses have always been well built. Some of them have been standing for more than a hundred years. They are adapted to the Russian climate. Only one story high, they are easily warmed. We will build all the new houses on the same plan — three rooms, all on one floor, a combined kitchen and dining-room, and two bedrooms."

"How about bathrooms?" I asked.

The Armenian architect smiled and said: "Separate bathrooms are not a custom in our villages. It is too cold in the winter. We will build communal steam bath-houses as before. We will also do our best to preserve our typical Russian art." He turned a book of color plates around to me and pointed at the one- and two-story wooden buildings with the Asiatic scrollwork in the front. "That is our Russian popular art," he said. "It is very handsome. It fits the country. When the war is over we will have the paint to decorate them, for our people love color. Some will be red with blue trim and others white with red windows and doors. Something cheerful for this cold climate."

"Do you plan to have garages attached to each house?" I asked.

Eophan shook his head. "No, our villagers will have the collective trucks and keep them in the collective barns."

"What about the churches? Do you plan to take them down?"

"No, they are part of our culture and scene. We will save many of them as museums and rebuild some of the most beautiful ones that the Germans have destroyed."

I asked him about his plans for the new Russian cities.

"Our new apartment houses will be more simple and severe. We won't build any more with fancy gables like a wedding cake. I saw some of your new apartment buildings in America. We will try to make ours like them." He paused and reflected. "Those kitchens — how much labor they save! I greatly admired them. . . . And those beautiful bathrooms. We will have them in our new cities."

I reminded him that the Germans had succeeded in making Russian villages and cities into "hedgehogs" of defense by mathematically placing their gun positions and making the wooden houses into pillboxes. "Is the new Russia going to think of defense?" I asked.

Eophan hesitated and said: "After this war I don't think there will be any for a long time." Then he nodded his head gravely. "But we are considering the subject of defense in our plans."

October 19 ⚑ The strange figure of Rudolf Hess has stalked across the world stage today. *Pravda*, the most important newspaper in Soviet Russia, has asked for the immediate trial and punishment of the famous prisoner of the British. Today's outspoken editorial asks whether Hess is a criminal or an "accredited envoy of the Hitlerite Government in England, enjoying immunity . . . and thus converting England into a haven for gangsters. . . ." Despite these strong words, the Soviet newspaper dropped the story next day. It was really a political form of demand for a second front rising out of Russia's disappointment. England has taken a firm line in answer to this form of needling.

The editorial was based on a note sent to the Soviet Union by the Czech Minister to Russia, M. Fierlinger and M. Garreau, member of the French National Committee, on behalf of the enslaved nations of Europe. The odd thing about the note was the fact that it was submitted to the Soviet Union ten months ago. It asked for a joint declaration regarding German responsibility for crimes against civilization.

Members of the diplomatic corps in Moscow explained to me that this flare-up of hard feelings is really the result of a diplomatic blunder. Britain sent Russia a note inviting her to serve on a war-crimes commission, but the Soviets say they didn't have time to answer before the British announced details of the plan. Specifically it provided for *post-war* punishment of war criminals. The Russians had considered the plan an open political matter and were offended when they were confronted with an Anglo-American *fait accompli.* President Roosevelt had also signified willingness of the United States to co-operate with the other United Nations on the matter. Hess's re-emergence into the news has turned out a tempest in a samovar.

October 20 ✒ I met one of the three women who wear the gold star of a "Hero of the Soviet Union" — Major Valentina Grizadubova.

There is of course no "nobility" in the Soviet Union, but the order of Hero of the Soviet Union entitles the wearer to have a small bust erected in his or her native town, and their perquisites include free railroad transportation for the rest of their lives.

Heavy-set, dark, and masculine-looking, Grizadubova is now the only woman in the Soviet Union to have led an all-male squadron of heavy night bombers. She won her award before the war, in 1938, when she piloted a plane with a woman navigator and a woman radio-operator on a record non-stop flight of 4,031 miles from Moscow to Siberia.

She wore a man's uniform with the collar wings of the Red Air Force and a Sam Browne belt and pistol. A member of the Supreme Soviet as delegate from Uzbekistan, Grizadubova spoke with the usual force of a Communist Party member. "There are many women in the Soviet Union who are fighting for their country," she said in a deep husky voice. "They are especially good in the air. The youngest girl in the Red Air Force is seventeen, and the oldest is a woman navigator of forty-five." She tapped her red-painted finger nails on the table. "We take volunteers only, and most of our women pilots received their training before the war started. My good friend Marina Raskova now commands a regiment of all-girl dive-bombers," she said proudly.

I asked what the Germans did to the girls they took prisoner. Grizadubova raised her eyebrows over her slanting blue eyes and said: "You can guess."

"Did you ever bomb Berlin?" I asked.

The bobbed-haired brunette shook her head. "I cannot answer that question," she said; "but the reports that the Germans have surrounded Berlin with very heavy anti-aircraft guns is positively true. My pilots have little trouble finding their targets, though. They know the way there well. They flew the same route in the civil service before the war."

"Do women react differently from men in coming out of a power dive?" I asked. "In other words, do women blackout more easily than men?"

Grizadubova smiled scornfully. "When a woman is in good condition," she said, "there is no difference between her and a man!" Then she turned to me and said: "I see you are a pilot. You are interested in flying."

I sheepishly explained that I had never flown a plane, but had spent a long time with the RAF in France.

Husky Grizadubova nodded. "Yes, I can see now that you are not a pilot. You ask too many questions."

October 21 　　　　　　 ✠ "Moscow will not go hungry this winter," said the Mayor of Moscow. Stocky and square-shouldered, looking something like New York's Mayor LaGuardia, little Vassily Pronin talked as though every fact was at his fingertips. We sat in the old cherry-red building of the Moscow Soviet in the Mayor's private office.

"We have figured it out," he said. "There is enough flour and meat to last the winter, but we are going to economize so that we will have a reserve for any emergency." He carefully rolled a cigarette out of typewriter paper and quoted an old Russian proverb: "If you go to war for a week, you must prepare for a year." Then he went on: "The factories raised enough on their farms to supply their canteens with cabbage, carrots, and potatoes for the next ten months. It's true we are a little short of butter and meat fats, but we think we'll have enough to feed every heavy worker sixteen ounces of meat a week. We'll have to cut out the butter and fat rations for all dependents who don't work, though — those between the ages of eighteen and forty-five, I mean."

I asked him why there had been such food shortages in the city during the past year.

"That was the fault of bad organization," he admitted. "The population of Moscow increased a half-million when we brought some factories back after the siege. Then we had thousands of people in from the Urals and Siberia on business trips. They brought their ration cards with them and got their food in special stores, but I'm afraid we overlooked that when we planned the food budget for the year. There were more people on official missions to Moscow from the east than we had counted on. So we had to cancel all the meat-ration coupons of the public for the last three months to make it up."

A carefully groomed waitress with waved blond hair walked in and served us tea and crackers.

"Is there any American food in town?" I asked.

Mayor Pronin scratched his head and thought. "Yes," he said finally, "there is some American chocolate."

Just then the waitress returned with a dish of what unmistakably were neatly molded cubes of American cane sugar. I put one in my tea without bothering to question the Mayor about it.

"As for heat and light," he continued, "Moscow will be kept warm. But it's a question of the weather in more ways than one. If we have an early freeze, we shan't be able to get in all the wood. If the rivers ice up early, we shall have a problem. We are rushing the wood into the city as fast as is humanly possible. About one third of it has already been delivered."

"What about Stalingrad?" was the last question. "Will it stand?"

"I am of course optimistic," said Pronin. "We have far-reaching strategic plans that may come to maturity. No matter what happens, we will be prepared." He looked out the window at the wet, driving snow. "Don't forget," he said confidently, "our reserves are trained for offense as well as for defense."

October 22 ⚑ There is always bustle and confusion attending the departure or arrival of trains or planes in wartime Russia, and today was no exception.

I said good-bye to Katya. She was silent and looked at me long with her large dark eyes. Then she quoted a line from Pushkin: "If you find one better than me, you'll forget me; if you find one worse, you'll remember." I thought I'd remember.

The plane was leaving at six in the morning. At midnight Intourist phoned me and a secretary said: "I'm sorry there's no room in the plane. You must wait for the next one."

Angered, I abandoned packing and hurried to see Mr. Palgunov at the Press Office. He phoned the airport and told me sadly that the Foreign Office had asked for six seats on the plane to Persia, but all were taken.

I explained that I had already announced over the air that I was making my last broadcast from Moscow and now I was faced with three weeks of idleness until the next plane was scheduled. He was even sadder. "What can I do if there are no seats?"

I walked slowly back to the hotel and went to Walter Kerr's room, disturbing a chess game to announce that I wasn't leaving after all. I explained that I would have to take all my clothes back, my underwear, wool shirts, fur hat and coat, boots, everything, in order to keep warm during the next three weeks.

With resignation, Kerr gave me back the bundle of clothes and I went to bed. At four o'clock in the morning the phone rang. It was Intourist again. A girl's voice said: "Meester Lesueur, if you are going to get on that plane you must be over at the airport at five thirty a.m."

Elated, I threw the bare essentials into the small canvas bag I had been carrying ever since the war in France in 1939. I looked down at my newly soled shoes and decided to sacrifice them, adding them to the wardrobe of cast-offs for the other correspondents. I stuffed them into the huge knapsack I was leaving behind and made for the airport in my slippers. I left a note for Kerr asking him to go ahead on the morning broadcast, for I was on my way home.

Hard-working, conscientious Walter Graebner of *Time* and *Life* had engaged an Intourist car and we sped out to the airport in the dark. A cold, wet snow was falling as we boarded the Soviet Douglas transport waiting on the field.

I felt sharp and confused emotions of joy and sadness as I looked down on Moscow. I was leaving, to return to lights and warmth while the people I knew so well remained behind in the drab, gray city for another long, dark winter of cold and hunger. Back we flew the way I had come a year ago, toward the Urals and the steppes and the dark pine forests. The plane droned at low level over the wooded hills of the Volga to Kuibyshev, some six hundred miles southeast.

The Grand Hotel at Kuibyshev was no grander than before. The Japanese correspondents still lived there, but the hotel manager told me that they didn't hold banquets any more; they had become quiet and somewhat depressed.

I thought the manager looked several years older than when I had seen him months before. Yet he seemed youthful enough as he proudly showed me the new bathtub installed in the past month. He took me to the window to point out the new street lights and the buses running in the street. From a crude, uncomfortable country town, Kuibyshev in a year of war had become one of the most important cities in European Russia. The gray-haired manager spoke of Kuibyshev's vast dreams, the dam across the Volga that one day would be the largest in the world. "When you come back," he said, "as I know you will, there will be a new Russia to greet you."

The food was good in the hotel dining-room — better than in Moscow. We stayed the night and took sandwiches for the rest of the long plane ride.

East we flew from Kuibyshev over the black-earth region of the steppes. Distances look insignificant on a small-scale map of Russia, but they are in fact very great, as Hitler learned to the cost of German lives.

Not a green leaf nor a drop of fresh water was in sight as we passed over the wasteland on the edge of the Transcaspian desert. The brown-burnt steppe was marked here and there by an old caravan track weaving between the salt marshes. We were on the east side of the Volga, where the defenders of Stalingrad knew "there was no land."

The Red Army colonel sitting in front of me pointed down at the ruins of an ancient city. "That below us," he said, "was once the capital of Genghis Khan." Then he pointed to the north. "And the smoke you see in the west, that is Stalingrad." I nodded.

The big ship put down at the top of the Caspian Sea at a small town which had been standing since time immemorial. The adobe huts had not changed down the years. Only the big airport symbolized the advance of the centuries.

We winged over the green of the Caspian Sea to Baku, the richest little city in Europe, the pot of gold at the end of Hitler's fleeting rainbow. It was a sea-level city of sand, thrusting skyward a forest of oil derricks like unshaved black stubble. A crowded electric train rumbled past the airfield as the pilot and some girl workers tied down our plane behind a wind-barrier to protect it from the sand-storm that swept off the Caspian Sea in a yellow cloud. It was the coldest wind I had felt in months. I knew it was piercing those thin German uniforms at Stalingrad. The mark of the East was on Baku, with its whitewashed Persian houses and its dark-skinned women goatherds with white shawls over their heads.

We stayed the night at the Intourist Hotel, easily the finest hotel I've ever seen in Russia. No two rooms were decorated alike, the walls were inlaid or painted in brown and white modernistic designs. In the morning we breakfasted at the airport. To my surprise the counter was loaded with unra-tioned candy and fruit, almost unknown these days in Mos-cow, a thousand miles away. When I left the hotel I had taken off my last suit of winter underwear and given it to the chambermaid. She was overjoyed. There was none to be bought by civilians in Russia.

Our big Douglas soared toward the high Caucasus that came down to meet the plain like giants. Below them was the bottom of a dried-up sea. Then we rose above the clouds to fourteen thousand feet and still we saw the snow-capped peaks of the Caucasus range thrusting through the mist like frozen waves of granite, just the way they were heaved up out of the earth a million years ago.

We flew low over the oases of northern Persia and suddenly zoomed up and circled the airfield at Teheran, the key-point of Russia's Burma Road.

I climbed out of the plane, stretched, and blinked at the glaring hot sand. I felt very pale and white with all the sunburned Red Army men around me.

A Soviet officer, red star on his cap, grinned and offered me a cigarette. "Are you from Moscow?" he asked. I nodded. He stood silent for a moment and then said: "How is Moscow now?"

I told him that it was snowing when I left; that the people were preparing for a hard winter; that air raids were almost non-existent, and the ballet and movies were playing as usual. Then I asked him: "What about Stalingrad?"

He looked at me long and proudly. "Stalingrad!" he repeated. "Stalingrad will never fall!"

New York, May 1943 　　When I reached Cairo, the war was at its turning-point. The British Eighth Army, made up of the finest-looking soldiers I had ever seen, cracked the Axis defense in depth at El Alamein. Then, with the Afrika Korps in retreat, the United States launched its first large-scale offensive of the war against Tunisia.

I found myself somewhat bewildered in Cairo. I couldn't decide which was the more artificial, Moscow or Cairo; the Russian capital, grim and gray, but possessing a strange atmosphere of exhilaration because of the elemental vitality of its completely involved people, or Cario, with a neutral people enjoying peace-time pleasures, yet filled with determined, battle-hardened troops.

I satiated my long-denied craving for fresh fruits and salads and picked up a convincing attack of dysentery. Somehow I resented the pleasure madness of Cairo and I found myself thinking of Moscow — the austere community life of the correspondents and its close friendships.

I was struck by the frozen, self-conscious faces of English and American men and women as against my memory of the mobile-faced, uninhibited Russians. Then I realized I had probably never lost my own Western look of self-consciousness in the midst of crowds of strangers.

Traveling across Africa in an American bomber, I ate the best food I had tasted in more than three and a half years: American Army food. I talked to scores of envious, home-sick American soldiers and airmen who wished they were going home, too. I promised to eat hamburgers and play jukeboxes for them; they were pathetically eager to enjoy just one more Saturday night back home.

It had taken me forty days to get to Moscow from Scotland a year ago. Now, twelve months later, I was flying all the way home from Moscow to New York in nine days. The new definition of time and space was startling, but I was home.

At first I was confused by the extremely well-dressed appearance of the American people. I wondered if, in the past, we had really drained all the brightest people out of Europe. Then visits to several American war factories convinced me that my people were not really very different from the workers I had seen in Europe. We just had the clothes and a look of happiness and an ability to laugh that Europe has lost for too many years. Nevertheless, if you put American clothes on Russian workers and transplanted them into our atmosphere for a short time, I know they'd soon be indistinguishable from the rest of conglomerate America. I was startled to see so many men doing what I now considered women's work.

The winter is over. It is over in Russia, too. One of the world's decisive battles has passed into history. Stalingrad and the Volga are in Russian hands. The Germans were beaten by three factors: superior Russian strategy, geography, and the supreme devotion of the Soviet soldier.

The Russians, greatest chess-players in the world, had never permitted the Germans to get sufficient numbers of troops inside the extremely long and narrow city of Stalingrad. The Red Army had massed large bodies of troops at both ends of the city. If the Germans sent too many divisions inside Stalingrad, the Russians brought pressure against one of the weakened flanks. If the Germans transferred troops to meet the new threat, the Red Army moved against their center or their opposite flank. The crack German Sixth Army was checkmated at every move. Geographically although Stalingrad was no more favored for defense than Chicago, still the Germans were unable to put the massed Soviet artillery out of action because their tanks couldn't reach it. It was emplaced across the Volga. It couldn't be bombed or strafed out of action.

No more need be added to the stories of the heroism and devotion of the Soviet soldiers. One needs only to remember that one regiment of heavily outnumbered Russian soldiers defended an area of rubble-strewn street no longer than a football field for weeks. A German advance of two hundred yards would have pushed the defenders into the Volga and might have decided the fate of Stalingrad, if not of the world.

Once more the Germans had miscalculated Russia's war potential. When the Red Armies finally encircled the crack German Sixth Army, it was the Soviets who had the greater number of tanks. The Red Army is losing men, but proportionately it is becoming stronger in numbers and equipment than the Germans. The Russian war factories evacuated east to the Urals and Siberia have settled down to work. Anglo-American aid is now being felt in Russia. The Red Army's power for offense is growing, and when the Soviets recover their Don Basin, half their war will be won. Russia's industrial cities on the European plain will no longer be short of coal and iron.

Another spring of war faces the world. Hitler's armies still lack their life-blood — oil. They may still search for it in the direction of Baku. But it looks as though this year not all the decisive land battles will be fought in the east.

In the months I've been home there have been strong indications of the lack of full understanding between Russia and her allies. I feel, however, that these incidents have served a worth-while purpose in bringing out into the open certain factors which might later have hit us with simultaneous impact. For instance, I didn't realize until I came home that the American public was unaware that the Soviet Union regarded the Baltic States as full-fledged Soviet

Republics. They were incorporated within the USSR in 1940 before Russia was at war or had signed the Atlantic Charter. The Soviets say that the people of the Baltic States overthrew their old governments by revolution and announced their desire to join the USSR. It was obvious in the Moscow press that it would not be the Soviets' policy to permit small and weak states to exist on her borders as a temptation for enemies to concentrate by fifth-column methods.

How far the Red Army will go to the west in pursuit of the Germans, I cannot say. I once asked this of Solomon Lozovsky, the Soviet Vice-Commissar for Foreign Affairs. He answered that the Soviets would be satisfied to drive the Germans out of the land of Soviet Union. He added that it was possible that some of the decisive battles "might take place across the frontiers."

Russia's continued pleas for a second front anywhere in Europe have another interpretation aside from the strictly military aspect. It appears as though the Soviet Union is satisfied to see the armies of Anglo-American free enterprise controlling the rest of Europe. There is little doubt in my mind that Soviet Russia is desperately eager to have an enduring peace to rebuild her devastated agriculture and industry, perhaps with the help of German labor, very likely with the aid of factories removed from the Reich as a form of war indemnity.

However, I don't think Russia will forget the millions of fellow Slavs in eastern Europe. A Pan-Slavic bloc of friendly governments along Soviet Russia's frontiers not only would ensure her borders but would outweigh Teutonic central Europe.

The future of Russia, more than any other power, depends to a large extent on her relations with bordering nations. The Russian land frontier, on a pre-war map, skirts successively Finland, the Baltic States, Poland, Rumania — and through Rumania the Balkans — Turkey, Iran, Afghanistan, India, China, and Japanese Manchukuo. I think we can assume therefore that Russia will always maintain a large group of professional military officers around whom a great army of compulsorily trained men can quickly be mobilized.

The migration of her European war factories to the Urals and beyond and the fixing of workers in their new homes has given Russia the long-sought opportunity to colonize her east. In my opinion the names of such cities as Kuibyshev, Magnitogorsk, Sverdlovsk, Novossibirsk, and Tashkent will one day be as familiar to us as Kiev, Odessa, Minsk, and Kharkov.

In other words, Russia is going to be both a great European power and a great Eastern power. I don't think that the future will see Soviet Russia becoming a democracy of the American type. After the war I think Russia will develop her own democracy on the lines of her present system, in which there is no private ownership of the means of production.

However, I don't believe that our two systems must necessarily clash. There seems to be plenty of room in the world for both of them to exist in peace. In the future, Soviet Russia may rival even the United States in industrial production. Her natural resources and population exceed ours. We cannot afford to lose Soviet Russia as a friend if we are to avoid a third World War.

TYPE NOTE

This book was set on the Linotype in *Bodoni Book,* a printing-type so called after Giambattista Bodoni, a celebrated printer and type designer of Rome and Parma (1740–1813). *Bodoni Book* as produced by the Linotype company is not a copy of any one of Bodoni's fonts, but is a composite, modern version of the Bodoni manner. Bodoni's innovations in printing-type style were a greater degree of contrast in the "thick and thin" elements of the letters, and a sharper and more angular finish of details.

The book was composed, printed, and bound by The Plimpton Press, Norwood, Massachusetts. The typographic and binding designs are by W. A. Dwiggins.